3CL3
CBS
5/18/03

THE MUSIC OF
WILLIAM
WALTON

Sir William Walton

THE MUSIC OF
WILLIAM
WALTON

FRANK HOWES

Second Edition

London
OXFORD UNIVERSITY PRESS
NEW YORK   TORONTO
1974

Oxford University Press, Ely House, London W.1

GLASGOW NEW YORK TORONTO MELBOURNE WELLINGTON
CAPE TOWN IBADAN NAIROBI DAR ES SALAAM LUSAKA ADDIS ABABA
DELHI BOMBAY CALCUTTA MADRAS KARACHI LAHORE DACCA
KUALA LUMPUR SINGAPORE HONG KONG TOKYO

ISBN 0 19 315431 5

© Oxford University Press, 1965, 1973

First published 1965
Second edition 1974

Acknowledgement is due to Stainer & Bell Ltd for permission to quote extracts from the Piano Quartet. All other works of William Walton quoted in this book are controlled by Oxford University Press. 'The Seeds of Love' is quoted by permission of Novello & Co. Ltd.

*Printed in Great Britain by
The Camelot Press Ltd, London and Southampton*

Contents

Illustrations

Introduction

THIS book of discussion of Sir William Walton's music is a revision and expansion undertaken at the publisher's request of two *Musical Pilgrim* booklets first published in 1942. In the twenty years that have elapsed the method of analysis, which is the recognized and indeed inevitable way of commenting on instrumental music of the so-called absolute kind, has received support from the public, which has found programme notes, record sleeves and 'symposia' of composers' works useful—otherwise they would not have bought them—and from philosophers, notably Mr Harold Osborne, who commend it from the point of view of aesthetics. Musicians regard it as an important tool in style criticism, which has been a late arrival in Britain. Although I have done a considerable amount of this sort of analysis I have never regarded the results as anything but a rather unappetizing form of literature, though Tovey did much to redeem it from total unreadability. Moreover structural analysis, which has been the basis of much of the musical appreciation that has contributed heavily to the increased interest in orchestral music, has recently been under fire as being inadequate, not searching enough and indeed not worthy of the name of analysis. We are invited to look more closely at the themes of sonata and symphonic movements and to search for an underlying unity in the contrast of first and second subjects, allegro and andante movements. This 'thematic analysis' is all to the good, and the book, *The Thematic Process in Music*, by Rudolph Reti does reveal quite astonishingly the mechanics of that unity in diversity which has always been the aesthetic glory of sonata form. The method of isolating a latent motif is not wholly new, since germinal motifs that are not latent but explicit—the opening three notes of Brahms's second symphony and the rhythmic shape of the opening of Beethoven's fifth symphony are classical instances—have long been recognized for what they are. Furthermore it offers strong temptations to over-stretch the evidence, but psychologically it is soundly based.

The psychological considerations are set forth in Mr Alan Walker's *A Study in Musical Analysis*, which spoils by a certain aggressive defensiveness some sound arguments from theory of knowledge and the fact of subliminal perception. There was no need for him to dismiss the structural analysis that at least has half a century of good service behind it as something obscurantist: the new thematic analysis carries the good work of structural analysis a stage further, and further subtleties of rhythmic analysis, of which he gives examples that go further than Reti, take us further still into the workings of the composer's mind. For one important function of analysis is to enable those who appreciate, but cannot create, music to see the musical process at work—Reti's book is well called *The Thematic Process*.

My dissection of Walton's music will, I hope, reveal in some measure how his mind works, and I have devoted a short chapter at the end of the book to a general account of his idiosyncrasies. As his music proceeds at high tension and his scoring is elaborate in detail, analysis, which maps out his movements and isolates details, may even indeed claim to elucidate performances for the listener and to uncover features that might otherwise be missed in the excitements of apprehending a performance. I hold too that discursive knowledge may, I don't say will, help understanding,[1] though I am ready enough to admit that the best justification of analysis is that it may satisfy curiosity about a work of art and that the apprehension of music is fundamentally intuitive. Indeed my aesthetic creed is that art is a kind of knowledge—knowledge of states of mind—and that beauty and emotion, which are certainly involved in art, are not the kernel of the nut. Knowledge is through perception and it is the skill to perceive which is hard to cultivate in oneself and still more to induce in others. Criticism is one device of proved value in the cultivation of perception, and criticism has tended to turn away from the adventures of the soul among the masterpieces—though the records of such adventures may be revealing to others—as too subjective in favour

---

[1] I have argued this in *Music and Its Meanings* (Athlone Press).

of analysis and technical study, which takes the emotion and the beauty for granted in the listener's response as the Pateresque critic did not, and deals with the cognitive aspects of the experience. It is true that ideally the cognition of a work of art is immediate and intuitive, but as in fact a symphonic movement is spread out over twenty minutes of time some means of sustaining attention must be found, as it has to be found by the composer himself when he uses his technique to elaborate his primary invention—technique is indeed thinking in sound. Analysis therefore has become a tool of criticism, just as criticism has become a tool of aesthetics. Mr Harold Osborne, in deploying these great matters for discussion in his two substantial studies in aesthetics, *Theory of Beauty* and *Aesthetics and Criticism*, applauds the use of analysis in music criticism and indeed gives to musicians the credit for pioneering in this branch of criticism. My analyses, therefore, though less concerned with evaluation than what I may have written in *The Times* and other journals about Walton's works and their performance, are a branch of music criticism. The German philosophers, who have always recognized aesthetics as a branch of philosophy comparable with logic and ethics, developed also under the same name the study of individual works of art, which could and no doubt did illumine philosophical aesthetics but actually led to art history, style criticism and analysis. These essays in analysis are therefore in essence style criticism.

The new method of thematic analysis I have been unable to apply with the rigour that Reti profitably turns on Beethoven, for one reason that the thematic polymorphism I discover in Walton's work precludes such neat and sure demonstration, and for another that it takes insufficient account of rhythm. After all it is agreed that if the rhythm and the notes of 'God save the Queen' are taken apart, the rhythmic outline is more readily identifiable than the melodic sequence without the rhythm. It is to Mr Walker's credit that he recognizes rhythmic and harmonic analyses—of which he quotes as an example the Neapolitan lurch in the first and last movements of the Appassionata sonata—have as much to contribute to our understanding of the latent unity of the contrasting elements as Reti's thematic process. In my analysis of

Walton's first symphony I have called attention to several of the pervasive elements, the kinship of Exs. 3, 4 and 18, and 24, the persistence of a four-note gruppetto in the themes of all movements except the scherzo, the use of a falling second as the essence of the first subject (Ex. 3) and of the first theme of the second subject in the first movement, of the fierce unison in the scherzo (Ex. 13) modified to a minor third in the slow movement (Ex. 15), and multiplied by two in the exordium of the finale (Ex. 18).

Melodic contour with minute variations of interval and rhythm is often with Walton the basic unification of the various appearance of a theme, as *Troilus and Cressida* shows in which Cressida's motifs are not leitmotifs but varying expressions of the same basic idea which stands for her and her plight. The praise motifs in the heathen procession in *Belshazzar's Feast* are another example of unity by contour.

It will, I hope, be apparent that though I have accepted the limitations of formal analysis as my main concern, to expound rather than to interpret, I am not in general fearful of evaluations or of postulating connexions between life and art. But Walton is reticent in spite of the violence of his expression and I find his contacts with the world not sufficiently clear or certain to warrant such psychological observations as are usually made in studies of this kind.

★   ★   ★

For this new edition I have added a chapter on the works composed between 1965 and 1972 as well as making a few corrections of detail. The list of gramophone records has been deleted since such lists are out of date almost before they are printed and most of the music is now available on record. A chronological list of the compositions has been substituted and one or two pictures have been added.

Biographical Note

WILLIAM TURNER WALTON was born at Oldham in Lancashire on 29 March 1902, the son of a singing teacher. At the age of ten he went up to a voice trial of probationer choristers at Christ Church, Oxford, and got a place. According to his own account this was the first manifestation of the luck which he has enjoyed throughout his life. His father happened to see the advertisement; his mother managed to get him to Oxford just in time for the competition after missing train connexions from the north. He sang Marcello's 'O Lord our Governor' to Dr Henry Ley, who was then the (very young) Cathedral organist, did some ear tests—ear training was a regular part of choir practices at Christ Church—and was accepted. He went to the Choir School in 1912 and stayed there six years.

Of his schooldays a few anecdotes have survived. According to Jack Taphouse, of the Oxford firm of music dealers, and Hilary Macklin, for many years secretary of the Associated Board of the Royal Schools of Music, who were his contemporaries, he showed his sardonic wit even as a small boy. It once took the form of ringing the breakfast bell an hour too early on April Fool's Day and getting the whole school out of bed—a joke which, however legitimate, the headmaster did not appreciate. To his teachers he showed the compositions which even then he had begun to write. Basil Allchin, at that time assistant organist at Christ Church, who used to teach him the piano, said that he covered reams of music paper, largely in the form of motets for double choir. From his earliest days his music showed strong individuality, and if his choirmasters were baffled by these juvenilia they encouraged him to go on.

His second piece of luck was the then Dean of Christ Church, Thomas Banks Strong—'Do you like your T. Strong?' was a familiar cartoon in Oxford in those days. Strong, who afterwards became Bishop of Ripon and later still Bishop of Oxford, was a considerable musician, who could play the piano and had a doctorate in music as well as divinity. He used to give the choir-boys the run of the Deanery on Sundays, and when Walton's voice broke he kept him on until he could matriculate him at the exceptionally early age of sixteen. This he did after consultation with Dr Hugh Allen, who was the most forceful and influential figure in Oxford music before he became Director of the Royal College of Music in 1919. Walton, as he himself has said, had no wish to become a cotton clerk in Oldham, and was glad to become an undergraduate. He did little work but revelled in the opportunity to read scores made available to him by the Dean and Allen.

It was not Allen's way to give systematic teaching, but he provided the necessary guidance to steer Walton through the Bachelor of Music examination. He failed Responsions (the official matriculation examination), however, and was sent down after a few terms. But while he was in Oxford, in those days at the end of the war when there were few people about, he met Roy Campbell, Ronald Firbank, and, again a lucky encounter, Sacheverell Sitwell. So a fertile friendship was begun. He went to Italy with the Sitwells and lived with them in Chelsea, where before long *Façade* was conceived and first performed. The Oxford connexion was ratified many years later by the conferment of an honorary D.Mus. in 1942 and an honorary Studentship (fellowship) of Christ Church. Other honours that came to him were honorary doctorates from Durham in 1937, Manchester in 1952, and Cambridge in 1955. He was knighted in 1951.

Of his early years Walton says, 'I had by this time (*circa* 1915) begun some tentative efforts in composition—settings of Shakespeare songs from the plays we happened to be studying, some organ pieces and a march for a wedding.' A couple of songs achieved publication, 'The Winds' (Swinburne) and 'Tritons' (William Drummond) and a part-song 'A Litany' (Phineas Fletcher). After Oxford he was entirely self-taught and is only credited subsequently with advice from Ansermet and Busoni, and instruction from Eugene Goossens in conducting, when it became desirable for him to direct performances of his own works. He was indeed a precocious talent and, apart from the benefit of being brought up in that fruitful nursery of musicians, the English cathedral choir, he had a minimum of formal training. Unlike other composers who had similarly picked up their training for themselves—Elgar and Boughton come to mind—Walton was not late in maturing sufficiently to make his mark as a young man. His Piano Quartet of 1918 was performed and subsequently published, and in 1923 he secured international recognition at the Salzburg meeting of the International Society of Contemporary Music. He produced a master work in the Viola Concerto when he was twenty-seven, and had written a powerful symphony by the time he was thirty-three.

There is a sense, however, in which he was not fully mature when he appeared before the public as a fully fledged composer. His early years as a musician coincided with the post-Armistice conditions which were marked by a furious passion for dancing, the vogue of jazz, a cynical wit, and an anti-romantic outlook. Walton was *persona grata* with the juries who chose the works for the International Festivals of Contemporary Music, and to them romance was taboo because it was not contemporary. Music, like manners, had to be hard-boiled. But in the thirties this prohibition relaxed somewhat and the relaxation coincided with the development of Walton's own temperament, in which there is plainly a strain of brooding and almost melancholy feeling that is quite different from the sharp intelligence and smart exterior which are other conspicuous features of his style. A comparison of the Viola Concerto with *Façade* shows this difference.

From his Christ Church days Walton took away as technical equipment no more than an ingrained ability to write for voices, but the helpful influence of the Dean, and his friendship with Sacheverell Sitwell, afterwards extended to the other members of that talented and artistic family, were of incalculable value to him, as he has publicly testified. His musical career did not, however, develop along the academic lines that radiate from Oxford. The landmarks in it are the appearances of his works in the programmes of the International Festivals of Contemporary Music, and it was from these meetings abroad that his fame began to spread through England, though the authorities of the Leeds Festival must have the credit for recognizing his significance and including works from his pen in their solidly orthodox programmes. After a String Quartet at the first of the I.S.C.M. Festivals at Salzburg in 1923, Walton's name subsequently appeared at Zurich in 1926 with the *Portsmouth Point* overture, at Siena in 1928 with *Façade*, at Liége in 1930 with the Viola Concerto, and at Amsterdam in 1933 with *Belshazzar's Feast*. By this time his position at home had already been established, since *Belshazzar's Feast* had had its first performance at the Leeds Festival of 1931.

The early performances of *Façade*, the birth of a masterpiece of artistic collaboration, constitute an event of historical importance. Sir Osbert Sitwell has described its early life amusingly and richly in the volume of his autobiography called *Laughter in the Next Room*. Soon after the uproar created at the Aeolian Hall by the first public performance of *Façade* on 12 June 1923, Walton appeared on the international stage with a string quartet at the Salzburg Festival of Contemporary Music, then just at the beginning of its career as an attempt to repair the breaches in communication between European musicians caused by the war. Walton was quite unknown yet to the English public, and his quartet in the circumstances described below (on pp. 1–2) did not make much impression. He himself describes it as 'mostly undigested Bartok and Schoenberg'. When it was played subsequently in London it was adversely criticized by Ernest Newman and eventually withdrawn. Walton now thinks the Scherzo had some merit but has no intention of reviving it.

During his Chelsea period Walton met Bernard van Dieren, Cecil Gray and Philip Heseltine, who formed an influential clique, Kaikhoshru Sorabji, the Parsee musician, and, most important for him, Constant Lambert, with whom he found much in common in his general taste and outlook upon music and with whom he formed a life-long friendship. It is worth remembering when in his seventh decade Walton is reproached for not conforming to a fashion, which after thirty years has had a come-back, of the avant-garde of the twenties, Schoenberg, Stravinsky, and the other gods preached by van Dieren's anti-academic, anti-establishment circle, it is from choice, not from ignorance or intellectual laziness. He was interested in all the ferment and dabbled in atonality and some features of Stravinsky's style—he himself points to the rhythmic complexity of his *Portsmouth Point* overture as an example of the latter. But he always was, and still is, too robust to follow any school, still less to become entangled in what, alas! cannot be denied was a very unhealthy company—the tale of suicide and early death need not be painfully recalled. Nor does he think it wise to follow Stravinsky's example in changing styles, since, as he says, Stravinsky is a phenomenon without parallel in the history of music. Before long Walton retired to live in the country the better to cope with his financial problems, which in the days before film composition and admission to the Performing Right Society were not easily solved by up-and-coming but not-yet-arrived composers. Walton with north-country directness acknowledges with gratitude the help he received from Dr Strong, the Sitwells, and finally a small legacy from Mrs Samuel Courtauld.

His 'arrival' was with the Viola Concerto, which won universal recognition as a masterpiece and assured his future career. This was in 1929. In 1931 followed *Belshazzar's Feast* in which he again collaborated with a Sitwell, the book being by Osbert Sitwell. For both these successes Walton owes something to Edward Clark, who was pursuing a progressive policy at the B.B.C. He it was who invited Hindemith to launch the concerto and he who mooted the idea of the choral work. Beecham took the latter into the Leeds Festival, though he left its direction to Malcolm Sargent.

The story of Walton's life is from this point onwards the story of his career as a composer, for he never embarked as Constant Lambert did on conducting, save of his own works. During the war he was obliged to compose music for use rather than his own pleasure or other commissions, that is to say, he wrote music for films—not however for the first time, since *Escape me Never* belongs to 1934. In 1948 he went to Buenos Aires as a representative

of the Performing Right Society at an international conference.
There he met Señorita Susana Gil and married her on 13 December
of that year. They have made their home on Ischia in the Bay of
Naples and, as well as making music, are, as Walton puts it,
'engaged in creating and tending a large garden (a comparatively
new and to me absorbing aspect of life), and managing houses we
have built (or rather my wife does).' From Ischia they descend on
England from time to time to direct or attend performances of
Walton's works, consult his publishers and keep in touch, or go
to America or elsewhere when the invitation comes.

CHAPTER I

Early Works

String Quartet (1922)

WALTON'S music first came before the public in 1923 when it was learned that the composer of the freakish extravaganza *Façade* had achieved an international reputation, to the extent at least of having a string quartet included in the first of the festivals of the International Society for Contemporary Music. *Façade* was produced in London in June; in August the quartet was played at Salzburg. Who was this William Walton? Whose pupil was he? The only clue to the category in which the new and unknown composer was to be placed was the company he kept: the other English representatives at the Salzburg Festival were Bliss and Lord Berners. The quartet was not favourably noticed—it was too long to keep the attention of a tired audience at the end of a long programme.

A correspondent contributed to *The Times* of 14 August the following account of its first performance.

It is a long work and it was very unfortunately placed at the end of a long programme. The impressions it gave at a first hearing were, first, that it might be considerably condensed, and second that some passages might be rewritten with a view to making the work more grateful for the strings to play. The Scherzo is the least effective part of the work. The lengthy treatment of an apparently meaningless figure of two notes lost the attention of the hall and this was never regained. The result was that by the time the latter part of the fugue was reached the restiveness of the audience made it almost impossible to listen intelligently A word of congratulation is due to the McCullough Quartet, who bravely and successfully overcame the many difficulties of the work.

At the end in summarizing the British contribution (Bliss and Berners) the writer adds as commentary on its unrepresentative inadequacy, 'No one grudges Mr Walton the performance of his quartet, but one may doubt the wisdom from the composer's point of view of forcing an immature work on the public notice.'

As to the restiveness of the audience and the bravery of the performers Sir Osbert Sitwell told the story of a diversion that occurred at the concert. The cellist got the spike of her instrument into a thing that worked a trap-door on which she was sitting. She began to go down, but was apparently rescued in time, since she 'came up smiling' while the audience rocked with laughter at the light relief. The quartet was withdrawn by the composer who recognized its immaturity after a couple of subsequent hearings in London.

Pianoforte Quartet

A still earlier work, however, the Pianoforte Quartet, composed some five years before, when the composer was only sixteen and therefore still more immature, refused to be suppressed, although the Post Office did its best by losing the sole manuscript score somewhere between Italy and London for two whole years. It eventually turned up unscathed and found its way into print through the Carnegie Trust, which at that time was subsidizing the publication of modern British music. Stainer and Bell in 1924 issued the work written in 1918–19 while the composer was still at Oxford. When it was played some years later at an ordinary chamber concert in London, some astonishment and relief was expressed at the mildness of a work from the pen of one who was becoming known as a forcible, and perhaps formidable, writer. Very naturally the quartet shows influences that have not been fully absorbed and it gives few signs of the way the composer was to develop. It is liable therefore to give a wrong impression to anyone who hears it without knowing its place in its creator's development, since it can hardly be called a characteristic work. Yet it does show some of his later characteristics, notably the fluidity of his themes, which are rarely heard in identical spellings at their various reappearances, powerful marcato rhythms, and a certain pungency in the harmony. And it is of extraordinary interest as the forerunner of the concertos, the cantatas, and the symphony. After the String Quartet, Walton abandoned chamber music for twenty-five years in favour of the orchestra, and this juvenile work has therefore this added claim to our attention, that, however little representative it may be, it is the first available example of Walton's writing for concerted chamber ensemble.

The quartet is dedicated to the Right Rev. Thomas Banks Strong, Bishop of Ripon. Before he became Bishop of Ripon, Dr Strong was Dean of Christ Church, and to him, as has already been related, Walton was indebted at the time when the quartet was written for his exhibition at Christ Church.

Putting aside all this critical apparatus the quartet captivates the hearer by its frankly youthful charm and its unabashed romanticism. There are two main streams in Walton's work, sometimes mingling, sometimes parting when one overlays the other. They are this romanticism, which put up its head in the Viola Concerto, and the sheer devilish cleverness which is always uppermost in the witty, the quick, the incisive music, and emerges in prickly rhythms, pungent dissonance, and a general atmosphere of electric sparks. The twenties were not favourable to romanticism, and after this quartet that side of Walton's musical nature takes a back seat for a time. In the Piano Quartet, however, he writes like a romantic, though not like a nineteenth-century composer, and more like a French than a German romantic. Or is that impression merely due to the medium being the same as that employed by Fauré?

The first movement is laid out in regular sonata form, of which the proportions are: exposition 120 bars, consisting of a first and a second subject each of 60 bars—such equality is unusual—a development of 56 bars, and a recapitulation somewhat reduced to eighty-odd bars, rounded off by a coda of 15. The development draws on both the first and second subjects, but does not elaborate them to any great extent, since each has been already expanded immediately upon its first statement in the exposition. The first subject is stated by the violin without any preliminaries—a sixteen bar tune in the Dorian mode over a double pedal point, tonic and dominant, held by the violoncello:

Ex. 1

It has an unequal counterpoise, a downward scale in double octaves from the piano:

Ex. 2

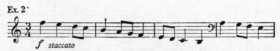

This retort, however, is not an indication that the treatment of the instruments is to be antiphonal. On the contrary, the general method is concerted, but the opening deployment is very adroitly managed with a separate entry for each instrument. Violin and violoncello begin, the viola adds its voice to the last three bars of the opening tune (Ex. 1) to give additional weight to the crescendo, and then the piano breaks in with Ex. 2. Thereupon Ex. 1 is re-stated with full harmony in chords and arpeggios. This process of expansion is carried further as the strings alternate between arco, pizzicato, and tremolando, and the piano between emphatic scales and flowing passage work. The theme breaks up in the process and imitative use of *b* from Ex 1 is the last stage in the link which leads into the second subject. Of this the outstanding feature is a quaver figure—*c* in Ex. 3, and as a preliminary to the statement of the second theme we have this figure played by the first violin over a hint in augmentation of the tune that is just coming played by the second violin. The tonal centre is now G sharp and the signature is actually changed for a few bars to five sharps. The new tune is announced by the piano in octaves:

Ex. 3

The conclusive G sharp is not sounded and the strings pick up the tune from the beginning. The treatment of this second subject runs on very much the same lines as that of the first. Much is heard of figure *c* and a new figure turns up from the first subject, *a* in Ex. I.

The development brings the two subjects into closer relationship, though it also asserts the ascendancy of the first. It begins with Ex. I still Dorian, but now in B, but the opening section of tune is rounded off with the quaver figure *c*. The tonality changes by blunt sequences of chords consisting of superimposed triads garnished in many cases with 'added' notes. The viola is generally busy with figure *c* mostly played tremolando, the violoncello shows an interest in Ex. 2. There is a moment when the rhythm breaks from threes into fives, an earnest of the restless dislocations of regular accents which were to electrify the score of *Façade* and still more of the *Portsmouth Point* overture. The four instruments subsequently break out into an argument of triplets against motifs *a* or *c*, which is only concluded by the emergence of motif *b* as the verdict. Thereupon the recapitulation follows.

The violin duly leads off tranquillo with Ex. I, but the theme is now accompanied by the viola in imitation, by the violoncello with a tremolando phrase built up out of *c*, and by the piano playing sequences of chords. It is no literal recapitulation, and after ten bars the theme shows traces of the influence of the second subject. The little complementary phrase, Ex. 2, is used as a link to the second subject which is now stated in three sharps. In contrast to what precedes it, where a strict diatonic Dorian in D veers to an Aeolian on A, the feeling of the new tonality is that of a clear A major, and the tune Ex. 3 is given out by strings in unison with a piano accompaniment harmonized in chords, all played loud. The compression is less severe than in the case of the first subject, but again the recapitulation is not exact and the order of occurrence to the various constituents is changed. In the coda the work runs down thematically, dynamically, and in texture. A drooping phrase based on *b* is passed from one instrument to the other, and life is only kept in the movement by some triplets which the piano takes over from the violoncello. It ends quietly on a plagal cadence in Dorian D.

The significance of a movement which is essentially simple and is always perfectly straightforward to the ear is the fluidity of the thematic material, the same kind of identity in difference which is the most marked feature of the First Symphony written seventeen years later.

The Scherzo is propelled from the start by a scratchy figure from the strings, such as he was constantly to use later:

Ex. 4
Allegro scherzando

The strings do most of the propulsion through the movement, the piano has the tunes. Of these there are two. The first is

Ex. 5

which, though you might not think it, is in C major, for the basic harmony, though much exacerbated with augmented triads, which are sometimes superimposed on one another, swings comfortably over a C-G-C bass. The second, which might have been written by Elgar and harmonized by John Ireland, has a grand swagger:

Ex. 6

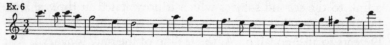

extended to twenty bars.

By way of compensation to the strings for dancing attendance on these two melodies they are given a fugato entirely to themselves on this subject:

Ex. 7

which, it will be observed, is again in the Dorian mode.

The structure of the movement is simple. After an introductory scamper based on Ex. 4 and full of the bizarre flashes that are typical of later Walton, Tune 1 (Ex. 5) emerges on the piano. This first subject is rounded off by a return of the scampering repeated notes, pizzicato notes, trilled notes and various pianistic flourishes that are released by Ex. 4. The second subject is the fugato Ex. 7. When this is finished the piano takes the lead with Ex. 6 plumb in C major. A middle section follows in which various familiar elements are bandied about rather than developed. In particular the snap of Ex. 4 and the six-eight rhythm of Ex. 5 pursue each other. A recapitulation sets in with Ex. 5 transferred to the violin. The fugato duly follows in the same tonality as before and Tune 2 gathers the movement to its climax in the more sonorous key of E flat. It is extended in length and might have gone on for miles if the strings, not in the best of tempers even at the beginning of the movement, had not interrupted and banged down a conclusion on it with which the piano is obliged to concur.

It will have been observed, no doubt, that Ex. 7, the fugue subject, is a revised version of the opening bars of Ex. 1. Other allusions to the first movements also occur, notably reminiscences of *a* and *b*. In this movement there is more of the pungency, both harmonic and rhythmic, that later came to be regarded as Walton's especial sign and signature.

The third is a slow movement, somewhat Brahmsian in character alike in its first melody, the general run of its harmony, and in the interpolation of an agitato episode.

The opening subject is shared between strings and piano:

Ex. 8   Andante tranquillo

This is richly harmonized and then counterstated with more movement and more figuration. A change in the violoncello part has been authorized since the score was published. When the tune Ex. 8 appears in the tenor it is played by the violoncello and not relegated to the pianist's left thumb. Since it is a tune made for the violoncello the alteration is pure gain, especially as there is quite enough triplet movement going on in the other parts.

This tune, Ex. 8, begins and ends the movement. The middle section, however, is not a correspondingly simple strain, though it does contain another melody:

This is plainly a tune for the viola. It is accompanied by chords on the piano and a series of harmonics, for which the composer appears in this movement to have conceived a sudden affection, on the violin. It is repeated in pure three-part string writing. Then the mood is disturbed with agitation at the approach of a long and rather dramatic allusion to the first tune of the first movement, Ex. 1. These three disparate elements are made forcibly to cohere by being placed firmly between the early and late statement of the main tune, Ex. 8.

In the finale the cub Walton shows the claws, rhythmic claws mostly but also some sharp-pointed dissonance, that the young lion was later to put out in the ferocity of *Belshazzar's Feast*. There is also a touch of extravagance in the writing for the instruments, which in point of fact is not fully effective, but does at any rate contribute an effervescing ingredient to the tartness of the mixture. The movement is constructed on the principles of the sonata rondo, the ritornello being a series of rhythmic kicks (*d*) which soon develop into an energetic tune, (*e*) of Ex. 10:

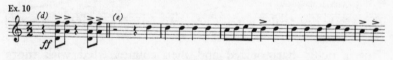

the essence of which is still more concentrated later in

It is characteristic of Walton's tunes that they develop as they proceed, like the Bergsonian conception of evolution in which the present as it unrolls itself from the past carries the past with it. So Walton's tunes are not, like folk tunes or Schubert's tunes or even Beethoven's, developable themes in the nature of statements. Rather are they self-developing ideas, which grow as they go. After a crisp statement of this ritornello a quite obvious transition leads to the first episode, a sustained tune for the violoncello in marked contrast to what has just preceded it:

Ex. 12

espressivo calando

When this has been amplified the ritornello returns, in which a version of Ex. 11 evolves all sorts of things out of itself, so that it almost doubles its original length. The second episode is a fugato on a subject beginning with and running to nine bars in length,

Ex. 13

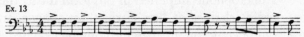

which is a variant of Ex. 10 *e*. This turns back into a new and more cursive version of the ritornello, in which the rhythm is syncopated and contorted. The first episode returns in a different key as a second subject, and brings with it also a non-fugal statement of matters arising out of Ex. 13, culminating in rushing quavers in three different octaves. Just before the final brief return of the ritornello, Ex. 10, there is a subsidence of the turmoil in which the piano reverts once more to the opening bars of Ex. 1 which thus haunt the work throughout its course. Apart from the direct quotations of *a* and *b* from Ex. 1, which we have noted as we have gone along, the little quaver figure in *a* has proved to be the germ of the whole quartet—a germ which persists through many mutations. This thematic identity in differences[1] is a basic element in Walton's style. It is so natural to him that he seems hardly conscious of it. In this quartet we see both the conscious recapitulation of the main idea of Ex. 1 and a more pervasive unconscious persistence of the quaver germ. Which is interesting both as musical thought and as showing how an intensely musical mind works.

[1] To which much attention has been directed by Schenker, Reti, and Alan Walker.

Façade

Façade, as originally planned and executed in 1923, was the name given to an entertainment devised by the Sitwells. On a curtain a monstrous head was painted (the original by Frank Dobson, a later one for the Siena performance by Gino Severini, and a still later one for a performance in May 1942 by John Piper) with an enormous mouth fitted with a megaphone through which some poems of Edith Sitwell were declaimed by a reciter to the accompaniment of Walton's music. The original megaphone was, according to Sir Osbert Sitwell, *Laughter in the Next Room*, pp. 183–4, a Sengerphone, called after the name of its inventor who used it when singing Fafner in *The Ring*. It was replaced in Piper's curtain by a microphone amplifier. In this form the scoring is for flute or piccolo, clarinet or bass clarinet, saxophone, trumpet, violoncello and percussion. In 1926 the composer revised and extended his work, in which form it was given at the Siena meeting of the International Festival of Contemporary Music in September, 1928. Already during the Russian Ballet Season of 1926 at the Lyceum an independent version as an orchestral Suite had been heard, which was put into the programme of the Leeds Festival of 1928. Subsequently a second Suite was made. These two Suites have since been utilized for a ballet by Frederick Ashton, who has taken ten numbers for a set of Divertissements. *Façade* therefore may be heard in three forms: (1) for reciter and chamber ensemble (recorded for Decca by the poet and Constant Lambert); (2) as the accompaniment to a ballet in the Royal Ballet and Ballet Rambert repertories, and (3) as two Suites for full orchestra, either separately or together, in which case some rearrangement of the numbers is officially recommended.

This is not the place for literary criticism, but for a true appreciation of *Façade* in its original form it is well to bear in mind that Edith Sitwell's poems are not written, as most poetry and all prose is written, to develop an idea or pursue a line of thought; on the contrary they play on words which are connected by free association, sometimes of assonance, sometimes of sense. Their train of

thought must not be too relentlessly sought; they must rather be
appreciated as nonsense verse is appreciated 'for the vagueness, the
sheer harmony of word' which is 'emphatically poetry—poetry
run mad, poetry on the verge of becoming music', as the Belgian
poet, Emil Cammaerts, once defined nonsense verse. The difficulty
of any nonsense verse which is not sheer airy-fairy fantasy is like
that of making music on bells, which are all overtones with little
or no foundation tone: Edith Sitwell's poems are made of the overtones of words. The flow of images is determined by exigencies
of rhyme rather than of idea: the sound makes the sense. The
addition of music is a substitute for ideas as the connecting thread
and its function is to unify the roaming discursiveness of the poem.
The possibilities of thus successfully combining two arts on a new
basis is best observed in No. 2 of the first suite, 'Valse', where the
rhythm of the dance-music makes sense of the poem by unifying
the scattered images of Edith Sitwell's word-picture.

The poem begins:

> Daisy and Lily,
> Lazy and silly
> Walk by the shore of the wan grassy sea,
> Talking once more 'neath a swan-bosomed tree.
> Rose castles,
> Tourelles,
> Those bustles—
> Where swells
> Each foam-bell of ermine
> They roam and determine
> What fashions have been and what fashions shall be.

The poems are spoken in level tones and strict time—they are
set in the score to pitchless notes of definite time-values—so as to
depersonalize the voice as far as possible, the megaphone and the
concealment of the reciter being further devices to achieve the
same purpose.

It may be convenient to tabulate the contents of the various
entertainments to which this versatile music has contributed.

I. *Façade Entertainment*
The poems are now grouped in the following order:

Group A. *Hornpipe*
En famille
Mariner Man

Group B. *Long steel grass*
Through gilded trellises
Tango—Pasodoblè

Group C. *Lullaby for Jumbo*
Black Mrs Behemoth
Tarantella

Group D. *A Man from a Far Countree*
By the Lake
Country Dance

Group E. *Polka*
Four in the morning
Something lies beyond the scene

Group F. *Valse*
Yodelling Song
Scotch Rhapsody

Group G. *Popular Song*
Fox-trot 'Old Sir Faulk'
Sir Beelzebub

This selection of twenty-one out of some thirty poems subjected at various times to musical treatment was made for the revival of 1942 and is definitive. The Fanfare, which does not appear in the above list, was in fact used in the earlier recital performances. 'Daphne', 'Through gilded trellises' and 'Old Sir Faulk' have an independent existence as three songs, essays respectively in the English, the Spanish, and the American styles.

II. *The Orchestral Suites*

No. 1. (a) *Polka*
(b) *Valse*

(c) *Swiss Yodelling Song*
(d) *Tango—Pasodoblé*
(e) *Tarantella Sevillana*

No. 2. (a) *Fanfare*
(b) *Scotch Rhapsody*
(c) *Country Dance*
(d) *Noche Espagnole*
(e) *Popular Song*
(f) *Old Sir Faulk* (Foxtrot)

The two Suites may be mixed and played as a whole, lasting twenty-five minutes. In this case the following order is recommended:

(a) *Fanfare*   (II.1.)
(b) *Scotch Rhapsody*   (II.2.)
(c) *Valse*   (I.2.)
(d) *Tango-Pasodoblé*   (I.4.)
(e) *Swiss Yodelling Song*   (I.3.)
(f) *Country Dance*   (II.3.)
(g) *Polka*   (I.1.)
(h) *Noche Espagnole*   (II.4.)
(j) *Popular Song*   (II.5.)
(k) *Old Sir Faulk*   (II.6.)
(l) *Tarantella Sevillana*   (I.5.)

III. *The Ballet.* (First produced by the Camargo Society at the Cambridge Theatre, 26 April 1931.)

(a) *Scotch Rhapsody*   à trois
(b) *Nocturne*   male solo
(c) *Yodelling Song*   a milking scene à quatre
(d) *Polka*   solo en pointes
(e) *Fox-Trot*   à quatre
(f) *Valse*   à quatre danseuses
(g) *Popular Song*   à deux hommes
(h) *Country Dance*   character dance for two men and a girl

    (*j*) *Tango Pasodoblé*   à deux
    (*k*) *Tarantella Sevillana*   ensemble

(*b*), (*e*) and (*h*) were later additions to the original seven numbers.

The musical differences are chiefly of scoring and texture. Thus the saxophone of the chamber ensemble is interchangeable with the cor anglais in the orchestral suites; in some instances the one is marked in the score as preferable, in other cases the other instrument is to be preferred. The Tarantella is noticeably shorter in the *Entertainment* than in the orchestral or ballet version. It will be best to devote my commentary on the music to its fullest, that is, its orchestral, version.

First Suite

    a. Polka. A cheerful rhythm over an oompah bass—an onomatopœic promoted to the status of a technical term by Vaughan Williams—pounds out a respectable tonic-dominant-subdominant foundation for the harmony. Snooks are cocked by all the woodwind together indulging in rapid scale passages, fragments of tune pop up from the various solo instruments, a satirical harmonic progression makes a grimace:

At last what it has been hinting at is shouted without disguise by the trumpet—the old music-hall song, 'See me dance the polka, See me clear the ground':

In the version with recitation the opening words are La-la-la-lo, La-la-lo-la, La (which reinforce the rhythm of the side drum) and the clue is declared at once

> See me dance the Polka
> Said Mr Wag like a bear.

The absence of words in the orchestral suite emphasizes the wit of the music.

b. Valse. This parody valse may put one in mind of Tchaikovsky, Strauss, and even Ravel (the orchestration of Forlane in *Le tombeau de Couperin*). It begins with a bogus piece of *Casse-Noisette*:

The general method of jazz accompaniment—broken figures, displaced accents, cross rhythm, back-chat instrumentation—is applied at once and intensified when the key changes to F. The tune of this part, when it emerges, is Viennese:

And the marcatissimo ebullition of leaping octaves and trills to which it leads is quite in the Johann Strauss manner. This longer second section is enclosed by a recapitulation of the short C major opening.

c. Swiss Jodelling Song. Three things go to this skit on what one feels is the German component of the Swiss scene—an exceedingly sentimental tune, a heavy Ländler rhythm, and scoring, which, for all its hints of cowbells on glockenspiel and xylophone, finally achieves the portable harmonium and zither of a German beer garden. The bassoon first announces the tune without accompaniment.

Various decorations are attached to it—trills from the flutes, a quotation from the *Ranz des Vaches* from the oboes, horn-calls from the brass, melancholy sighs from the woodwind in turn. After this orgy of sentiment the song is concluded by a pert cadence in two keys:

d. Tango—Pasodoblé. There are two music-hall tunes at the back of this Tango, one explicitly stated and the other suggested. 'I do like to be beside the seaside', which is caught up by the composer from the word 'seaside' in the text exactly as Edith Sitwell catches up herself, is played on the cor anglais. It is accompanied by a South American syncopation—lazier than the North American variety employed in the Valse—on the bassoon:

This is how the dance begins. It is interrupted by a gobble-gobble noise which in the original was spoken, but in the full orchestral version is made of trills on strings and ascending broken thirds on the wind rising to a scream. The key changes from E flat to G, and a new, livelier oompah rhythm is started up, against which a tune from off the street is spat out in chunks. Tempo primo and the old key return but before the 'Seaside' tune comes back we hear another:

Is this just a tango tune or is it an allusion to 'Get out and get under the automobile'? Or is that too far-fetched?

e. Tarantella Sevillana. The two chief rhythms of six-eight time are started up at once:

and

which, as played by the wind, is pointed by acciaccature prefixed to each note. The form is that of a Minuet and Trio. The first Minuet is quite short. For the second the key changes from four sharps to four flats; Ex. 9a in various modifications becomes the main tune with a strong thrummed accompaniment on the main beats either underneath it or in alternation, and there is no holding it. For the Trio the key reverts to E major and a tune derived in the last resort from Ex. 9b is slung across the chief non-stop rhythm:

A great deal more rhythmic mischief is going on—indeed in all these dance movements the score bustles with ingenious figures here, there, everywhere and all the time—but it would be confusing to set it out in detail. Certainly in the Tarantella it passes much too swiftly to allow the ear to linger over the piquancies presented to it and as quickly pushed aside by others equally pointed. The work owes its brilliance to this finely jewelled detail of rhythm and orchestration.

The Trio contains, as a trio should, two ideas, and then, after a moment when the stride broadens to 9-8 time, the first Minuet is resumed and developed at greater length than on its first statement and so becomes sufficiently emphatic to provide a conclusive ending to the suite in any of the permutations in which it may be played.

c

Second Suite

a. Fanfare. This movement, Sir Osbert Sitwell tells me, was inspired by a travelling showman with a devil in a bottle at Palermo.

It is a short fanfare in C with a bias towards the Aeolian mode which begins as though, after a single trumpet call, it was to be a summons to attention by a drum and fife band. But it soon adds horns and trumpets in canon—the antithetical use of the two brass instruments is a persistent feature of Walton's scoring. Alto saxophone and/or cor anglais participate but the double basses are silent. In any version of *Façade* the Fanfare leads straight into

b. Scotch Rhapsody. The suggestion is of a Highland reel. The woodwind give out molto vivace a dotted-note tune. After a couple of bars the strings pizzicato and the side drum snap out strong accents at irregular intervals. The central tune which is passed round from one instrument to another as in a partnership of jugglers is this:

Ex. 11

The movement is short. Percussion is copiously used and considerable subtleties are demanded: thus the side drum player is instructed to play on the wood and the cymbal player with a wire brush.

c. Country Dance. Here is more suggestion. We expect pipe and tabor. The tabor begins, but it is not a drum; instead a violoncello pizzicato is made to sound like the rustic drum. The other strings soon give it more volume as flute and clarinet begin their piping. The element of parody is not conspicuous in this number and there is no suggestion either of a traditional English

Country Dance or of a tune from Playford's *The Dancing Master*. The number was composed as an afterthought for the ballet in which it is used as the innocent accompaniment for a dramatic sketch involving a Maiden, a Yokel, and the Squire. The main tune which is stated in canon by flute and clarinet is a very good example of the way in which Walton achieves unity without symmetrical repetitions of pattern: the elements recur but with their various features in different places:

The scoring is exceptionally simple; the strings do nothing but accompany, most of the time pizzicato, the tune which flits from one of the four ordinary woodwind instruments—no sophisticated saxophones here—to the other. The texture, though contrapuntal, is kept very clear; air-holes and breathing spaces break up the melody so that it has to be passed like a football along the forward line, and often enough only mere fragments of it are in the air at any one moment.

d. Noche Espagnole. English simplicity is followed by Spanish exoticity: by the tango in the ballet and by *Noche Espagnole* in the suite. In either case the contrast of treatment is complete. Cor anglais, saxophone, and brass return and the percussion player picks up his most picturesque instruments—castanets, tambourine, and triangle. In the original version the title of the poem to be recited is 'Trio for Two Cats and a Trombone', but none of these instruments actually appears in the score. Various suggestions, however, are contained in the poem, which begins:

> Long steel grass—
> The white soldiers pass
> The light is braying like an ass.

Mouth organ, trumpet, drum, 'the martial cornet', castanets and the 'sound on the onycha' (which however is really a smell[1]) are poured out by the poetess in a riot of imagery and picked up by the composer.

The military evocations are disposed of first by a trumpet call, accompanied by the castanets that stand for 'the tall Spanish jade', who is the heroine of the poem. Soon, however, a swaying figure on the clarinet leads to a free rhapsody on the saxophone over a tango rhythm on the strings. The texture is enriched to a tutti, there is some intricate rhythmic elaboration of the steady pulse of the dance, and the music becomes as voluptuous as its title suggests.

e. Popular Song. From languor we return to healthy vulgarity. It's wonderful what a diminished third can do to an honest tune, and a hiccup to a regular four-bar phrase. The tune is a tune as far as the cadence at the fourth bar, thereafter it becomes an outline sketch of a tune with side drum and cymbal to fill in the gaps. A jazz treatment is thus imposed on a tune that might have come from a music-hall or perhaps from Sousa:

Ex. 13   Grazióso

Observe the diminished intervals on the strong beats; observe the economy which uses the same melodic figure many times over to make up a tune, a feature which is at once the strength and weakness of popular tunes in that it helps to impress them quickly on the casual ear and equally quickly tires it by too much repetition. There is no fear that a composer of Walton's resource will allow

[1] Sir Osbert informed me that his sister found it defined in an old dictionary as 'a shell with strings'; a primitive musical instrument. The shell also produced the smell, an ingredient in incense.

it to go beyond tickling the ear. He provides it now with a descant above on the flute, now with a counterpoint below on the saxophone, and as in 'Noche Espagnole' keeps the tune in a perpetual state of transference from one solo instrument to another.

f. Old Sir Faulk. This is a fox-trot, but it also exists as a song, one of a trilogy composed by the composer to poems in the original *Façade* but not, with the exception of 'Sir Faulk', included in the orchestral suites. The direction to the singer of the song is 'nello stile americano' and to the accompanist, 'sempre molto ritmico'. It is in fact an elaborately scored piece of jazz. 'Old Sir Faulk' is scored for orchestra and not for jazz band. It suggests, but does not imitate, the dance orchestra, but it goes so far as to borrow the percussion and the saxophone of the typical dance band. The drummer should provide himself with 'traps'; bass drum, side drum, cymbal, and Chinese blocks are used. The trombone is asked for a quasi-glissando and has the following solo:

Ex. 14

The saxophone is told to 'slap' his tongue and the horns to flutter theirs; the trumpets put on wa-wa mutes alternately with ordinary mutes. So is the orchestra enriched with jazz effects, so is the jazz band made more resplendent with orchestral tone colours. This is parody inverted.

The general atmosphere of the music is one of incisive, yet not cruel, parody; it has mockery without malice; wit is used as a criticism of style; virtuosity in the use of rhythms and tones epitomizes the taste of a decade in fifty bars of modern music.

Sir Osbert Sitwell has described with a wealth of amusing detail in evocative prose the origins and first private performances of *Façade* in the fourth volume of his autobiography, *Laughter in the Next Room*. The title arose out of a private joke—someone had called his sister clever but only a façade. The distinctive form had its origin in some technical experiments Dame Edith was making with words in dance rhythms. The curtain was evolved in

Dobson's studio while the artist was painting a portrait of Sir Osbert. The music was composed with Walton's fastidious care for detail in sessions with the poetess declaiming her verses. The first performance, which was private, was at 2 Carlyle Square in the Sitwells' drawing-room on 24 January 1922—Sir Osbert gives this date categorically though he elsewhere speaks from memory of the rehearsal for it on the previous day as being a cold day in February. The public performance at the Aeolian Hall which led to something of an uproar was on 12 June 1923. The press reports according to Sir Osbert were angry and contemptuous, and he quotes an example. But *The Times* had a notice, that reads to me like the work of A. H. Fox-Strangways, which characteristically ignores the rumpus and is indeed almost dull.

Miss Edith Sitwell and her brothers have always been apostles of what has been called *épatism* and on Tuesday afternoon at the Aeolian Hall they carried their assault on the accepted things a step farther. Their entertainment, called *Façade*, consisted of a recitation of her poems by Miss Sitwell to an accompaniment of four wind instruments, violoncello and percussion, devised by Mr W. T. Walton. The poems were read in monotone with great rhythmic emphasis through what was called in the programme a 'Sengerphone', which protruded through the mouth of a monstrous head painted on the curtain by Mr Frank Dobson. The object was, as Mr Osbert Sitwell explained, to prevent the personality of the reciter from getting between the poem and the audience. That much was achieved; but it is almost impossible to make words clearly audible through a megaphone unless they are spoken slowly and distinctly. Mr Walton's accompaniments obviously owe a great deal to Stravinsky and are for the most part too spasmodic. Here and there he succeeded in throwing a gleam of light on the words; and when he had definite dance-rhythms to build up he produced clever results.

The next public performance was at the Chenil Galleries in Chelsea on 27 April 1926. The war-time revival at the Aeolian Hall on 29 May 1942, when it was preceded by Schoenberg's *Pierrot Lunaire*, restored to intermittent currency the original or *Entertainment* form, which had for a time been eclipsed by the popularity of the Suites.

CHAPTER II

Larger Orchestral Works

Symphony No. 1 in B flat minor-major

THE classical symphony was an elaborate structure based on key. Architecturally speaking there was room in its design for a luxuriant variety of thematic material disposed with a good deal of individual variety, but always ensuring coherence by a balance of contrasted tonalities. The composer was able to effect such a balance by means of harmony. The resources of harmony were constantly enriched by the increasing subtlety of the composer's imagination and by the ability of the listener's ear, lagging a little behind maybe, but none the less steadily advancing, to appreciate the logic of harmonic progression. During the nineteenth century this harmonic development went beyond its structural functions and began to be used decoratively: chromatic harmony, in fact, for all its own dazzling possibilities, weakened the structure, just as encrustations of decorative plaster tend to weaken an architectural design. It ultimately undermined the stability of key and the extravagance of its development led to exhaustion. At the end of the century composers began to feel that tonality, after a useful and enormously fruitful career of three centuries, was finished as an organic principle of design. They began to look elsewhere—to the old modes, to non-harmonic counterpoint, to the simultaneous use of several keys whereby a new kind of tonal balance was effected, and even to the rejection of any kind of centre of gravity in favour of purely arbitrary schemes of construction. After the second world war serialism, proposed by Schoenberg a quarter of a century previously, became the favoured principle of structure. This atonality seems very much like trying to abolish gravity and attempting to build from the roof downwards. At any rate there is a certain amount of evidence to show that the ear, as a psychological organ of apprehension, demands by its own nature some sort of tonal centre as a base from which it can make its explorations into the imaginative possibilities of sound. If harmonic development has weakened the unifying force of key, it has only thereby increased the need for some other rallying point for the ear.

Walton wrote his First symphony in 1932–5 when there was a good deal of restless experimenting after new principles of cohesion for instrumental music that aspired to long flights. He was prepared to use the most far-fetched harmony, which in vulgar parlance means strong and acute discord, and he had therefore to obtain some cohesive agent capable of bearing the disruptive strain to be put upon it. His choice fell on the simplest, the most primitive and the most direct—the pedal-point. He puts down a note, or maybe a chord, in the bass and does not allow you to lose sight of it for a moment—it is his sheet-anchor, his tonal centre, his tonic.

It is worth while, therefore, to look at the bass of the first movement and observe its behaviour independently of what is going on above it. For the sheer amount of tone produced from a thick and heavily scored texture of dissonant harmony and self-willed contrapuntal lines requires a more drastic assertiveness on the part of the bass, if single-handed it is to control the tonality, than when it progresses harmonically, contrapuntally or thematically as in classical symphonies. A bass note is put down and sustained for long stretches. When it moves it shifts stiffly on to a neighbouring note or gravitates by uneasy passage towards a new tonal centre. Even when, as at [14] the bass enunciates a theme (a version of Ex. 9 below) it is only a momentary occurrence lasting eight bars between fixture on C and fixture on F. Again, even in the middle section, which retains some of the harmonic mobility of the classical development section, the bass is ever resisting freedom of movement, and asserting by mere persistence the broad tonality of the movement. At one point (between [25] and [30]) a pedal chord moves up the chromatic scale, but it manages to lever itself back on to F and thence to the B flat pedal-

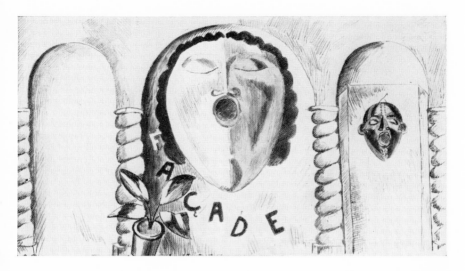

Plate 1   Two designs for the *Façade* screen
(a) By Frank Dobson for the 1923 performance at the Aeolian Hall
(b) By John Piper for a performance in 1942

Plate 2 The composer as a young man

Plate 3   The composer in 1973

point that marks the beginning of a compressed recapitulation at [33].

This extended use of the pedal-point entails a very different treatment from that of a bagpipe's drone. It permits of reinforcement by a dominant pedal sounded either simultaneously, as in the opening of the symphony, or in alternation with it, when it has the usual projective force of dominant harmony. It may take the form of a chord, as in the instance already quoted of a moving minor sixth. It may also be strengthened by oscillations on either side of the main note, as for instance at the point just before [4] where the tuba throws in its weight in order to move the centre of gravity to C:

1st Symphony
Ex. 1

which only differs from an organ-pedal G in being more emphatic.

This method of regulating the harmonic flow of the music by a stiff bass is like the determination of a river's course by the corners of its banks. Its main direction is clear, but it winds and divides itself into reaches. The reaches vary in length; each is self-contained while it lasts, but at the next corner a new view is revealed. So this symphony flows clearly in B flat minor, with a double pedal of tonic and dominant to assert the fact at the opening and the close, for the pointed figures of Ex. 2 constitute a double drone with an

Ex: 2

ictus. The use of the dominant, F, to give a rhythmic kick to the pedal point should be noticed, for F is to occupy the position of mediator between the main and the subsidiary tonalities. At the risk of tedium to the reader, but as a direction post to those who have a score at hand a further paragraph shall be devoted to the goings-on of the bass.

The second subject of the exposition is to cluster round C, and this new tonality is approached by twelve bars of its dominant G, as we have just seen in Ex. 1 above. C is now maintained continuously for twenty-three bars. When it is relinquished the theme, Ex. 7 below, contrives still to maintain the tonality by circling round the note C. The bass now begins to drop and dwells for a time (17 bars) on E. The next section of the movement which constitutes the central section of the second subject (beginning at [11] 'a tempo agitato') is securely pinned to C by alternations of pedals on G and C. The third section, after [15], is clearly in some sort of F, rising, as the middle section of the movement is approached, to F sharp and thence by stages to B, which dominates the first half of the development. F natural recaptures the latter part of this section, and so acts as a dominant preparation for the return of B flat at [33] for the recapitulation, which, with the coda, is anchored to the tonality of B flat with very little movement of the bass.

We have then, broadly speaking, a tonal scheme in which the balance is struck between B flat minor and a chromatic kind of C. We have also a formal scheme, tripartite, as in the classical symphony, but thematically more closely knit and more continuous in development. Analysis along orthodox lines, so far as it is possible, is advantageous in, so to speak, a geographical sense—it enables you to know where you are in the movement. It also provides a framework in which various kinds of balance can be struck—a balance of themes, of keys and of sheer length as between one section and another. This symphony chiefly differs from the classical symphony in the disposition of its first and second subjects—using 'subject' in the accepted sense of a mass of thematic material. Thus the first subject is short (63 bars) and compact; but its main theme, Ex. 3 below, dominates the movement by refusing to be confined to its place in the tonic key in the exposition. It draws attention to itself when the key changes, just where one would expect new material to take the stage; it does the same thing again in the third section of what from its place in the scheme one would call the second subject group, and it echoes through to the end of the section in a new theme (Ex. 10) that is ultimately derived from itself (Ex. 3). By thus quelling each new theme as it appears Ex. 3 maintains its supremacy. If allowance is made for this very important modification, it is permissible to analyse the movement as in sonata form since its structure is tripartite, and its musical subject matter is an abstract argument of themes and a balance of tonalities. The key and thematic issues, however, are not fought out together, as in the classical symphony, but independently, though overlapping each other.

The key scheme we have already examined. We now have to look at the thematic material. As soon as a drum roll has conjured a B flat out of silence and the horns have confirmed the key, the second violins reaffirm it in their fashion, which consists of a light but markedly rhythmic figure in two pieces—*a* and *b* of Ex. 2 above. At once a tune is announced by the oboe, a tune reminiscent of Sibelius, as indeed is all the first subject, a fact which suggests that the starting point for the symphony in the composer's mind was the work of Sibelius which was the dominating influence in England at the time it was written. Walton's views on Sibelius, however, soon outgrow the scope of an essay in musical criticism and develop a spacious argument entirely of their own, conducted in a language that is entirely the composer's own. The Sibelian tune which constitutes the first theme of the first subject is this:

A pendant to it, which assumes great importance later on, is tacked on by the flute and immediately accepted by the oboe:

and a further pendant is linked to this by the bassoon:

which also becomes important, notably as discharged by the trombone at [13] where the bass moves decisively to C and in the recapitulation at [36]. Meantime the violonçello has dropped a hint of the bass it means to develop:

Ex. 5

In an augmented form this becomes (at [1])

Ex. 6

poco marcato

of which the importance is the interval of the seventh. For the seventh characterizes one of the second subject themes and it is the limiting outline of the chord of the diminished seventh, a chord universally reprobated by post-romantic composers, which is nevertheless to be found at the heart of this modern symphony—though not in the finale.

Key is usually regarded as the main determinant in an orthodox sonata form of the arrival of the second subject, though there is the case of Beethoven's Piano Sonata in A, op. 101, where the new key is established before the new theme arrives, and it is possible to conduct an academic debate on how long the first subject lasts and where the second subject begins. In this symphony, as already indicated, a similar legalistic quibble arises if attempts are made to analyse it on orthodox sonata lines, for when the secondary tonality of C has been reached and held by a pedal C, the first theme to be heard is the first subject (Ex. 3) loudly proclaimed by all the woodwind and subsequently reaffirmed by the strings.

There is no doubt, however, that we reach the end of a section at [7] and a new tune, the first of the second subject group, is announced by the violins and a couple of solo violoncellos playing in unison:

Ex. 7

mp sostenuto   poco f   f

This tune in its counterstatement develops a triplet figure:

Ex. 7a

which makes it readily identifiable in subsequent appearances and the gruppetto *f* enlarges itself to contain five instead of four quavers.

Under the tune Ex. 7 the second violins and violas have in alternation a new accompanimental figure:

Ex. 8

in which the prongs of the fork *g* spell out the chord of the diminished seventh. And in this disguise the chord permeates the music, until at [10] a new theme (containing prominent sevenths) appears:

Ex. 9

This is the second constituent of the second subject. The third is an agitato passage which issues in a fantasia on the chord of the diminished seventh with the first subject—Ex. 3 *c*—hurled against it. (The tonality at this point is a firm C.) Next comes a version of Ex. 9 stated by all the basses including the tuba, but excluding the trombones. Finally a portmanteau tune derived from the first subject, an amalgam of Ex. 3 and Ex. 4, rounds off the exposition:

Ex. 10

The middle section begins with the first subject Ex. 3 in A flat, but the tone is damped down to a pianissimo. This next part of the movement is to provide the contrast of comparative quiet and reduced speed and impetus. After Ex. 3 comes Ex. 9 on the bassoon, which, when joined by the flute, presents Ex. 4 in the form of Ex. 11:

and so provides a text for considerable discussion. The time is further slackened after [22], and an episode marked 'espressivo con dolore' follows in which the same motif, Ex. 11, is heard from the oboes, with violoncello, horn and bassoon in turn making sympathetic comments on it in contrapuntal solos. The background, however, is the mutter of strings played tremolando, a source of unrest that very soon restores animation and power. Ex. 9 is next recalled by the horn [25]. At [26] Ex. 3 c sounds its alarm once more, and the bass in minor sixths climbs chromatically from D and B flat to A and F with the tonality pivoting round A until it returns to F (with suitable supertonic alternations on C) for a return to B flat. The recapitulation is projected not only by all this thorough preparation in the bass, but with a catapult-like force derived from a climax of trills, tremolos, and short powerful figures. Thus the middle section is a steadily developing dynamic crescendo.

The recapitulation thus launched is condensed to half the length of the exposition. All the main themes are recalled—Ex. 3, Ex. 7 and Ex. 4, and then summarily and powerfully Ex. 9 in its horn version. There is a sudden interjection of crashing dissonance by the whole brigade of brass at [41]. This interruption precipitates the coda, which poises first on an A flat pedal before moving to B flat to conclude the movement, as it began, with Ex. 2 and an emphatic chord of B flat major.

The interest of the second movement is not thematic or structural, but rhythmic and dynamic. And the rhythms and stresses are applied to produce an emotional effect uncommon in music—malice. This Scherzo is headed 'presto, con malizia'.

Now ill-will is not one of the sentiments which music finds it easy to portray. The only method it has at its disposal for doing it is the creation of organized disorder. It is hard to conceive of evil otherwise than as the negation of good, of which the mind has a direct intuition. The nature of goodness is broadly speaking apprehended as a harmony—in its literal sense of a fitting together. Evil is a disruption of that harmony. Music itself is a system of harmonious relationships, i.e., of sounds that fit as to euphony and rhythm. When it is called on to portray the opposite of the good it does so by disrupting its own harmonies (again using the word not in the limited technical sense, but as representing every kind of melodic, contrapuntal, rhythmic way of fitting sounds together). To deceive the expectant ear by a displaced accent is therefore the first fall from innocence. Jagged and broken time-lengths, irregular groupings, wilful misplacements become sinister, and their forceful iteration is damnation itself. So does Vaughan Williams portray Satan in *Job*.

Walton inherited from Stravinsky the method of scattering bar-lines and drumming away at gritty chords on all the wrong beats. His early work is full of the prickly, restless energy that was set free by the disintegration of normal organic rhythms—*Portsmouth Point* is the conspicuous instance of such a release of high-tension current and *Belshazzar's Feast* uses the same means of generating forceful expression in the interests of drama. In this Scherzo the drama is not specified, but one constantly feels that the curtain is up, and that the furious forces will become persons contending on a stage. It is not ballet music, but one expects it to become that at any moment.

The tonality is a Dorian E with the flattened seventh made prominent by inclusion wherever convenient in the tonic chord. As in the first movement, which also uses a prominent flattened seventh in its tonal scheme, this tonality is established and the general rhythmic run of the movement opened out by an animated drone of tonic and dominant, E and B. The first theme—for there must be themes in which to embody rhythms in any music above that of a rhapsody for drums—is a gruff sequence of thirds, distinguished by internal syncopations and harmonic false relations:

Ex. 12 Presto

This is repeated by the violins with various adjuncts and flying commentary from other parts of the orchestra. Between this and the next obvious theme occurs a swift episode of angular rhythm —threes and fives in alternation. Soon comes the savage tune

Ex. 13

six bars to be extended to eight on subsequent appearances. There is here a thematic relationship with Ex. 3 of the first movement both in the repeated notes and in the contour, and there is also an amusing recrudescence of the chord of the diminished seventh when the violins and cellos in all seriousness and solitude play 'sul tasto' (i.e., with the nasal tone of finger-board production):

Ex. 14

There is no formal recapitulation, but both Ex. 12 and Ex. 13 are heard more than once in the headlong course of the movement and at one point [76] they occur together.

It is difficult to describe the devices by which the pieces of agitated rhythm are forced under pressure into a continuous torrent. It is easier to take a glance at the score and observe how their order rooted in disorder stands, if one may borrow and distort a Tennysonian phrase to account for the *malizia* already discussed. There is just before the final climax one further piece of wickedness. The whirling atoms of rhythm, which usually come together to make a crescendo of tension, get softer to make a quite appreciable and very misleading diminuendo. But the withdrawal is only *pour mieux sauter*, and the movement clatters to its close with every instrument going at it hammer and tongs.

In the slow movement attention reverts to themes and their behaviour, but it is a melodic rather than a structural interest that engages the listener—and the analyst. There are certain superficial similarities of method to the first movement. Tonalities are established in the same way by persistent bass notes used as centres of gravity. Development is even more continuous, and one theme seems to evolve out of another without the paraphernalia of sonata form, and in spite of the absence of familiar direction posts an equally organic unity is achieved. The movement grips the more for being less violent than its predecessors. It is very much more contrapuntal in texture, and seeing that the themes change their outline as they grow—the sign manual of Walton's style—they are mostly etched in the decisive lines of woodwind solos. Indeed there is a moment in the middle (at [88]) where the violins make an entry that is arresting because they have had hardly any melodic work to do up to that point. It has the inevitable rightness of something not consciously missed before, but now obviously needed.

The moods of violence and malice are passed; the slow movement is ruminative and tinged with melancholy—it is so marked. And so a feeling of romance is engendered which looks back to the viola concerto and forward to the violin concerto, though the harmony remains sufficiently astringent and the counterpoint sufficiently independent to avoid all suggestion of anachronism or incongruity with its present surroundings. The chosen tonality is C sharp, equidistant by a minor third from the B flat of the first movement and the E of the second.

The flute announces the parent theme over a pedal point:

Ex. 15

D

This theme, if taken by itself, would gravitate to F sharp minor, but the main tonality, propounded by the pedal in the opening bars and confirmed by its reassertion in the last, is C sharp minor. This is an instance of a tendency towards bipolarity of keys to be found already in the earlier Sinfonia Concertante. Tonic and dominant no longer stand in their old fixed relation to each other, but rival one another in importance—after all, even in Beethoven there are instances of their simultaneous assertion. But Walton's practice seems rather to be due to a liking for modal ambiguity as a means of obtaining intensity of effect.

It will be observed that the melody, Ex. 15, has a curious tendency to resolve its dissonances not upon harmony notes but on the unison. Its pattern is that of Ex. 4, which has a far-reaching influence on the whole symphony: the quaver gruppetto is important in that it influences the contour of the other themes. The next two appear together over a lightly held pedal G sharp:

These are very soon followed by a tune that is obviously a development of the oboe theme of Ex. 16:

which is repeated several times by various instruments and finally answered by the string entry already referred to. These solos proceed quite quietly and the tranquillity is not disturbed by the entry of the drum playing a pedal C in triplets. Pianissimo: but it pervades the flow of the music, and triplet figuration is maintained after the bass is changed and a quasi-recapitulation begun with the reappearance of Ex. 15 on woodwind, horns and strings in octaves. Before this happens, however, the sinuous figure *g* of Ex. 17 threads in and out of the texture calling attention to the flat-sharp oxymoron of the last two F's in figure *g*—a very characteristic Waltonism.

The reprise, when it comes, is interesting for the fact that the tonic key is not established either with or by the first subject (i.e., Ex. 15), but is reaffirmed when the turn of the second subject comes. The first subject is recapitulated in F. The tonic key of C sharp for the second subject (the double tune of Ex. 16) is established in the usual way by a pedal. This pedal lasts till the end of the movement with only a moment's intermission for a rhetorical, and indeed passionate, appeal in reiterated chords just before the music broadens out to a quieter mood of final resignation. At the very last the flute recalls with a sigh the essence of Ex. 15.

Finale

The last movement of the symphony was composed some time after the other three, which had even had their first public performance before the composer had decided how to bring to a logical and emotionally satisfying conclusion the many vigorous issues and the conflicting moods which he had let loose in allegro, scherzo, and slow movement. Recourse to the technical procedure of fugue was probably the easiest way of resolving the deadlock. For, in any form of composition, literary, musical or pictorial, the 'how' and the 'what' of expression cannot be separated in the artist's mind, so that he can seek the solution of his problem of their complete integration by either route. If the more common way is to cast about for the best way of saying something which he has in his mind to say, it is still equally possible to concentrate on the choice of a medium or a method, with a resultant clarification of the content of his thought when he has found it. So here. The technical decision brought with it the right expressive content.

Certain changes were dictated by the adoption of fugal procedure: the pedal point is necessarily more restricted in function and the treatment of the main themes becomes more stable and less polymorphic. Incidentally there is less pre-occupation with the interval of a seventh in this movement.

It may be noted in passing that Vaughan Williams made the same decision to write a fugal finale in his F minor symphony which was roughly contemporary with Walton's. There, too, the ordered summary of a fugue was found to be the best way of resolving violent emotions.

The organic connexion of the finale with the rest of the symphony, however, apart from the superficial testimony of the ear is attested thematically by the prominence and persistence of the following motif:

Ex. 18

Ex. 18 is not a quotation but a formulation of the main subject of the movement, and the initial octave swoop from the little C to the big C stands for various forms of anacrusis. Its relationship to Ex. 3 *d* and still more to Ex. 4, of which it is a kind of inversion, in the first movement, and its rhythmic resemblance to Ex. 17 of the slow movement link the last movement securely to its predecessors. So does its tonality—B flat once again, but more major than minor.

Structurally, the movement falls into four clearly defined sections: a forceful exposition in two parts, two fugal, or at any rate highly contrapuntal, middle sections, and a recapitulation of the introductory maestoso of the exposition for epilogue—the rest of the first section, 'brioso ed ardentemente', is not recalled.

We begin, then, maestoso in Walton's most ceremonious manner and in B flat, with our faithful servant the pedal-point to put us securely on our tonal feet before we are caught by the vigorous blast of the quick brioso section, which is to become feroce before we are through it. Over the B flat sounds with no uncertain voice Ex. 18 written out in longer notes and with a

double anacrusis, namely a swirling scale from the strings and a
striding arpeggio from the wind. It is repeated time and again
with a diminution of itself by way of emphasis and punctuation:

From this massive enunciation of a pregnant text the composer
breaks into a fiery harangue, consisting of short motifs welded
together by the sheer speed and violence with which they follow
one upon another. But however fast and far they go, Ex. 19 in
some form or another snaps in on them. Otherwise, apart from
this recurring figure, there is not much resemblance in the thematic scraps when microscopically viewed. Project them, however, in sequence, as they are here propelled through the orchestra
(often in antiphony between wind and strings), and they form a
coherent thematic line with, of course, a supercharged vitality.
It is thematic material shot out of a volcano to form a stream of
lava.

The stream suddenly breaks at [112] and starts again in a trickle
marked, as is appropriate to volcanic activity, focosamente, i.e.,
fierily. This livid trickle is the subject of a fugue:

It is enunciated by second violins and violas with such extra
tingle as quick up- and down-bows and semi-quaver rests can impart to this bold outline. Its pungency is also increased by reinforcement at various points with doublings from the woodwind.
The subject at subsequent reappearances sometimes wears a new
nose and a different tail, but from the last beat of the first bar to
the end of the eighth bar it is constant and 'real'.

So, the subject having started firmly in E flat, the answer duly follows in the eleventh bar in B flat. The counter-subject appears in slightly varied forms, but its essence consists of forward semi-quaver movement followed by an octave drop:

Ex. 21

The third voice enters with the subject in the bass. Upon the conclusion of this statement the first bar of the subject, figure *h*, is taken and worked in imitation, with the brass, hitherto silent, putting in their oar. A middle entry in D follows in the soprano voice with the bass pursuing it in imitation at a bar's distance, until the whole thing breaks off with a loud snap as the lines of contrary motion converge. A calm episode now supervenes. The oboe plays this theme:

Ex. 22

which is as close-fisted as the fugue subject was open-handed. But observe that the new theme follows the general melodic outline of the old, though its contours are much flatter, and the little cadence figure *j* recalls similar turns of phrase in the previous movements. Fragments of the fugue subject, Ex. 20, are heard in counterpoint with Ex. 22, which is soon repeated a minor third higher. The strings appear to become uneasy at the continuation of this seeming depression and begin to murmur 'sul ponticello'. Their agitation brings horn and trumpet to the rescue. They loudly proclaim the first bars of the subject (Ex. 20 *h*) in the tonic key and in augmentation. It is enough: the subject in full sweeps in with all the majesty of trumpet and trombone in octaves, and after much jubilant reiteration of *h* we are ready for the next stage in the movement's progress.

The time changes to 3/8 and the tempo to vivacissimo. When

the change of mood has been sufficiently established a new fugal movement is started with this version of Ex. 22 as its subject:

Ex. 23

This time fugal procedure is very informal. The subject is accompanied right from the start with a counterpoint. Its answer appears a diminished fifth higher and no further complete statement is made of it. Instead we hear recapitulatory hints of Ex. 20 *h* and something even more fundamental:

Ex. 24

which on inspection turns out to be an allusion, several times repeated, to Ex. 18 from the introduction of the movement. Soon indeed we have a complete restatement of the first fugue subject, Ex. 20 (though written out in the notation of the second, i.e. in 3/8 time). Entries of *h* in stretto lead to a considerable climax, which, however, is not broken off but is dispelled in a diminution of time and speed to the final section.

The maestoso part of the exposition returns in full power, and Ex. 18 sums up both finale and the symphony as a whole in its concise and cogent diatonic declaration of faith.

Thus the composer, after taking the unprecedented step of allowing an 'unfinished' symphony to come to performance (as it was by the London Symphony Orchestra on 3 December 1934, when Sir Hamilton Harty conducted the first three movements) succeeds in resolving the problem that had given him pause. The first complete performance was given at a B.B.C. Concert at Queen's Hall on 6 November 1935, under Sir Hamilton Harty.

It is worth noting that the instrumentation employed for the symphony is that of the orthodox full orchestra and makes no demands for additions to the wind (such as the saxophone), luxuries (like the brass bands in *Belshazzar's Feast*), nor special percussion until the last movement. Two each of the woodwind, four horns, three trumpets which incidentally are 'in C', three trombones, and tuba constitute with drums and strings a modest 'full orchestra' for a modern work. The extra percussion required in the finale is an additional set of timpani (two players), cymbals, side-drum, and gong. The drama of *Belshazzar's Feast* with its large choir of voices had demanded a much enlarged orchestra capable of producing special effects (which are sometimes dispensed with in performance); the purely musical issues of the symphony can be adequately presented on a more modest orchestra, hardly larger till the finale than that used by Brahms.

Symphony No. 2

Between the First and Second Symphonies was a gap of a quarter of a century, in which the substantial but still smaller works like the overtures and the Partita, itself a kind of sinfonietta, had kept the composer's hand in at orchestral writing, but apart from *Troilus and Cressida*, and to some extent the concertos, Walton's range of thought and imaginative span had not been fully stretched. When the Second Symphony came the first impressions were that if the composer was attempting once more to scale the heights either he had failed to achieve his purpose or the height scaled was not after all so high. It was, it seemed, a smaller symphony, to the hostile critic not significant, to the friendly critic rather in the position of Brahms's Second vis-a-vis his First Symphony, or like Nos. 4 and 8 in the Beethovenian canon. To begin with it is not so long, playing under half an hour; to continue it has only three movements. The mastery was there of course, more easy and assured than ever, but did it not perhaps fail to conceal an inner poverty of imagination, a lack of compulsion? Though the symphony went round the world it did not get a very warm welcome at home in Britain. True, the critical fraternity was off on one of its periodical bouts of whoring after strange (though not necessarily false) gods, Bartók, Stra-

vinsky, Schoenberg, Webern, anybody but honest English, to
which Vaughan Williams while he was alive had kept them at
least respectful. I cannot plead guilty myself to a public under-
estimation of the work, though between the first performance at
Edinburgh on 2 September 1960 and the time when the Cleveland Orchestra's record and a full score for purposes of this study
were acquired I must have had some private reservations like
those I much deplored in my colleagues' reactions to *Troilus
and Cressida*—that it neither broke new ground nor scaled the
heights. To that reproach I would always answer, 'Why should it?
No one demanded that of Haydn or Mozart; it is a post-Beet-
hoven aesthetic to demand advance or novelty as essential to the
validity of a new work. Every work of art exists in its own right.'

If I had such reservations I now think that the Second Symphony
is a work that does not in spite of a lucid design yield its full
meaning, all its beauties and the qualities that determine its value
on a few hearings. Familiarity breeds respect. I say this, although
I also say arrogantly enough that in a long career of professional
listening I have rarely revised my opinion of a new work for the
better, but only sometimes have concluded that a work has been
overpraised. What I said[1] was this:

The compact new symphony bears Walton's unmistakable finger-
prints, the electrical discharge of energy in short and rapid figures, the
urgent melodies depending largely on the interval of the seventh, the
tight but withal clear contrapuntal web, and the mastery of orchestral
effect. Its emotional roots seem to be apprehension (in both senses) of
the turbulence of our lives, meditation upon it, and resolute action,
which, after the conflict presented by clash of tonalities, succeeds in
containing that disquieting turbulence.

The last movement is the longest and most elaborately organized:
the exercise of the will is conducted in a powerful passacaglia and its
decisive stroke in a fugato. The first movement is thus a brutal exposition in a kind of scherzo recalling the con malizia marking of his first
symphony. The slow movement weaves melody in and out of melody
poignantly and urgently. Nothing showed Mr Pritchard's skill in reading the composer aright more than the beauty he extracted from this

[1] In *The Times* of 3 September 1960.

central movement by sheer elucidation of the texture, though the excitement of the piled-up tension in the complex finale was realized so surely as to bring immediate acclamation from the audience. Here at last was something by which to remember this festival [the Edinburgh Festival].

The suggested emotional programme seems sound enough, though the attribution of the turbulence may be too specific. Walton always writes as though composition is a safety valve for a tremendous internal pressure. Internal pressures however must in part be caused by the world in which the person lives, and though Walton is personally reticent and has never written programme music outside his films he no more than any modern person lives in an ivory tower, even though Ischia may seem something like one. But what seems to escape one in this symphony is its individuality, its subtler beauties, its individual flavour, which is superficially lost in the general Waltonian characteristics enumerated in my first paragraph of the *The Times* notice.

The facts about the symphony are that it was commissioned by the Royal Liverpool Philharmonic Orchestra which reserved to itself the right of its first performances, but generously, or perhaps in requital of the honour of being asked to appear at an Edinburgh Festival, waived its claim to a first performance in its own city.

It is scored for a large orchestra of triple woodwind, the usual brass, two harps and a piano, besides a large battery of percussion requiring four players (excluding the timpanist). The vibraphone is important in that it colours the sonority at several points in the symphony, a kind of icy pervasiveness made more frosty by piano and celesta. There is a Bell in D which emits one note only during the course of the symphony—at the very end, [326] in the score, to introduce the last twelve bars of coda.

The movements are severally differentiated by their plumage—the xylophone for instance is not used till the finale, the cassa chiara which is a side drum to be distinguished from the tambour militaire only by its size and clarity, i.e., its opacity ratio, is also reserved for the third movement. Walton is very particular about niceties of effect to be obtained from the subtle use of membraphones and idiophones, but the terminology is less certain than his intentions. Walter Piston in his book *Orchestration* says of the snare drums: 'Identification of the various kinds of snare drum indicated in scores is often problematical. The names have different meanings in different countries, so that translations in printed scores are sometimes misleading and this is further complicated by divergent usage by both composers and performers.' Walton demands four varieties of *caisse* or *cassa*, tambour militaire, caisse claire, gran cassa, and tamburino. Timpani of course, being of definite pitch, come into another category.

The surface, or what I have called the plumage, of the music is of course integral with the substance. But owing to our (legitimate) use of the word 'superficial' we are inclined to think of the superficies as something separate from the substance, which of course it is not—the surface is merely the topside of the substance. But in this symphony the pungent, astringent, acidulated flavour —one could go on all through the limited vocabulary of the sense of taste from sherbet to ginger beer and peppermint in search of an epithet that would even faintly convey the sound-quality of the music—is integral with the thought, as a simple excerpt from the opening bars will show. A chord of G, i.e. tonic and dominant G and D is to have a top constituent—one must not call it garnish for it is part of the substance—of B flat and C sharp. The first important motif spells it out explicitly.

Here is the germ of the whole movement, as can be shown by the new method of precipitation by the process of thematic analysis, which leaves out the rhythm and concentrates the intervallic essence into these cabalistic formulae:

of which the interpretation is as follows: A is the abstract of Ex. 1 above, the essence of the first subject, B is a similar abstract of the second subject Ex. 6; *a* is an octave, *b* is a Waltonian sharp seventh, *c* is an augmented second or a minor third, *d* (in B) is the G and D which underlie Example 1. It is wonderful what you can do with this sort of analysis if you have enough faith and ingenuity. Anyhow, these pungent intervals, sharp sevenths and sharp seconds, are not only thematic germs but gustatory flavours. Taste them and see how Walton serves them up. In a swift surreptitious anacrusis (down, though, instead of up) the clarinet burbles

The flute and the first harp follow on the strong beat with

though this is to misrepresent the harp in that he has an arpeggio of nine notes spread over two octaves, and his companion, the second harp, plays a stolid chord making a kind of clonk. At the same time the squealing E flat clarinet puts the same sequence of notes in a different order as do the trumpets and trombones with the omission of G and the addition of A:

Violins and violas also play, alla corda and divisi punta, various combinations of the same notes and intervals. The celesta does the same with different figuration and the piano soon adds its quota.

The impact on the ear of all this sharp glitter makes one suspect the presence of the vibraphone, as in the Cello Concerto and Vaughan Williams's Eighth Symphony, but no, it is reserved for a single note in the coda. All these instrumental parts are carefully marked with dynamic, expressive and technical directions.

So minute an analysis of a few bars is intended to show not only how highly polished is the score and how careful the composer is in the minutiae, but how closely thought and manner, substance and effect, are integrated.

Structurally the symphony is straightforward. The first movement can be analysed as a sonata form with a very obvious bridge passage between first and second subjects, consisting of a fining away to a single strand of violin and viola cantilena. The first subject itself starts with Ex. 1 and grows a number of short ejaculatory, congruent phrases that under pressure of pace, accent and consistent figuration (notably in the celesta part) build up into a coherent paragraph. The key centre round which the tonality ebbs and flows is G, a tart G with an F sharp, C sharp, and B flat in its final chord—there is a parallel for this sort of acidulated tonality in Roussel's Second Symphony, in which also a common chord is inflected with some higher harmonics.

The second subject begins with the phrase of which the abstract has already been given in the formula B of Ex. 2 above. Its melodic shape is

Ex. 6

and it is doubled in the Elgar manner with woodwind taking different shreds of it, a sort of *Klangfarben*; indeed, the clarinet takes over from the viola before the end of the phrase, which actually is left open so that pieces of it can be handed around. But not for long; a new idea is introduced agitato. This is noisy with glissandi, percussion, brass, and short snaps and stutters on the strings. A codetta dominated by an aspiring figure epitomized thus by the piano:

leads to the middle section, which is signalized by greater speed—vivace.

This development is concerned to build up a central climax out of the motif

which it will be observed is made up of the intervals of the major seventh, the minor third and the octave, that otherwise put together occur in Ex. 1 and with less resemblance in shape in Ex. 2, by means of a sustained and huge crescendo: the texture is fined down at the beginning and is going full blast with all brass and a great deal of percussion at the end. The two semi-quavers in Ex. 8 become quadruplets and quintuplets. Ex. 1, sometimes extended, appears on violins or wind at various pitches. By the time a brioso section is reached ('poco più mosso') the wind is breaking into trills and the strings have resumed their snatching figure (originally marked 'talone') in a new shape till the whole orchestra boils like milk and, as always happens with milk, boils over in a trumpet solo:

which is an expansion of Ex. 1. It subsides into the recapitulation, in which the first subject is half the length of its exposition. The second subject is rather longer than in the exposition. Indeed Ex. 2 is extended to a whole paragraph of violin melody running on into the agitato section. This in turn is extended into a further development or codetta before the arrival of the Coda, which begins quietly with a horn solo and then repeats Ex. 1 over and over again for emphasis. Some brusque chords give way to a quiet ending and the chord of G minor acidulated.

The slow movement recalls the lyricism of the Viola Concerto and is brimming with ideas of great immediate beauty; it might be a symphonic poem or even at its climax an operatic scena. Its form is organic, i.e. each idea grows out of its predecessor, though there are two elements recapitulated, one the key of B with cantilena and counterpoint for strings, and the other the theme

Ex. 10

pp Bassoon

which is at once repeated by the horns and soon after transferred to the violins, where it is rounded off with a descending arc of melodic tissue. The reference to it near the end of the movement is brief.

A few bars of neutral introduction played in by bassoon, bass clarinet, cor anglais, and flutes leads to a chord of B major flavoured with a major seventh—there is actually a key signature of five sharps—out of which grows this affecting strain played by bassoon, cor anglais, and oboe:

Ex. 11

Oboe
Cor Anglais *pp*
Bassoon   Horns

Then enter strings with solo counterpoints from flute, oboe, clarinet over them for eight bars. Then a passage of florid can-tilena for violins beginning

Ex. 12

Vln. I

Next a change of key to F major and the beginning of a quiet

throb from the two harps helped by clarinets, over which the
flutes utter bird calls that awaken some agitato, tremolando,
sul ponticello noises. From which emerges Ex. 10 over a thrummed pedal point in D. From this tranquil passage an ominous
murmur from the timpani playing, of all improbable intervals,
major seconds and minor thirds, leads into an agitation that
begins quietly with triplet chords on upper strings and celesta, but
is whipped up by harp glissando and percussion—the vibraphone
articulates its ambiguous tones and the cymbalist takes a wire
brush to his perturbing instrument. The rest of the orchestra
joins in to create a sudden fortissimo, which is only dispelled by
the return to B major. Here we have strings, joined by harps
playing arpeggios, but the cantilena (flute and violin), when it
comes, is not like Ex. 12. Gone are the arabesques and in their
place a smoother melodic line. Still, the second violin does inter-
vene and the line does grow more florid, as the first violin leads
to another dynamic climax. Its last phrase is echoed by flute and
oboe and modified by the horn as the texture is thinned and the
momentum reduced. Ex. 10 now makes its brief reappearance
and disappears into a haze created by muted brass, chords on the
piano, and arpeggios on the harp and cellos. The tremolando
started by the violins affects the piano, the celesta, and the vibraphone. The cellos and one double bass linger on an honest, well-
spaced triad of B major.

This sort of narrative catalogue of the contents is an unsatis-
factory form of analysis. If analysis is to be at all useful it should
resemble a map rather than a news report of an event or developing situation. But with organic growth it is not possible to sketch
a map, though it might be possible to sketch a tree, if only trees
did not differ so vastly among themselves from a may bush to
a poplar. The tree, rather than the map or architectural plan, is the
analogy for one of these organic musical structures, such as are
found in the late quartets of Beethoven. But the simplest pattern
for a musician of what is meant by organic structure is a tune
in which there are no recapitulations. Such is the folk-song
'The Seeds of Love' as Sharp collected it from the vicarage
gardener down in Somerset. Here is no AABA, but ABCDE, in

which each phrase is projected as an outgrowth from the one
before:

Ex. 13

Walton working on a large canvas with an immense apparatus
with which to decorate his design has created an organism in
which the only mechanical aid to coherence and unity is the recapitulation of Ex. 10, though some resemblances are traceable
between sections, as in the B major passages for strings. Otherwise
the web is seamless and continuous. The mood, however, is not
so consistent, and some may feel that the agitato sections, in
which the linear orchestration dissolves into a haze, provide too
much contrast. Others, however, may feel that, just as a building
has to have a roof and even a chimney, so a movement of music
laid out on a flat plane with the interest concentrated on melodies
that behave like a river should nevertheless have a hill or two in
the landscape, if only to give a feeling of breadth by the presence of
another dimension. Walton nowhere in his works relies heavily
on the mechanics of sonata form—even less than did Elgar or
Vaughan Williams—and his thematic repetitions are often fluid
and varied. His music is founded on tonality but there is less use
in this symphony than in his first of the pedal point as a determinant of key at any given moment. Still, this is a symphony in
G with a slow movement a third away, as often in Beethoven.

The finale requires little analysis since it is in the form of a
Passacaglia, of which the outlines are clear for all to hear, but
what fills out the outlines shows the mastery which is concealed
by its sheer effectiveness. It is more extraverted than the previous
movements: its interests more purely musical, as the phrase goes
for lack of a better.

The theme (14 bars) is announced in a gigantic unison by the
full orchestra—unison, i.e. in the usual sense that means octaves,
and full to include piano and harps but exempting the flute

E

from general service in return for capping five high notes. Here
it is:

Ex. 14

None other than a 12-note series, rather like the one that
Britten uses in *The Turn of the Screw*, i.e. used as a *canto fermo* but
not as a source of harmony. This series, incidentally the same
beginning as the series on which Berg bases his Violin Concerto,
spells out a chord of G minor to be swung into the major by the
trilled B natural, made doubly sharp by the C sharp in the trill
itself. The flattening of the fifth and the second degrees corrects
the equilibrium and gives a daub of chromatic colour to this stark
ground bass. Ten variations, a fugato and a coda with two tails
follow the enunciation of the ground.

Variation I is marked 'con slancio', 'with impetuosity', launches
itself with a woodwind scale passage of anacrusis, occupies precisely its 14 bars, is heavily scored with woodwind and celesta
trilling the theme like mad, while trumpets and strings add a
strong counterpoint in figuration suited to their respective abilities.

Variation II is marked 'scherzando' and plays hide and seek
with the theme, which is concealed in the staccato chords of horns
and trumpets, most of the notes occurring in the first horn part
and removed from the bass line, which does its best to appear
irrelevant, while some tart chords are bandied about in antiphony.
The theme itself is broken like a mediaeval hocket for an odd bar
or two here and there, so that the total variation is extended to
17 bars.

Variation III, 14 bars again, is more orthodox and begins with
the theme in the bass or at least in the horns with the harp to
double it at the octave below and the bass clarinet to take on the
ardours of the trilled notes. It is marked 'l'istesso movimento' and
is lightly scored with a flowing counterpoint in the oboes in
thirds. The strings murmur sul ponticello and pizzicato.

In variation IV (grazioso) the theme returns to the bass (strings, who are bidden to play vibrato). A sprightly counterpoint is assigned to the bassoons playing in thirds.

Variation V is marked 'agitato' and the theme is given to the piano, helped out at the end by tuba and harp. The percussion now takes a hand with big drum and xylophone (glissando).

Variation VI has no expression mark save for a quicker metronome rate. The trombones take the theme but hand it over half way to the horns. The strings again take up the snatching sort of figure which they used in the first movement. There is no regular counterpoint but activity among harps and drums including the caisse claire again, which had appeared in the first variation

Variation VII is marked 'impetuoso'. It is the retrograde inversion of the theme used as a bridge between Variations VI and VIII, and contracts itself into only ten bars.

By way of compensation Variation VIII runs to 23 bars. It is marked 'tranquillo' and its characteristic is the use of chords. The first three notes of the theme spelling the G minor triad are played as a triad (with the fifth, sixth and seventh notes of the theme played as a triad in the second bar on the trumpets) reiterated on vibraphone, celesta, and second violins very high; after the D flat (no. 7 in the series) the theme buries itself and the variation fades away on tremolando strings marked 'flautato'.

Variation IX is slow and only ten bars in length. Against a complicated pattern of repeated chords on strings the theme is transformed upon the horns, while the bass line steadily marches down hill in slow counterpoint to it; harps and woodwind add light decorations.

Variation X, risoluto, opens with a flourish and ends with the last A flat prolonged with trills, flutter-tonguing and tremolando to make an approach to the Fugato. It runs to 21 bars and the theme is variously disposed on trumpets for the G minor bit, on woodwind and horns for the middle notes, and the same reinforced with trombones for the conclusion of the theme.

In the Fugato there is more than meets the eye and more than

the ear will take in at the speed at which it goes. The 12-note
theme Ex. 14 is now rewritten thus:

This, however, is not enough: by way of codetta—it could hardly
be called a counter-subject or a second fugue subject, though it
recurs—the series is written out again for oboes and second
violins, the oboes playing quavers and the violins semiquavers.
The series, however, is slightly deranged as appears in

The answer enters at the fifth above but not quite orthodoxly
as the fifth is an augmented fifth. The next entry is also the answer,
appearing at three octave levels. It is followed by the Codetta
Ex. 16, violin version on violins and flutes with only intermittent
accompaniment of chords, which runs its full length of six and a
half bars. Then the subject enters in the bass with itself in canon
one quaver behind in the treble—a sort of stretto. When it ends,
it is extended in some free writing that is to catch up the semiquavers of Ex. 16 and lead into the Coda (of the movement not
the fugue). This is marked 'scherzando', though the trombones
and the piano, both syncopated, join in, over a dominant pedal.
A coda to the coda hurtles along presto in two-four time (though
soon reverting to three-four), with the timpani and big drum and
side drum propelling it into a series of glissandi. This would seem
to be the end, but, as in the First Symphony, Walton breaks off

for the brass chorus to make a final dissenting declaration before
the rest of the orchestra clamps down firmly on repeated chords
of G major.

Variations on a Theme by Hindemith

Variation writing and a very much diluted form of serialism
are the chief developments in Walton's more recent works. All
that he takes from serialism is the idea of using a predetermined
order as a strut, either with or without the full complement of
twelve notes, in his structure. Any form of serialism, except
Schoenberg's stringent formula, implies variation—serialism is a
development of passacaglia. Variation too would appear to be
closely akin to creation whenever thematic evolution, as expounded by Reti, is the way the composer's mind works. Composers' minds do not always work that way, as for instance when
they find a good tune for a short strophic song or a simple dance.
But even when a set of variations is written on such a simple
square tune, as for example by Brahms in his Handel and Paga-
nini sets, we are aware of different degrees of similitude between
original theme and subsequent variations. It is an old philosophical
problem, this of identity in difference—how indeed can a tune be
varied without losing its identity? In metamorphosis, as when
Daphne changes into a laurel, there is a loss of identity, but mere
change, as when my hair goes white in the night through seeing a
ghost, does not involve loss of identity; the hair is still there, only
different. There is the limiting case of the cricketer who thought
he had the same bat for twenty years, though he was accustomed
to have a new blade every other year and a new handle in the
alternate years. But normally a thing cannot be said to have
changed unless it remains the same thing, and all well conducted
sets of variations conform to that canon of identity in difference.
Composition with themes, as when Beethoven spins a symphony
out of four notes ♪♪♪ | ♩, is thus very near to variation. Sym-
phonic writing involves antithesis, contrast, accretion, interruption, repetition and other basic processes besides thematic evolution

and variation. But all the great symphonic composers have had recourse to the unitary forms of variation and fugue as a relief from the ternary form of the sonata: Mozart, Beethoven, and conspicuously Brahms, who all in their different ways experimented also with combining the unitary and the ternary, Mozart in the Jupiter Symphony, Beethoven in the finale of the Eroica and in the A flat sonata Opus 110, and Brahms in the Fourth Symphony. The easier way, however, is to make a set of variations serve as one movement in the complete sonata or symphony as Walton has done in the Cello Concerto, or to do it on the grand scale as a self-subsistent work as Brahms did in the St Anthony Variations, and as Walton has done in his Variations on a Theme by Hindemith.

This work was written one may suppose as a tribute of long friendship, and indeed the payment of a debt, from one composer to another. Hindemith, whom Walton had met at that historic Salzburg Festival of 1923, intervened decisively at the first major crisis of Walton's career, when he undertook the performance of the viola concerto after Tertis had turned it down. More than thirty years later Walton makes this public gesture and includes Mrs Hindemith in the dedication along with her husband. That the gesture was appreciated is shown by the following letter from Hindemith to Walton, which is quoted here by kind permission of all parties. Hindemith's regretted death at the end of 1963 alas! disposed of his intention to play the work himself.

Vevey, poste restante.

July 29th '63.

Egregio Amico:

Finally our criss-cross journeys came to an end and we could sit down in front of the exhaust of our grammophone and play your piece, score before us. Well, we had a half hour of sheer enjoyment. You wrote a beautiful score and we are extremely honoured to find the red carpet rolled out even on the steps to the back door of fame. I am particularly fond of the honest solidity of workmanship in this score—something that seems almost completely lost nowadays. Let us thank you for your kindness and for the wonderfully touching and artistically convincing manifestation of this Kindness (even old Mathis is per-

mitted to peep through the fence, which for a spectre like him seems
to be some kind of resurrection after artificial respiration!).—I am glad
that George Szell had a great (and well deserved) success with the piece
in the States. I also shall put it on my programs as soon as possible. I
wrote to the Oxford Press people that this could only be the case during
the next season, i.e. starting autumn 1964, since I received the score at
a time when all programs for 63/64 were settled and could not be
changed. I hope this will be all right with you, and I shall do my best to
become a worthy interpreter of WW. Again my and Gertrude's
heartfelt thanks! —We shall be in Naples around the middle of
October and we hope to see you.

Love to you both

as ever, yours

Hindemiths.

It is also a tribute of another kind, a birthday celebration for the
Royal Philharmonic Society on the occasion of the 150th anniversary of its first concert. It was played for the first time at the Royal
Festival Hall in London on 8 March 1963, the composer conducting, one hundred and fifty years to the day since the Society's
first concert at the Argyll Rooms in Regent Street.

The impression the Variations made then was that Walton had
widened his range of mood and modified his restless tension by
intercommunion with Hindemith. For he had not just taken a
tune by another composer, as Beethoven did from Diabelli,
Brahms from Handel, Britten from Frank Bridge, and used it as
a starting point for an exercise of his own imagination and skill.
To begin with he had not taken a tune, nor even a theme, but a
paragraph. The text of the discourse is the opening section of the
second movement of Hindemith's Cello Concerto (1940), which
runs to no less than 36 bars in andante tempo and is not at all a
tune in binary shape. Furthermore Walton has stated it with
Hindemith's own harmony, merely changing the solo line from
cello to other instruments. Even the cello line of the original is
not unbroken, so that this introduction to the movement is like
an independent composition in which the orchestra does not
merely support but punctuates and develops the argument of the
solo. The Times suggested in its notice (not written by me) that

the variations were like a discussion between the two composers about other composers' music and mentioning Strauss's *Salome*, Elgar's *Falstaff* and of course Hindemith's own *Mathis der Maler*, from which a quotation is made. The idea was confessedly fanciful but it remarked in a striking way what was abundantly apparent at the first performance—that somehow these· variations had an interlocutory character that was something new in Walton's output and indeed in all the variousness of variation writing.

The other quite new factor was the use of the serial order of Hindemith's first twelve notes to provide the tonal centres for the several variations. This is indeed to use tonality as a structural element in quite a new way, rather like Britten's bold use of a serial order for the fugal entries in his *Cantata Accademica*. The tonalities (safer to call them that than keys) sit lightly on the variations but each one of them ends on its appropriate note in the series. The series itself, however, does not comprise the complete chromatic scale, since G natural is missing and its place taken by a repetition of A. The composer elects to use the tonality of A for his sixth variation instead of his second, i.e. at the second appearance of the note in Hindemith's tune, no. 8 instead of no. 3 in note order. We therefore have the following numerical pattern for the delectation of any numerologist who cares to make a puzzle, do a sum or seek any metaphysical significance in one and the same note having three different numberings:

Ex. 1

These 4 bars contain the main thematic idea that is to be varied, but other elements in Hindemith's paragraph have to be noted, first the accompanimental figure, Ex. 2 which is easily derived on Reti's method from Ex. 1:

Ex. 2

second, an orchestral figure at the end of the cello's first sentence:

which is repeated in three sequences and constitutes a landmark that turns up in all of the variations; third, the continuation after Ex. 3 of the cello's solo which builds up the character of the theme.

This is half of the material, i.e. Exs. 1 and 4 followed by Ex. 3 and its sequences making 15 bars all told so far. The second half begins with Ex. 1, now transferred to the orchestra while the soloist accompanies, followed in due order by Ex. 4 transposed. But instead of any repetition of Ex. 3 we are given a long tune (13 bars) made up of Exs. 5 and 6 run together—there is a tiny cut at the join:

Ex. 5 is accompanied by tart chords which emphasize its syncopated character, Ex. 6 by Ex. 2. The bracketed phrase at the beginning of Ex. 6 is not only striking and important but is related to a similar melodic idea, derived from contiguous triads,

to be found in *Mathis der Maler*[1] and subsequently to be quoted
(see p. 60). Hindemith's complete theme for what in the concerto is also a set of variations (albeit on two themes) thus contains ample material for extended variations.

The complexities and ingenuities, the differentia and the iden-
tities, can now be set out for everyone's greater convenience in
catalogue form:

Hindemith's exordium is transcribed literally, as already mentioned, with only the elimination of the solo cello. Its tonality is E
mixolydian, and it runs to 36 bars andante con moto. The timing
given is 1′ 48″, i.e. nearly two minutes of music.

Variation 1. Vivace. Unstable time signatures. A scherzo. It ends
on the second note of the theme, G sharp. Strings marked
'spiccato' start the theme and the music of Ex. 3 follows. The
next phrase (on flute and oboe)

Ex. 7

is the first violin counterpoint to the theme Ex. 1 at its second
statement (7 bars after 17 in Hindemith's score). The rest is made
up of another descending phrase from the scale of G, still another
in the reverse direction from the last two bars of Ex. 5, and finally
something from Ex. 6 (*x*). Thus the variation remains in touch
with the theme as a whole.

Variation 2. Allegramente (rather fast by the metronome
marking). Goes to F sharp (note 3 of series). A toccata type of
movement with syncopation supplied by the horn. Bare fourths
are a prominent harmonic feature. Exs. 1, 3, and 4 seem to be the
chief sources of the material till the second part, when Ex. 6
asserts itself.

Variation 3. Larghetto. A siciliano movement ending in B
(note 4 of series). Material is from Exs. 1, 3 and 6, scored mostly

[1] Prelude Engelkonzert. The Chorale *Es sungen drei Engel*, bars 5 and 6 contains this
Ex. 6a.

Ex. 6a

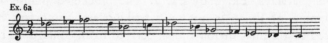

for strings and so mildly harmonized as even to permit consecutive chords of the sixth.

Variation 4. Con slancio (i.e. with impetuosity). Moto perpetuo. Ends in C sharp. Harmonies in thirds are used as lubricant though there is enough grit in the glancing dissonances to generate propulsive energy.

Variation 5. Andante con moto, i.e. the tempo of the original theme, which is followed pretty closely throughout, though the opening tune (on woodwind) is in fact a retrograde version of Ex. 1 and its continuation (in bars 5 and 6) is an inversion of Ex. 4, both transposed. A new feature is a bass in running quavers that strides along legatissimo:

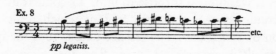

of which the chromatic tangle in the first bar evolved fortuitously into Bach's familiar signature motif (which is in fact implicit in Ex. 5), appearing towards the end on flute and horn:

(B flat = B, B natural = H in German nomenclature.)

Variation 6. Scherzando in 5/4 time. Ends on A. The theme is dismembered, and small bits of it bandied across the orchestra spurred on by side drum, tambourine and harp, and by a series of glissando surges on the xylophone and anything else that will do them. This is very much a variation on the iambic rhythm which is prominent throughout Hindemith's long tune.

Variation 7. Lento molto. Ends in C. Over a rocking figure based on Ex. 1 three bars of Ex. 4 are heard in the horns in harmony. An elaborate version of Ex. 3 is worked on strings. The lilting figure persists in an attenuating texture until the harp (and upper strings) start playing crochet chords, 1-2-3 in a bar, which is what Hindemith does in the concerto when at the point 32 in his score he reinstates the theme (Exs. 1, 2 and 3). To crown this incantation Walton quotes a phrase from Hindemith's *Mathis der Maler*, and marks it with inverted commas, so that there shall be no mistake.

Ex. 10

Of it Walton writes: 'This quotation from *Mathis* was taken from the opera and not the symphony, and occurs on page 221 of the piano score, four bars before 47. Though the first bars of Ex. 6 seemed naggingly familiar it was quite some time before I spotted the connexion and, from what Hindemith wrote me, it was quite a surprise to him.' Its context in the opera is the second scene of the sixth tableau which deals with the temptation of St Antony. The essence of Ex. 10 is the quotation of three triads in descending form, E major, C major, A flat major, E major equidistant from each other by a major third. This basic idea is to be found pervading much of *Mathis der Maler*, both opera and symphony, and it resembles parts of the cello concerto's theme—to the composer's surprise.

Variation 8. Vivacissimo, which ends on B flat. The woodwind chatters on a flattened-out form of Ex. 4 and the strings in due course deal with Ex. 3 suitably adapted to the context.

Variation 9. Maestoso is short (10 bars only) and leads into the finale, but it reaches F, the last unused note of the series. It is less a variation than a tremendous flourish for the fugal conclusion.

Finale. Allegro molto ending firmly on E. The fugal form of the theme is only worked on strings, to which it is by shape best fitted:

Ex. 11

The fugal entries are not in orthodox order at the distance of a fifth. The first is on A flat, a minor third higher; the third is on B a semitone higher still though actually pitched in the bass octave. The fourth entry is a redundant entry on F, augmented in time value. The equivalent of Ex. 3 follows this fugal exposition. The second part of the theme, Exs. 5 and 6, is now treated, suitably transformed into semiquavers, as a kind of recapitulation. The gathering momentum requires a new time signature at the climax, so we have $\mathrm{d} = \mathrm{d}.$ lo stesso movimento, nine crotchets to the bar. But a diminuendo immediately supervenes and the Coda marked 'tranquillo' begins a new and broader statement of the theme, of which most appears. The horns play Ex. 1 in augmentation and the first section is finished off by trombones. The terse figure of Ex. 3 is transformed into a rhapsodic cello solo which hands its arabesque over to the violins which in turn transform it into the last part of the theme Ex. 6. A solo trumpet, echoed by a solo horn, plays the *Mathis* theme, which after all turns out to be Ex. 6 in a more straightforward rhythm and on this note of fulfilment the Variations end quietly.

For the moral of *Mathis der Maler* is fulfilment. Mathis was torn by the conflicting pulls of politics and his art. When Hindemith wrote it many Germans were facing that agony of conscience. Hindemith was his own librettist and he read the lesson of the Mainz painter of 1525 as an injunction that the artist had better use the gifts God has given him instead of trying to be a not very good soldier. So Mathis pulled out of the Peasants War and went back to his studio, where the vision he had of the temptation of St Anthony became one of the subjects on his great altarpiece for the monastery of Isenheim.

The influence of Hindemith has pervaded the Variations subtly as well as by the overt allusions and derivations herein noted. Hindemith is a composer in whom the balance of intellect and imagination, obverse and reverse of our mental apparatus, leans towards intellect. Perhaps for this reason, though these psychological balance sheets can only be speculative, his sound texture tends to be grey. The mixture of a little grey pigment with Walton's vivid palette produces a more restful, or should we say a less restless, score than is natural to Walton. The actual scoring is not markedly different, but there are fewer of those sharp rhythmic subtleties and dynamic markings. Many composers have exchanged compositions with each other for mutual study and eventual influence on each other, Byrd and Ferrabosco, Brahms and Joachim, and in a rather different way Holst and Vaughan Williams, but this conversation between Hindemith and Walton has no actual parallel. Altruism by borrowing sounds like a paradox, but Walton by politely giving the last word to Hindemith in this close colloquy has enriched himself by acquiring a new tone of voice.

Partita for Orchestra

When Vaughan Williams invited a few of his friends and admirers to hear a run-through on the piano of his new Eighth Symphony, which, it will be recalled, carries no programme, not even indirectly, and is for him unusual in that functionally it is an exploitation of orchestral tone colour apparently for its own sake and is a 'small' symphony, some of us suggested that it would more appropriately be called a sinfonietta. He would not hear of it, saying, 'No one will pay any attention to it if I do that.' Walton confronted with a similar situation in which he wanted to produce a symphonic work without the serious implications of a symphony, a shorter work, a 'small' symphony, hit on the happy idea of calling it a Partita, but did not feel constrained to copy the eighteenth-century model in the number of movements—Bach's partitas normally contain six. But he did borrow the idea of beginning with a toccata and ending with a gigue. Between them he put a Siciliana—he uses the siciliana as a light contrasting movement also in *The Quest* and as the third of the Hindemith Variations.

The intention to avoid seriousness and aim at diversion—he might have equally well called it a divertimento—is avowed in a programme note which, under pressure from the Cleveland Orchestra and its conductor George Szell who commissioned the work, he provided for its performance by the Cleveland Orchestra on 30 January 1958. He wrote:

Two major difficulties confront me in responding to your kind invitation to contribute a few words about my new *Partita for Orchestra*. Firstly, I am a writer of notes and (to my regret) not of prose. Secondly, it is surely easier to write about a piece of creative work if there is something problematical about it. Indeed—so it seems to me—the more problematical, the greater the flow of words. Unfortunately from this point of view, my Partita poses no problems, has no ulterior motive or meaning behind it, and makes no attempt to ponder the imponderables. I have written it in the hope that it may be enjoyed straight off, without any preliminary probing into the score. I have also written it with the wonderful players of the Cleveland Orchestra in mind, hoping that they may enjoy playing it. If either of these two hopes is fulfilled, I shall be more than happy.

The work is in three shortish movements and their titles explain themselves. The orchestra used is normal, with no unusual 'extras'. Since the first and third movements are predominantly vigorous and use full orchestra for a good deal of the time, I have designed the middle movement, the Pastorale Siciliana, which opens with an unaccompanied duet between solo viola and solo oboe, as a complete contrast in mood and texture.

Need more be said? Something can be said since analysis is our purpose.

Toccata means a thing touched as compared with cantata, a thing sung, sonata a thing sounded (i.e. played). The term came into use at the beginning of the seventeenth century when the keyboard instruments were developing, on which the performer's touch was an important element of display and of the effect of impact on the ear that could be produced by repeated notes of equal length. Walton observes the principle of repeated equal impacts—somewhere or other there is quaver motion going all the way through. He begins by giving to strings (second violins and violas only) chords of this shape, marked 'alla corda', i.e. on the string for emphasis to give the 'touch' effect:

Ex. 1

which shortly change to

Ex. 2

in which the bowing is modified, and again, when a second subject appears (Ex. 6) we have the violas doing this in octaves:

Ex. 3

or later still the horns and trumpets this:

Ex. 4

And so it goes on with endless ingenuity and without intermission save for a point of climax.

Over this continuous movement a tune is spun of which the rhythmic shape of (*a*) is important:

Ex. 5

Vln. & Oboe

which is repeated by the horns who share the quavers.

At poco meno mosso (fig. 3) against Ex. 3 and pizzicato in the strings above and below the violas, another idea starts up, but it too soon turns into running quavers:

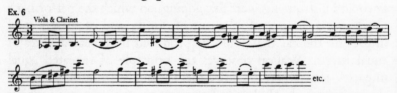

Ex. 6

Viola & Clarinet

After a slight ritenuto we come to the second subject proper, using the terminology of sonata form. Thematically there is not much to it, but the key change from E to its dominant (with five sharps in the score) and some flamboyant orchestration, trills for wood-wind, held-notes on trombones, upward swishes on the harp, marks a change of orientation in the moto perpetuo. The identifiable part of the theme is

Ex. 7

Vlns. with Horn support

This in turn is repeated with changed allocation among the strings and the music becomes quieter. Cellos and basses are now given a theme, triplet and trill, of their own, which is not unobserved by the heavy brass, which, trombones and tuba, assert one of their own in long white notes.

The recapitulation begins not with Ex. 5 but with Ex. 6 which is followed by a recapitulation now in the tonic of Ex. 7. The first theme is only indirectly alluded to by references to (a) and the movement ends with trills and a run full tilt into the buffers.

The Pastorale Siciliana has an altogether Mediterranean flavour, like that of *Siesta*, of an eclogue. The sun shines, and sometimes burns with a sharp shaft of semiquaver string scrunches, a speciality of Walton's scoring, like this (though this is not an exact transcription of what oboes, clarinets, trumpets, violins and violas actually do, each after its own aptitude):

Ex. 8

the sea laps in compound time sometimes nine, sometimes six but not twelve quavers to the bar; the shepherd pipes, of course, with rare versatility, picking up the oboe first (naturally) but being equally at home on clarinet and horn, and the pastoral scene dissolves at the end in a mid-day blazing shimmer produced by vibraphone and the violins playing this:

Ex. 9

Vb.
Str.

fz   *poco*

Harp   Celesta

F

This is not just a colour effect but the key to the tonality of the movement which is the resultant of a clash between C minor and E major. In this as in the choice of the instrumental protagonists at the opening of the dialogue—for it begins as Theocritus does with dialogue—the movement recalls to mind the similar opening of Vaughan Williams's *Flos Campi*, where oboe and viola conduct a conversation in different modes with different centres (E Dorian and F minor to be specific in which E natural clashes with E flat and A natural with A flat). Walton gets his clash between E flat and E natural and an enharmonic ambiguity of G sharp and A flat. So he begins with the viola accompaniment establishing a rocking motion in a figure starting with and emphasizing the leading note, D sharp. Over this he introduces his oboe tune:

This tune is extended to 10 bars and then starts to repeat itself with a fuller accompaniment of harp, horn, and muted or trilled violins. But the oboe, instead of burbling on, jumps to a loud high note and stays there till it hands over the siciliano to clarinets, flutes, strings, and bassoon which elaborates it with semiquavers. Percussion now takes a hand, celesta, glockenspiel, and triangle flicking, or rather flecking, the score with flashes—perhaps the shepherd is a shepherdess who has a mirror in her hand.

She changes her tune and her instrument; a new dialogue begins with a differently shaped phrase over a different accompaniment, a rocking pedal point on A:

Ex. 11

Activity dies down and flares up; a solo flute has a cadenza (accompanied) in Sicilian rhythm. Then the first subject, the oboe tune of Ex. 10, returns but now transferred to the clarinet with the solo viola underneath doing something different in semiquavers. The key sounds like a tart C minor, which moves to E minor, established by a momentary clearance of the harmony on to a chord of its dominant. By now the tune, passed to the strings, is being repeated as in the exposition but with a different accompaniment consisting of trumpet and harp off-beat chords and counterpoints of woodwind too varied to be specified—that is a feature of Walton's style that his procedures are not to be summarized: he is endlessly and fastidiously varied in his details. The second subject duly recurs on woodwind over its rocking pedal on E flat. There is a horn solo and another flash più animato before the dissolution. A binary dance form.

Gigues too are binary dance forms, but the Giga Burlesca with which Walton finishes his Partita is not quite so simple in structure —it is more of an irregular rondo. But the rondo tune is evolved instead of being stated. In its complete form it is as follows:

Ex. 12

But this is its last, not its first, appearance. Its constituents are projected piecemeal low down in the pitch register on violas, cellos, and bassoons (including the double bassoon), these for instance

and others such as repeated notes on muted trumpets. They spread upwards in pitch, and the speed makes them cohere into a fast gigue with innumerable on-beat and off-beat devices to impel the rhythm and by a build-up of every department of the orchestra to produce a climax in 52 bars. The first episode is an amalgam of flying fragments, gruppetti of chords, a cross rhythm in the trumpets, wind playing in thirds, horns doing a downward glissando, strings scratching divisi at oscillating chords and then at last a tune not in jig rhythm:

This on paper looks like a modified E minor just as Ex. 12 is a modified E major, but the feeling is more like A minor as indicated by the change of signature. It is in fact E modal, but not one of the regular modes (sharp 3, flat 6 and 7).

Now another tune in Walton's best vulgar manner of *Façade*—this time on the horns:

A series of chromatic scales up and down, consecutive seconds many of them, leads to the first clear statement of the main tune, i.e. a trumpet version of Ex. 12 which is bandied about in the orchestra and ultimately presented on the upper strings and upper wind in unison and octaves, definitely in A minor, followed forthwith by Ex. 15 at its old pitch and tonality on horns but repeated by violins in A flat. At last comes Ex. 16 preceded by a horn version of itself. The eye will detect in the score some familiar features, those 4-note gruppetti, those rising chromatic scales of dissonant seconds, the pizzicato bass on strong beats and many of the figures contained in Ex. 16, e.g. those burlesque triads on trumpets. There is plenty of percussion to pep the conclusion. Among it the composer prescribes 'cassa chiara'. What is that? Answer: side drum, for which the French term is 'caisse claire' as an alternative to 'tambour militaire'—the usual Italian is 'tamburo militaire'. The 'clear' does not seem to imply 'without snares'.

The high spots are obvious: the burlesque element is of the kind found in Façade, an ordinary-sounding popular tune with a rhythmic twist or two in it that not even a jazz composer would think of. The piquancy is derived from the detailed markings, the pointillist scoring, the virtuoso writing for individual instruments, notably horns and trumpets, which the composer directed at the Cleveland players. When the record of the Partita and the Second Symphony was made Walton wrote to Dr Szell expressing his delight at the 'quite staggering virtuosity of the performance'.

CHAPTER III

Concertos

Sinfonia Concertante

THERE are four concertante works, of which the earliest, the Sinfonia Concertante for piano, has withdrawn its claim to solo concerto status. It is, however, most suitably considered here in the context of the three concertos for string instruments.

It is neither a symphony nor a concerto, but its design in three movements brings it within the generous connotation of that elastic term, 'symphony', and the virtuoso writing for the solo piano in its first edition gave it an obvious superficial resemblance to a concerto. There was no need therefore to quarrel on *a priori* grounds with the title, which, considering how lax is music's terminology, gave a fair indication of the work's nature. But a certain dissatisfaction remained and in 1943 the composer revised it in the direction of greater clarity. The piano part was simplified and the new score changed the title of the work to 'Sinfonia Concertante for Orchestra with Piano Obbligato'. This was in fact the second revision, for the work was originally conceived as a ballet and was tried out provisionally for piano duet. Some inflation of the material was unavoidable when it was heavily scored for large orchestra (with three each of the wind), and the changed version suffered from a certain intractability as a result of the change of aim from ballet to symphony. Thus, the appendage to the finale of a coda harking back to the first movement and consisting of a mixture of elements from both first and last movements is a little artificial, but it is saved from arbitrariness by a latent relationship in the thematic material of all three movements. Walton has described how in his Chelsea days with Constant Lambert they had been drawn to Diaghilev's Ballet and how he himself hoped to write a ballet for it, especially after Diaghilev attended the revival of *Façade* at the Chenil Galleries. But 'when I approached Diaghilev,' Walton writes, 'he was sympathetic, but said I would be able to do one better in a few years' time.'

So the idea of a ballet for Diaghilev was dropped, but the music was plainly too good to waste. It was therefore retrieved by a change of purpose, similar, though opposite to that which had made Stravinsky, also under stimulus from Diaghilev, turn his Concertstück for piano and orchestra into *Petrushka*. The slow movement in particular had to be salvaged, for in it appears for the first time in a mature expression the composer's streak of deeply romantic feeling, hitherto buried under smart and brilliant dialogue but destined to emerge even more fully developed into the light in the viola concerto.

The date of composition in the new symphonic form was 1927, and the dedication is to the Sitwells, a movement apiece to Osbert, Edith and 'Sachie' respectively. The first performance was at a Philharmonic concert at Queen's Hall on 5 January 1928, under Ernest Ansermet with York Bowen as the pianist.

Structurally it is not in any of the set orthodox forms, but it is lucid and easy to follow because the themes are pithy and clear-cut. That they are also more stable in shape than is customary with Walton may be due to their original designation for dancing. The characteristic tendency to polymorphism of themes, however, persists in so far as themes in each movement seem to be variations of one basic idea. Observe, for example, the kinship of Exs. 5, 6, 7, and 8, and compare them with Ex. 13 and with Ex. 18, which is at once an epitome and an augmentation of them.

The first movement is prefaced by a massive introduction (maestoso), quasi-Handelian in the tread of its themes and in its general motion, but far from Handelian in harmony. The opening chords as played by the piano and duplicated by the strings, are full of 'added' notes, which thicken the texture, of which the main strand is this theme:

Ex. 1 Maestoso

There is a balancing phrase and then the pattern is torn across
by some impertinences, chromatic chirrupings from the wind,
little staccato snatches from the strings, pizzicato interjections and
the like. This is the 'bright young thing' of the day warning us not
to mistake Ex. 1 and its subsequent counterpoise too pompously
or too soulfully in spite of the marks cantabile and rubato. There
are more twitterings and a repetition of Ex. 1 which dies down and
clears out in order to project the main movement with the greater
impetus. This lull contains the phrase

Ex. 2

which perhaps accounts for a vague recollection that I came away
from the first performance under the impression that Elgar had
influenced the composer in the new work. At any rate that is all
the Elgar I can find in the score today.

The piano in double octaves and the horn announce the first
tune of the 'allegro spiritoso' in canon:

Ex. 3   Allegro spiritoso

This D major tune is harmonized by a chord not of tonic or
dominant but of G. Bias to the subdominant (or flat) side of the
key becomes a definite shift in that direction when the sharps are
cancelled, and B flat and A flat basses appear in the thrusts of re-
partee which form the link between the statement in D and the
counter-statement in D flat of Ex. 3. The link now leads to a
second subject 'poco meno mosso' in A minor:

Ex. 4   col 8ve

by the piano, announced and briefly extended by the woodwind until another link, this time of staccato chords in semiquavers, leads to a third subject. This is not presented at once, but evolved from the two bars of a droning, hurdy-gurdy figure started up by the piano alone:

The tonality of this second subject is interesting. Both Ex. 4 and Ex. 5 pivot on or around an A. The tonality of the passage dominated by Ex. 4 is an Aeolian A disturbed by a strongly placed B♭, which suggests a bias towards D minor. But the flat is cancelled in one of Walton's quite characteristic oscillations of modality, and the feeling of the passage as a whole denotes A as its tonic, but leaves the mode ambiguous. In Ex. 5 A still persists as a powerful harmonic influence, but it has now become a sub-dominant since the tonal centre has clearly shifted to E. Ex. 6 is definitely in E minor.

Ex. 5 is taken over from the piano by the strings so as to leave the solist free to make a little waif of a tune out of its semiquavers. At least it did in the first edition, but this is one of the passages that has been rewritten. In the new version there still remain some reflections on the melancholy of plagal harmonies in a key like E minor and what finally emerges is Ex. 6:

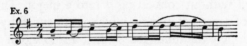

The second link passage of staccato chords leads to a modified recapitulation of the first subject, Ex. 3, played in unison by wind, splashed with chords from the piano. This works up a power-ful climax, after which the piano has a quiet reference to Ex. 6 and then leads into a clattering coda with Ex. 3. A good deal of counterpoint has been removed in the 1943 revision and the last section has been tightened up.

The slow movement was slimmed but not reduced in the revision of 1943—indeed it was lengthened by one bar at the end where the last chord is held for an extra bar and a half. The introduction:

Ex. 7 Andante comodo

was transferred from the solo piano to the orchestra. The piano writing at the recapitulation of the first theme (Ex. 8 below), which originally was so elaborate as to require three staves for its adequate notation, is simplified so to an arabesque. A few small counterpoints and doublings in the wind were eliminated, but the rewriting was less drastic than in the first movement.

The two introductory bars again propound an ambiguity of key. The treble is in D minor, the tenor might be in E minor or A minor, and a pedal G holds them in equilibrium until it moves to A, which it treats as a dominant, at the moment when the main theme, enunciated by a solo violin:

Ex. 8

declares itself gently, but decisively, for D minor. It is, however, a D minor with a third that may be sharp, and a sixth that also may be sharpened without converting it into a major. The effect is a minor key of great poignancy, which is enhanced by the instruments which play the tune (Ex. 8), first a solo violin and then an oboe and then again a cor anglais. The internal rhythmic organization of Ex. 8 is determined by the movement of the harmony, as can be seen from the bass line, which proceeds consistently thus:

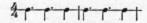

The third statement of the tune finishes on a firm unison D at the twelfth bar. A counterbalancing theme is thereupon stated in conclusion of the first subject. This consists in the first place of some sliding consecutive sixths with a hint of false relationship in their uncertainty whether to be sharply or flatly inflected—an idiom forecasting that of the Viola Concerto. To them is shortly added another one-bar-long motif:

Ex. 9
Flute

which by repetition (with varied prefixes and suffixes in the manner that was to become Walton's most noticeable mannerism) almost becomes a tune. This section has all the qualities of a bridge passage here because it leads to a middle section in which the key is different (a sort of G minor), the signature is changed (momentarily, at any rate, to 3/4), and a new, though obviously related, melodic idea is taken up. But a glance at the recapitulation shows that Ex. 9 is to become much more important than merely a bridge, because it is to bear the responsibility for winding up the movement on a note of great intensity.

The new G minor tune is also a one-bar affair and is likewise closely related to its predecessors:

Ex. 10
Oboe

It is repeated by bassoon, by violins, by clarinet, and elaborated in a horn solo. A sudden pianissimo recalls Ex. 7. With it goes a swaying octave figure:

Ex. 11
Oboe   Horn

which is not new, but is an orchestral counterpoint to Ex. 7 in its present and previous appearances. The interesting thing about it is that it is derived in the last resort from the string figure which accompanies Ex. 4 in the first movement and the piano's opening figure in this movement. Thus heralded by Exs. 7 and 11 the pensive tune of Ex. 8 returns in a richer texture on the violins doubled at the octave below by violas and accompanied by very elaborate arpeggios on the piano and semiquaver figures from the woodwind. At its second statement it goes into D major and is played at three-octave pitches by first and second violins and violas, one above the other. After a third statement (still on the strings) in the first version a passage in sixths, used before as a bridge, led into a grand simultaneous restatement of Exs. 8 and 9, with Ex. 11 now made into a majestic bass part and the piano contributing a running commentary of semiquavers. But this excess of contrapuntal ingenuity was removed in the revision, and the movement's lyrical beauties were allowed to appear in greater simplicity.

What is needed in a third and concluding movement is a burst of high spirits and not too much contemplation or counterpoint. So Walton writes a Stravinskyish sort of movement with two principal subjects (in F and B flat) rounded off with a coda in D major, based on the introduction. The movement begins allegro vivo sempre scherzando with a discordant cadence and a fanfare in F. After this introduction the piano gives out the first main tune of a rondoish nature, accompanied by bassoons playing hop-scotch:

Ex. 12

This six-bar theme, which derives its propulsive energy from Ex. 3 and its characteristic curve *a* from Ex. 6, is extended by the orchestra, with much neat passing, in the footballer's sense, between the forward line of the woodwind. Its suggestion of a rondo is not taken úp—the movement is no rondo because what follows is not an episode, but a very substantial second subject, so substantial and elaborately organized as to defy summary description. We may, however, specify the following elements: the heavy brass play chords of D minor off the beat, the violins interject a new idea

Ex. 13

and the piano gets busy with passage work like this:

Ex. 14

The woodwind, assisted by the xylophone, spouts—spits perhaps would be the better word—some syncopation:

Ex. 15

The brass punctuates this performance with

Ex. 16

and finally, some bars later, come two other more sober elements which are ingeniously interlocked by manipulation of their phrase lengths:

Ex. 17

which is perhaps distantly related to Ex. 4, and

Ex. 18

which is an augmentation of the basic idea common to the two previous movements. Exs. 17 and 18 form a kind of middle section between two statements of Exs. 14 and 16—Ex. 15 does not appear at this point. We thus have a second subject, itself a structure in simple ternary form, which leads without any development section or other episode to a compressed recapitulation. The first subject, Ex. 13, reappears in F, shortened and lightly stated by woodwind instead of piano. The second subject is even more curtailed: only 4 bars of Exs. 14 and 15 and their context are allowed to signify their formal attendance, when the interruption of the fanfare from the beginning of the movement precludes all possibility of further reference to Exs. 17 and 18, which, after all, had enjoyed considerable latitude of expression when they first occurred in the middle of the movement. The fanfare is elaborated and leads to a brief piano cadenza which in its turn heralds the return in D major of the Introduction of the first movement. This coda, however, is no simple transfer; the composer makes it integral with the finale and a unifying force for the whole Sinfonia.

We have Ex. 1 on flutes, trumpet and violins at the same speed as at its original appearance, though it is now written out in notes of double value. So much at least was clear in the first score, since the metronome mark was 60 the beat, which was a crotchet in the first movement (the 3/4 tune) and a minim (3/2 tune) in this finale. But it rather looks as though the composer intends it now to go more slowly since he indicates that the conductor should beat it 'in 6'. He has also removed some counterpoint in augmentation. The drums roll and the piano plays massive chords, but the commotion only last for five bars and tranquillity returns for a picturesque episode probably intended to recall the ethos of the slow movement, though there is no direct thematic allusion to what has gone before. In the new version there is a moment of sheer floating sonority on a chord of D (of a sort) created by string harmonics, glockenspiel, and horns over an ostinato figure in the bass of the piano. This episode in its turn is soon swept aside by the final recurrence of the opening fanfare of the finale. This coda, therefore, is compounded of many elements from different sources which in a short space cohere together themselves and give coherence to the whole work. The new ver-

sion is certainly an improvement on the old, which was overladen
both with counterpoint and thick scoring. Matter and manner
are now better adjusted to the dimensions of a piece of more
modest intentions.

Concerto for Viola and Orchestra

IT is generally agreed that in the Viola Concerto Walton gave the
most characteristic expression of his mind. Each of its three move-
movements is strongly defined, and they contain between them
most of the idioms, stylistic tricks of speech, the peculiar
dynamism and the sharp orchestration that are the superficially
recognizable features of his work. But their basic unity is unusually
marked. It is not in any case a discursive work; the usual extended
Allegro movement, which opens a concerto and bears the main
burden of its argument, is missing. The longest movement comes
last and gathers into its more ample embrace the conclusions of
the first two movements. Literal quotations, such as may provide
a mechanical unity, are not in Walton's normal way of going to
work—the conclusion of the Sinfonia Concertante is exceptional
in this respect. You will hardly find him recapitulating a theme
strictly and his tunes might be called Protean or Bergsonian with
equal justice: they turn up in many different forms and they re-
create themselves as they proceed. But the organic unity of the
whole is forcibly brought home to the listener—he may even be
able here and there to put his finger on a piece of connective
tissue, such as the double-stopped sixths in the finale which recall
the first movement—because it has been fused in the crucible of
the composer's mind.

The work was composed during 1928-9 and received its first
performance at a Promenade Concert on 3 October 1929, with
the composer conducting and Paul Hindemith, the German composer and violist, playing the solo part. It was chosen by the jury
for performance at the International Festival of Contemporary
Music at Liége in 1930, when Lionel Tertis was the soloist and
the composer again conducted it. The inner history behind those

facts was revealed by the composer himself in the autobiographical article which he wrote for the *Sunday Telegraph* of 25 March 1962. It is worth retelling for its human interest. Walton writes:

It was Beecham who suggested my writing a viola concerto for Lionel Tertis. When it was completed I sent it to Tertis, who turned it down sharply by return of post, which depressed me a good deal as virtuoso violists were scarce. However, Edward Clark, who at that time was in charge of the music section of the B.B.C. and was rather the William Glock of his day, suggested we should go to Hindemith. So I duly conducted Hindemith in it at the first performance at a Prom in 1929. Tertis came and was completely won over, and he played the work whenever he had the chance.

The scoring is not unduly elaborate; the ordinary full orchestra with three each of the woodwind is employed, but very careful directions are given to secure the finer shades of orchestral colour and intensity.

Many years later, in 1961, the composer revised his score, reducing his woodwind to two, second players to take piccolo, cor anglais and bass clarinet respectively when required, and eliminating double bassoon and tuba altogether. He did, however, add a harp, an instrument he likes to use for purposes of colour and texture. Here he employs it to replace with its more effervescent tone some of the deep bass and some of the arpeggio figures of strings and woodwind. The changes of scoring naturally produce some changes in figuration and, particularly in the third movement some of the instrumental assignments, notably of the horns, whose parts are reduced in various ways. There is no difference of substance, though a trill may be added here, and there a rocking figure substituted for a counterpoint or other accompaniment, and in one place an anacrusis has quadruplets substituted for triplets. The harp, however, has a considerable part to play including some glissando figures. The general effect is to lighten the texture, i.e. without altering the colour to make it less opaque. The revised version was first performed at the Festival Hall in London on 18 January 1962.

The first movement is marked 'andante commodo' and is really the slow movement. Its plan is a regular but slightly condensed sonata form. Like many concertos since Mendelssohn, who dispensed with the classical opening tutti, it begins with an exposition stated by the solo instrument—the soloist in fact dominates the situation and the orchestra is content for the most part to add imitative counterpoints. The texture indeed is strikingly contrapuntal; the woodwind for instance is mostly employed to draw solo lines across the web, and passages of homophony for the full orchestra never last for more than a few bars at a time. After the first theme has been stated in a kind of A minor and a point has been made of a motif marked with a false relation—I quote its first appearance on the flutes at bar 13:

a second theme is given out in a new rhythm (simple triple instead of compound triple, which sometimes stretches itself to seven beats in the bar). Of this the predominant tonality, as determined by the melodic centre and the main emphasis of the bass, is F sharp. Then comes the development which is more incisive in contrast to the predominantly lyrical character of the exposition. At one point the solo is itself so worked upon as to demand the expression-mark 'martellato'. When the soloist returns after a brief orchestral tutti he resumes his suaver manner and plays the second subject now harmonized in double-stopped sixths (both with and without false relation). A second and longer tutti leads into a compressed recapitulation in which the two main themes are stated but once and the soloist makes his final observation in the falsely related sixths of Ex. 1.

Such is the ground plan. Now for the details. A dark background is immediately provided for a dark-hued solo by imitative phrases played by orchestral violas and first violins on their low strings and then by clarinet in its hollow-toned chalumeau register. In the third bar the soloist enters with

a theme whose passionate character is quickly proclaimed in its continuation:

This solo is drawn out in long arabesques against a background purposely obscured by tremolando and muted violins, through which are obtruded broken pieces of this undulating sort of melody and the falsely related sixths of Ex. 1 sharply etched by the wood-wind in turn. A short bridge passage, consisting of double-stopped parallel sixths on the solo viola, virtually unaccompanied save by a rumble in the bass, leads to the second subject in a new rhythm

announced by the soloist over a spare accompaniment:

A tapping with the point of the bow on the violins imparts a touch of asperity and animation to a stringendo passage which makes the movement become for the time being more restless, as it heads for the development in which the first subject (Ex. 2) appears in a more angular form. The solo viola submits it to still another change which breaks away into a run of semiquavers, while above it the wind play phrases from the second subject (Ex. 4). A very brief tutti leads to a reduction in speed and the soloist proceeds to treat the second subject in double-stopped sixths (without false relation). These consecutive sixths, either with or without false relation, are a basic idea of the movement:

This reassertion of F sharp minor makes it the main key of the development section. The remainder of the development, in which the solo plays no part, packs many events into a simultaneous tutti. The flute, oboe, and cor anglais do this:

Ex. 7

The clarinets take up the tapping quavers which they soon hand over to the four horns. The strings make scrubbing-brush noises sul ponticello, while the bass makes great heaves in this rhythm:

Ex. 8

sevenths, octaves, and ninths being indiscriminately thrust up in the effort. When the energy is exhausted the soloist introduces the recapitulation, in which each of the constituent ideas, viz: the first subject (Exs. 2 and 3), the second subject (Ex. 4), and the consecutive sixths (Ex. 6) are simply restated. As the movement ends the false relation in the sixths is once more made prominent.

The second movement is generally described as a rondo with the feeling of a scherzo. Its main theme certainly starts off crisply and briskly as though it might make a rondo tune, and it crops up time and again, sometimes where a rondo theme might be expected to recur. But the music will not fit into the scheme of a simple rondo: the two episodes stand next to each other without the intervention of the rondo tune, if one tries to analyse the movement that way. Then, too, there is a large development section in which the orchestra asserts itself and temporarily refuses to let the soloist have things all his own way. But neither is it a sonata-rondo as Beethoven understood the form, in which the first episode is equated with a second subject and ultimately recapitulated. The movement has an irrepressibility which will not lend itself to confinement within a formula. As always in Walton one tune becomes another by a process of creative evolution and the unity of the movement is organic rather than mechanical. Still, in this Scherzo we have a basic idea which recurs ritornello fashion (Ex. 10) and we have two contrasting ideas (Exs. 11 and 12) so that some schematization is possible. I view its ground plan as a modified sonata—the chief modifications being in the dimensions of the development, which is much expanded, and of the recapitulation, which is considerably compressed and curtailed.

The first idea develops from a mere germ:

Ex. 9

and grows like lightning to some forty bars in length. Its tonal centre is E minor with the supertonic more powerful than the dominant—the tonic chord in fact is

Ex. 9a

The rondo-like tune, which constitutes the first idea, is stated thus on its first appearance:

Ex. 10

Underneath this a restless bass goes out on the warpath. It is inclined to group itself into three quavers as it paces up and down the scale, but every now and again it misses a note or two, and when it picks itself up it finds itself counting twice three are five. This five-beat grouping necessitates some changes of time signature—1/4, 3/4, 3/8, 5/8. These irregularities are directed to be played 'con molto preciso'.

The transition to the second subject momentarily banishes this rhythmic unrest and while the orchestra goes pat-pat, pat-pat— though even here the accent gets misplaced before the passage is finished—the viola runs up the scale and plunges into a four-level-quaver bit of tune:

Ex. 11

though it quickly relapses into semiquavers and leaves the orchestra to carry on with quavers. The displacement of the accents prepares the way for a new idea in American rhythm:

Ex. 12

This bit of jazz—note how the soloist snaps at it with (*a*) as it thrusts it way upon the scene—is the first part of the second subject and asserts the tonality of A major-minor. It includes an explicit statement of the five-note group, another persistent feature of the movement, emphasized by presentation in contrary motion. The second constituent idea of the second subject asserts a flatter tonality, F major. Its beginning is marked by some three-note chords in syncopated rhythm on the solo viola (see Ex. 13 below for its shape and character), and its close by a solo statement of Ex. 12. Ex. 10 now returns in its original key. Is it a rondo coming round again, or is it the beginning of a development section, such as Beethoven would have written with an immediate reference to the first subject? The latter is the better analysis of the structure, though development is not a suitable description of the musical process involved, since the themes do not expand and flower as in Beethoven but contract, thereby, however, losing nothing in force. Ten bars of Ex. 10 are succeeded by the transition, which leads now to D major, and the second idea of the second subject—the chorded passage:

Ex. 13

This is an orchestral tutti, corresponding to the second big tutti in a Mozart concerto. The soloist joins in with allusions to Ex. 10, and an extensive review of the various rhythms and motifs ensues at unabated speed, culminating in another orchestral statement of Ex. 13, this time in a key signature of six sharps. This is the climax which eventually gives way to a recapitulation beginning for all the world like a rondo with Ex. 10 in E minor. What follows is a condensed review of the chief material, with many modifications of the soloist's figuration. The second subject, however, having had two orchestral statements of its larger component (Ex. 13) in the middle section, is content with a single ghostly restatement of its shorter member, Ex. 12. But the soloist will not tolerate a ghostly ending and, seizing the main thematic ideas, Exs. 9, 11 and the four semiquavers of Ex. 12, brusquely finishes the movement with a résumé in six bars:

Ex. 14

The third movement is the longest and discharges a function the precise opposite of most classical concerto finales: it gathers up the mercurial emotions of the first two movements and reveals their serious purpose. An epilogue (not so named) definitely recalls the opening of the concerto and sums up, not so much the finale, as the whole work in a passage of eloquent and serious discourse, whose mood is almost one of resignation. The process of gathering up what has gone before distends the form of the finale and expands its emotional range from a grotesque beginning to a sublime conclusion. Its dramatic scheme is the opposition of a persistent theme of strongly marked character against less obvious, more fugitive, but equally persistent, elements from the first movement. The main theme, very dry in its first statement on the bassoons, begins thus:

Ex. 15

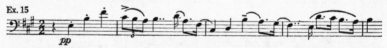

The dotted figures break into triplets before the soloist enters at the eighth bar and picks up the tune a fifth higher. This hint at fugal style is duly taken and there is a proper fugato before the end. Another hint is perhaps more like a pun and refers not to what is coming, but to what has gone; the Scherzo opened with an upward motif spelt F sharp, B, E, the finale opens with an upward motif spelt E, B, F sharp. Walton mostly avoids literal repetitions, but he is fond of allusions that conceal themselves in slightly wider or narrower intervals, slightly longer or shorter rhythms. So here, though we have his assurance that he was not consciously aware of the connexion.

The key is A major. The tune Ex. 15 is stated, and of course extended with more dotted-note figures and triplets, three times. The orchestra's two enunciations are 7 bars long, the soloist's which comes between them, sandwich fashion, is 13 bars long. The key changes to A minor and a squirming figure constitutes a transition to a second subject of a totally different character. The transition, amounting to another 13 bars shared between both parties, is constituted thus:

Ex. 16

The second subject is in two pieces, both of them more lyrical than anything that has been heard for some time:

Ex. 17

and

Ex. 18

which is like unto it, especially in the common shape of their second bars. But we have had double-stopped sixths before in the first movement. Also in the first movement we had a second subject identical in shape, but slightly different in melodic interval—compare Ex. 4. So this is the point at which first and third movements come to grips.

An extended development follows, the processes of which are almost conventional; imitation, canon even, and augmentation are used. The augmentation allows the soloist some florid runs and trills, the equivalent of the old-fashioned 'second solo'.

When Ex. 15 appears in order to begin the recapitulation, its key is A minor and its opening phrase employs different intervals and different degrees of the scale in Walton's most characteristic manner:

Ex. 19

ff Str. & w.w.

This brief statement by the orchestra leads quickly to the buzzing triplet transition, Ex. 16, which the soloist takes over single-handed. This too is reduced in length, and Ex. 17 is soon once more upon the scene, this time in C and played by horns and woodwind with the solo viola descanting above them. When Ex. 18 follows, a little late owing to the fascinations of double stopped sixths, it turns off into something like a cadenza, supported only by chords. This ought to be the conclusion of the matter, but it by no means fulfils expectation, for it leads instead into a new and even longer second development, beginning in the remote key of F major. The first subject is again under discussion, the keys are impermanent, so that it would give the wrong impression to call the whole of this long passage to the end of the movement an epilogue. Emotionally, the epilogue does not occur till the key and the theme and the tempo settle down to what they were at the beginning of the movement, and much has still to happen before that point is reached. What does happen is first a reconsideration of Ex. 15 and then a decision to treat it in fugato with certain modifications of its rhythmic outline. This leads naturally to a big and heavily orchestrated climax in which the soloist has nothing to say. When it is over the tone dies away, the soloist re-enters, the key is back once more at A major. Ex. 15 returns, but is completely subdued by the super-imposition of Ex. 2 from the beginning of the concerto. The falsely related sixths of the first movement also recur and assert their influence in the very last cadence of all, in which the solo viola sustains A and C sharp while the orchestral violas softly clash C natural against it in three pizzicato chords. There is just a touch of acerbity in the reverie over these tunes from the past, and the oboes intensify the poignancy by a soft but acute sequence of thirds.

Is it a melancholy end? Not really, for the main feeling is one of accomplishment and acceptance. The lingering farewell is, as it were, covered by the falling twilight and the boat glides out to sea in calm. But the viola is like Jessica: at the sound of sweet music it is never merry.

Concerto for Violin and Orchestra

The Violin Concerto was commissioned from Walton by Jascha Heifetz, who reserved it for his own performance exclusively for two years. In the spring of 1939 the composer visited the violinist in America to incorporate into the solo part Heifetz's own suggestions for presenting the substance of the music in the most effective light that violin technique could cast upon it. The last touch was put to the score in New York on 2 June 1939. Six months later (on 7 December) it received its first performance at Cleveland, Ohio, under Artur Rodzinski. It was subsequently given with success by other conductors in America, including Eugene Goossens, who recorded it with the Cincinnati Orchestra and Heifetz in the solo part. The concerto's journey to England, where it was first performed at a Philharmonic concert at the Albert Hall on 1 November 1941, did not escape the hazards of war. Heifetz's own proofs bearing his own bowing and fingering of the solo part were lost in the Atlantic, but a photographic copy made in New York as a precaution was safely delivered by air to the Oxford University Press in London. A set of gramophone records was also lost in transit, so that neither the composer nor Henry Holst, who together undertook its first presentation to an English audience, had heard the work before the concert.

The first movement of this violin concerto resembles the first movement of the Viola Concerto in being the slowest of the three; it is deeply felt but of less weight and substance than first movements used to be, thus reserving for the finale not only the summary and conclusion of the argument, but the greatest length and the symphonic range of an allegro movement. The actual tempo of this predominantly lyrical movement is 'andante tranquillo'. The key is definitely B minor. The solo instrument leads off with the first theme without any opening orchestral tutti, as in most modern concertos. The orchestra, however, has just enough time, before the soloist begins, to establish an accompanimental figure of a decisive rhythmic shape:

Ex. 1

The very first motif of (a) infects the whole movement, though the Scotch snap is pervasive rather than emphatic. The figure (b) is maintained with constantly varying instrumentation: the clarinet is succeeded by the muted viola, and the second violin takes a hand when it passes into its range; to and fro it goes on these shifting tints of what is basically the same sombre tone colour while muted horns hold the softest possible chord. This being the background, the tune stands out in relief without raising its voice above the mood of noble and dreamy (sognando) melancholy—A. The tune, however, is only one part of a composite first subject. Below it the bassoon and cello spell out a long-breathed counter-theme in the tenor which must not be overlooked—B:

Ex. 2

The opening leap is naturally an octave to strengthen the effect of anacrusis, but the interval that gives its character to the melody is the seventh, as can be observed not only in the second and third occurrences of this significant leap, but elsewhere between the pivot notes of the swaying tune. For its full statement it takes the orthodox 16 bars.

The architectural ground-plan of the first movement is a very much modified sonata form, in which sheer quantity and geography override, but do not dispense with, the classical principles of balance of subjects and balance of keys.

Geographically speaking the exposition of the first subject, which runs from the opening to figure [5] in the score and quantitatively occupies 44 bars at a tempo of 'andante tranquillo', is exactly counter-balanced at the close of the movement from figure [22] to the end by 45 bars of the same thematic material at the same tempo. The middle section of the movement between [5] and [22] is divided geographically by a cadenza. Quantitatively, however, the cadenza belongs to the first half of this middle section, since we find the following proportions: from [5] to [9], which comprises the second subject of the Exposition, is 30 bars; from [9] to [15], containing the first part of the development and the cadenza, is some sixty-odd bars (bar lines give out, naturally enough, amid the excitement of a cadenza); the stretch from [15] to [19] which deals with the development of the second subject and other matters, is also something over sixty bars long; from [19] to [22], where the recapitulation begins, it is just over thirty bars. So we have a formal lay-out, almost like that of an Italian garden, thus:

44 bars	30 bars	about 65 bars	65 bars	30 bars	45 bars
Start to [5]	[5] - [9]	[9] - [15]	[15] - [19]	[19]-[22]	[22] to end

In terms of sonata form the movement can be analysed thus:

Exposition: first subject in B minor, Ex. 2, A and B, as far as figure [5]; second subject in E flat minor and E minor, Ex. 3, figures [5] to [9].

Development: first subject, cadenza, second subject, orchestral tutti, and third solo from [9] to [22].

Recapitulation: first subject in B minor and reference to, but no complete restatement of, the second subject, from [22] to the end.

Now to the contents of these various components.

The chief melody, Ex. 2A, is stated by the soloist, while the bassoon and cello play the counter-theme, Ex. 2 B. When this is done the orchestra takes its turn in announcing the main theme, or at any rate the first part of it, Ex. 2 A, though the soloist soon claims it once more. This restatement of the theme begins to veer flatwards rather curiously, with the result that the second subject arrives in the 'wrong' key. This more flowing but shorter-phrased tune, Ex. 3 below, appears with a signature of six flats, i.e. the key has missed its mark by a tone and a half, so that we are landed in nine degrees of flatness, and the general pitch of the music lies a diminished fourth instead of a perfect fifth higher. This is carrying out on the greatly magnified scale of key-interval an idiosyncrasy constantly found in Walton's melodic intervals. The substitution of an octave for a seventh in Ex. 2 is a mild example; a more striking instance is to be found in the Viola Concerto's first movement (see p. 83), where ninths and sevenths alternate with octaves.

Arrived, then, at this oblique-angled key the movement announces its second theme promptly upon the orchestra. It is a simple theme derived from y in Ex. 2 B climbing and declining in two-bar phrases:

Ex. 3   Flute & Strings   Oboe

mp ━━━━━   mf ━━━━

The accompaniment is an arpeggio figure of a conventional shape in quavers consisting of flowing triads, but containing an alien note—notably a seventh in a strong position. This feature (triad with added note) is found also in the soloist's figuration. The solo violin, when it comes, as it does almost immediately, to make its statement of the new theme (Ex. 3), tires of the remote obscurity of E flat minor and decides on the sub-dominant minor of the main key for its highly ornamental version of this second theme. The signature is changed by cancelling all flats; the key, however, is not C but rather a very unstable E minor. The general character of the music is now restless, and almost every chord of the harmony contains a discordant seventh. The interval of the seventh, in fact, is the basic germ of the music. There is much tempo rubato until the soloist broadens out on his G string in a little codetta which thematically seems to be an epitome of Exs. 1 and 2:

Ex. 4

poco allargando quasi ad lib.

This is the signal for the development section to begin.

At first sight the tune propounded by the horns and later echoed by the soloist a semitone higher is not an obvious relation of Ex. 2 A:

Ex. 5

But scrutinized more closely it will be seen to bear the main features—the emphatic anacrusis, the octave leap, the contour of bars 2 and 3 being the equivalent of the second complete bar of Ex. 2 A, and the quavers the equivalent of the triplet figure in the second, sixth and tenth bars. It is in fact all but a note-for-note repetition of the first 7 bars of Ex. 2 A, but varied in rhythm, texture and pace (which is quicker).

The next text for discussion is a version of Ex. 2 B propounded by trombones at [11]:

Ex. 6   *con 8*

Trb.   *pp*   *mf*

and presently repeated by trumpets and woodwind. Just before the cadenza (at [13]) 2 A reaches its most remote transformation:

Ex. 7

Trpts.
ff

After the cadenza it is the turn of the second subject, Ex. 3, to be enlarged upon. Enlarged it is, in the technical sense of augmentation. It is accompanied by a conventionalized five-note figure derived from the opening of Ex. 2 A over an um-pum-pum bass. This broadening of the theme, the steady maintenance of a symmetrical accompaniment and the general lowering of the dynamics, make a welcome lull—is it not a common function of second subjects to modify the aggressive character of their more masculine partner? However, the first subject is not to be silenced. At [18] the soloist plays 2 A in outline very high up; at [19] 2 B launches an orchestral tutti very low down; at [20], a phrase of 2 B, hitherto not very prominent, viz. its last three bars, emerges; and the entrance of the solo after [21] is also based on this passage and leads into the recapitulation.

This recapitulation is very complete, as far as the first subject is concerned, the orchestra taking A and the soloist B to begin with and subsequently reversing roles. A new accompanying figure, consisting of descending semiquavers and chromatics, adds a sort of anxious urgency to the surprise. Near the end to the movement there are two short allusions to the second subject, Ex. 3, just sufficient to make it felt amid the attenuation of the main theme and of the general texture.

Second Movement

Technical virtuosity is a proper and indeed a necessary ingredient in a concerto. In this second movement the violin goes through its paces at a pace 'presto capriccioso alla napolitana', and since the listener to an actual performance will be far more aware of what the violin is doing than of any thematic or harmonic peculiarities upon which the orchestra may be engaged, so the score reader will be wise to look at the solo line first. There are no formal puzzles to trouble him since the movement is a reasonably regular scherzo with a trio. The Trio is a self-contained section labelled a Canzonetta.

Tonality is not quite so straightforward, since the main theme is characterized by the interval of the augmented fifth, which is subversive of key. But the second theme is in C sharp minor comfortably enough. It consists of a sustained double-stopped cantilena—like the parallel sixths in the Viola Concerto. The trio is in a kind of flat C major. Its tune, Ex. 16, is in C major by inspection, as the mathematicians say. But it is harmonized over an A flat and a B flat, and when the soloist starts to play triplets over it, As are always flattened, and Bs, though they only occur as grace notes, are still flat. So that the mode is not mixolydian (for although its third is sharp, its sixth is flat), nor is it Aeolian (since though its sixth and seventh are flat, its third is sharp), nor is it Dorian (again because its third is sharp and its sixth flat), but is a hybrid mode with one sharp and one flat tetrachord. An ambiguous but sharp-flavoured tonality for the Scherzo is offset by a flat C for the Trio.

This precarious tonality (which first feels like F, then is tugged towards B flat but is ultimately shown to be A) is thrown at the listener like a question in the opening phrase:

which the soloist then proceeds to spell out in the reverse, upward direction and in a form more apt to his bow:

One can hear the accents as the flying bow skims up the arpeggio with these periodic pressures on the strings. It is instructive to set out the violin's varied statements of this theme, since such a table shows both the kind of technical exploits which Heifetz invited and the characteristic Waltonian inability to tolerate identical statements of his themes. Here they are:

(Even the incidence of the 'hairpins' of expression and the number of notes grasped in a single stroke of the bow are different.)

Its final appearance is as Ex. 10 with the first bar played tremolando and sul ponticello.

From these quotations it will be seen that close study of this movement will provide ample interest in matters of detail, but the pace is such that the effect on the ear is one more example of that sharp, bright, dangerous, and flickering tone characteristic of Walton's music, which one is inclined to attribute to his scoring, but is really inherent in its substance. The ambiguity of key is an instance of this superpiquancy. When one hears Exs. 8 and 9 at the beginning of the movement the tonality deludes the ear into thinking it as F with a sharpened fifth. In the opening bars there is no B flat, but when the violinist counterstates the theme B flat is not only present to his arpeggio, but the whole passage is harmonized over a bass that swings from low F to B flat as from dominant to tonic. Is the key then F or B flat? The question is not answered nor the ambiguity resolved, since a bridge passage turns

aside into E major—this is where Ex. 11 occurs. Here also is where
the orchestra asserts itself to present its version of the theme:

Ex. 14

But in the final restatement the crucial phrase, Ex. 8, leads quite
decisively to a close in A, and one can see that A would round it
off on its previous occurrences. So we find ourselves moving from
a first subject in A to a second in C sharp minor. Here is the
second subject over a waltz accompaniment:

Ex. 15   Con molto rubato

After this the first theme recurs in the form of Ex. 12 over a
muttered string accompaniment.

The tune of the Trio is announced first by the horn of the
orchestra. The soloist ultimately gets it and plays it two and then
three octaves higher. Here it is with its sub-fusc bass:

Ex. 16   (Canzonetta)

This is a slower, more lyrical section and elicits from the soloist,
before it is over, some more double-stopped cantilena. The
Scherzo returns in the form of Ex. 13 and recalls briefly its second
subject in double-stopped sixths as well as the tune of the Trio
before the crisp restatement of Ex. 10 brings the movement to its
end on that elusive, but at last disclosed, chord of A. The Neapolitan Scherzo, with its hints of the Tarantella, and the canzonetta Trio give an Italian character to music which was in fact
composed in that country.

H

Finale

In this movement, expanded to contain a long reference to the main tune of the first movement as well as a cadenza that grows out of it, there is comparative economy of material. The two principal themes are sharp-pointed, the one gruff and the other shrill—though naturally they change their tone, if not altogether their temper, in the course of the movement:

Ex. 17

and

Ex. 18

Ex. 17 leads off in the orchestra, is taken up by the solo violin in double stops, is harmonized in solid chords and shared between the two parties in short antiphonal lengths. Ex. 18 follows immediately, but soon makes way for the sort of more stable melody one expects in a well conducted second subject:

Ex. 19

This rhapsodic utterance, marked 'flessibile', is appropriately accompanied by violas and harp, a romantic combination controlled however by the establishment of a regular pattern. It lasts longer than its appearance on paper would at first sight suggest, since the tempo is three times as slow as that of Ex. 17 and Ex. 18, which must be regarded as together constituting the first subject. The section beginning with their alternation and elaboration is the development, which starts promptly as soon as Ex. 19 has fully extended its cantilena.

Owing to the difficulty of describing musical events in words the account of what happens in the development sections of symphonic movements is usually scanty. Yet it is just precisely what happens to the themes which have been so carefully delineated that constitutes the chief intellectual interest of sonata form. Here it must suffice to note that by having a double-barrelled first subject the composer complicates his plot and increases the possibilities of adventure for his themes. In the first movement the two components of the first subject occur simultaneously; here in the finale they are stated in succession until the middle of the development at [59], when they are put in counterpoint one against the other by soloist against orchestra. They go further: they augment and diminish themselves (in the technical sense) as they parley together. Augmentation, it may be observed in passing, is very extensively employed in this concerto as a means of securing internal cohesion.

There is a cadenza in the middle of this development, as correspondingly in the first movement, but it is short and not sufficiently demonstrative to challenge comparison with the big cadenza which occurs later in the movement at the conventional place within sight of the end.

The violinist's trills lead now to a change of time and of key for a restatement of the second subject, Ex. 19, which is taken here instead of later in the recapitulation for a reason that will appear when that point is reached. It is fully stated in the tonic major key of B by the orchestra, while the soloist descants over it a slowed down version of Ex. 17, thus linking the two principal subjects.

This more expansive moment of high-flown melody over long-drawn counterpoints from woodwind and strings speaking in pairs (violin and flute, violoncello and clarinet, violin and oboe) and soft mysterious tremolando accompaniment, brings the development to an end. A particularly brusque and low-pitched version of Ex. 17 over a rolling three-note pedal marks the beginning of the Recapitulation.

The marked rhythms of Ex. 17 and Ex. 18 are excellent landmarks, but they are both only the starting points of quite lengthy extensions, in which the solo violin may indulge in passages which develop many other rhythmic features, sometimes for instance steady crotchet chords, sometimes steady triplet quavers. But the orchestra holds on to Ex. 17 and Ex. 18 as to the reins of the movement. Instead of the recapitulation of Ex. 19, which received a full and more than usually (for Walton) exact restatement in the development section of the movement, we find a passage of similarly lyrical character, which turns out to be the main theme of the first movement stated in the double-stopped parallel sixths that Walton is accustomed to use in his string writing for the purpose of intensifying his melody. After a few bars of the intruding theme, Ex. 17 steals in quietly in the bass, making rather a dry sound on bassoon and pizzicato violoncellos in contrast to the luscious sostenuto of the solo instrument, but knitting these two distant ideas together.

The tonality of the passage is interesting. The tune is at the same pitch as in the first movement, i.e. in B minor—no doubt the more certainly to recall it to the mind of the listener—but the signature now is one of three sharps, and instead of a tonic triad for background we have a chord of the ninth over a pedal E. On this the basses sway arpeggio-wise to and fro to F sharp and B, gravitating towards E, but finally coming out into a bright B major for an accompanied cadenza. The accompaniment is poised quite in the conventional manner over a six-four chord on F sharp, while the cadenza itself is occupied in turn with Ex. 19 played slowly in thirds, with Ex. 17 also in thirds, proceeding after a pause to Ex. 19, and finishing with flourishes ultimately derived from Ex. 2 A. From cadenza to coda: the orchestra resumes Ex. 17 'deliberatamente accelerando poco a poco' until, with a fanfare from the brass, the movement passes into a quick march over a striding bass which bears the concerto to an end that may justly be called triumphant. For the final page is simple and clear-cut in rhythm and decisive in tonality: to make the sharpness of B major sharp beyond a doubt the final chord is a tonic seventh.

The relationship with the first movement is established through the kinship of the first subject of the first movement with the second subject of the finale, i.e. of Ex. 2 and Ex. 19. The use of a subject based on Ex. 17 as a counterpoint to Ex. 19 ensures the unity of the finale. All three themes are assembled in the cadenza, which thus has unusual structural importance, where they are seen to be congruent with one another and with some of the figuration that the soloist has employed in his task of carrying the whole movement with hardly a bar's intermission to its climax and conclusion.

Concerto for Violoncello and Orchestra

Walton disclaims all ability to play an instrument and recalls the piano lessons of his boyhood with wry amusement. Yet concertos for instruments bulk largest in his output. He wrote his Cello Concerto in 1956 to the commission of Gregor Piatigorsky. It has some natural kinship with the other two concertos for strings, more particularly the Viola Concerto with its similarly dark tone, poignant feeling and double-stopped sixths, though equally naturally it contains gruffer passages proper to a bass instrument with rosin flying off the bow. As in everything he does the score is calculated to the last detail. The orchestration is full, though so disposed as not to smother the solo, as can easily happen when the instrument is of low pitch, but third players for the extremities of the woodwind family are not required. Three players, however, are required for percussion, which includes a vibraphone, and there is a part for celesta. The cello has a reputation for melancholy—was there not once a parody of Maeterlinck which ran 'Ah sad, how sad, sadder than a cello solo'?—but this concerto has the energy characteristic of the composer, energy generated in his usual way by dotted notes, doubly dotted notes, demisemiquaver rests on strong beats and, for the cello itself, copious streams of semiquavers.

The first movement is the least energetic—its mark is 'moderato'. It starts with a splash, as of a stone dropped into a pool, a chord on the vibraphone and harp, trills on a viola and an oscillating figure on the wind and upper strings. After two bars the soloist enters. His part is meditative, though ranging widely through the cello's compass; it ends with a protracted diatonic cadence, of which the last bars drop through five octaves. The middle movement looks like a scherzo but is marked 'allegro appassionato' and is in fact not only the core of the work but the most substantial and the most highly, if unconventionally, organized movement of the three. For a parallel to the finale one would have to look far. Variations of a sort to be sure, but the idea of antithesis, which is of the original essence of concerto form though it has not been greatly in evidence so far in this concerto, is here exploited to the extent of solo instrument and orchestra having alternate variations to the exclusion of the other party. It ends with an epilogue, in which the device of quoting from the previous movements is used in moderation to ensure the conscious recognition of the thematic unity of the work as a whole, hitherto probably only perceived subliminally. This underlying unity is not easily demonstrated in music-type because of Walton's tendency to vary his themes in detail, to write a sixth for a seventh for instance while retaining or bending their shape. The interval of the seventh in various guises is one such element of unity in this work; a pair of demisemi-quavers variously organized in dotted formation to give a kick of impetus is another. Impetus in fact is the main source of the unity and coherence of the concerto.

The lay-out of the first movement is determined by the dis-position of the solo part, which consists of seven paragraphs. These paragraphs are mostly ten bars in length, but No. 3, which constitutes a middle section of rhapsodic development, is a full 16 bars long, and No. 5, which is a substitute for the recapitula-tion of No. 2, is extended to eleven and a half bars. The key of the movement is a clear C major acidulated with some discordant high overtones. The tonality moves to E major and G flat (acidulated variety, by false relation of D natural and D flat) as secondary centres. Both the flux and the temporary stability of the tonality is achieved in Walton's usual manner of a very firm bass, mostly triads but sometimes pedals. The harmonic feature which accounts for the acidulation of the keynote in the first bar and emerges as a false relation in the coda—compare the Viola Con-certo—is a clash and an ambiguity of semitones, as shown in Ex. 1:

Ex. 1

A flat is an added sixth to the chord of C, which gives it a slight, very slight curdle, but above, D sharp alternates with E natural, as in Chopin's second Prelude, to create instability. The underlying harmony, however, is as firm as a rock, proceeding as it does on a sequence of unhurrying triads:

Ex. 2

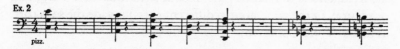

If Ex. 2, together with the first cello theme above it, Ex. 3 below, is regarded as the main subject A, then the structure of the movement is ABCADA=Coda, where B and C are counterpoises to A which, with their contrasting but essentially congruent thematic material, establish secondary tonalities. The congruence of the material may be seen if the main theme is dismantled. Its character is of a long continuous and sustained melodic line. Yet it is no symmetrical tune like a folk-song or Handelian aria but a compound of elements, some rhythmic, some intervallic, some motific that have been spun into a continuous thread, in which it would be hard to insert phrase marks over the bowing slurs anywhere before the penultimate bar:

Ex. 3 Moderato

To enumerate: there is the interval of the rising fifth (*a*), diminished, augmented or perfect; the dotted-note figure (*b*), appearing first with a demisemiquaver in its tail recurs with larger values: and a gruppetto of four semiquavers (*c*) makes two appearances with a triplet between them; the significant intervals all rise, fourths, fifths, sixths, sevenths including an augmented seventh at the cadence. In themselves these features have no significance—

after all all music must do something or other—but they recur in other orders in the other themes.

By contrast there is at the end of the middle section a striking counterpoise: the intervals are turned down hill and double-stopped to emphasize the fact, the gruppetti also run down or are inverted, and false relations (i.e. inconsistent inflection sharp, flat, or natural, of the same note in different parts) invade the solo part, as in the Viola Concerto:

Ex. 4

This feature from Ex. 4 reappears, transformed, augmented (in the technical sense) and in canon, (see Ex. 17 below) carried over a switchback of the cello's whole compass, as the coda and conclusion of the movement. The middle section is marked 'a tempo tranquillo (pochiss. meno mosso)'. The second episode, which remains to be accounted for, is simpler than the other sections with less rhythmic movement—the solo line indulges in octave leaps and the orchestra in succulent thirds on divided strings. It is not differentiated by a tempo mark. There is no cadenza in this movement.

The form of the second, central movement is that of an eel out of water, a large electric eel, and the only thing to do with it is to cut it up into lengths. This is not difficult, since under the smooth surface of the skin it is articulated into three sections. There is a great wealth of thematic material to be accounted for, and not all of it occurs where one would expect it. The first subject, call it A, contains three distinguishable ideas, an incisive affair of semiquavers:

Ex. 5

a suggestion from the opening bars:

and a more expressive cantilena, though only in one-bar phrases:

An allusion to the first idea Ex. 5 rounds it off, making 22 solo bars out of a total of 30 for A. The basic tonality is C sharp minor for thematic analysis shows that Ex. 5 is in essence a descending scale of C sharp minor in its plagal form:

Now follows a development of A, nearly 30 bars long, which is capped by a phrase in harmonics for the cello:

This recurs near the end of later sections.

Just before the sixtieth bar at [6] in the score the cellist is silent and the orchestra embarks on a kind of military march, but the cellist soon takes a hint from its ta-tantara-tan figure to embark on a new theme, which constitutes the chief member of the second group, B:

of which the basic tonality is A minor. Some stormy dialogue between solo and orchestra follows in which the cello throws off a phrase of triple stopping that recurs thrice later:

The cellist has two more ideas to throw at the orchestra, one brusque:

the other like a quotation from *Troilus and Cressida*:

Exs. 9 and 11 complete this section of 60 bars.

The third section recapitulates the second beginning with Ex. 10 now in E minor and invoking in turn Exs. 11, 12, and 13, but putting in a short cadenza, half accompanied, half solo, just before the reappearance of Ex. 13. Ex. 9 is also in attendance. All the material between [7] and [13] is reviewed again between [14] and [20], i.e. B is recapitulated at once.

The last and shortest section recalls but does not quote in full Ex. 5 of the first subject. As final coda the cello runs up the scale of C sharp minor from bottom to top—a harmonic on high C sharp—marked 'col legno' and 'throwing bow' for the last glissando.

The form is therefore what the Germans call *Bogen* ABBA + Coda, but as the last A is only a token recapitulation the movement is not so symmetrical as the formula suggests and the bow is less regular than Cupid's.

The third movement presents no comparable problem of analysis: it is a set of variations and the events are easily distinguishable. The composer entitles it 'Tema ad improvvisazioni' and its improvisatory character is stressed by the fact that two of the variations are given to the cello without accompaniment. The theme is announced at once by the soloist over a very light accompaniment of little more than pizzicato strings, though its statement is rounded off by 6 bars of orchestral postlude, in which

allusion is made to the motif

Ex. 14

This is the decisive rhythmic feature of the theme, no simple tune, this, but a highly organized cantilena:

Ex. 15

which goes from C minor to C major by a series of evasions, deliberately breaking off on F sharp to leave itself neutrally in the air while the orchestra finishes off the sentence and is equally evasive about its rhythm in spite of the apparent assertiveness of Ex. 14.

What follows are a quicker variation of the theme played by the orchestra while the soloist decorates it, an even quicker variation for cello solo, one quicker still for orchestra alone, then another rhapsodical variation for cello solo. The final section is an epilogue with allusions to previous movements. The relations of the variations to the theme are far from obvious owing to Walton's partiality for thematic polymorphism enhanced no doubt by the idea of quasi-improvisation and to the plasticity of the theme itself, but there is no doubt about their relevance or the unity of the complex whole.

The first variation goes into triplets and compound time. For this the soloist had already given warrant by what he does in the last bar of the theme Ex. 15 and in the link which he supplies between the theme and its first variation. This is an unbarred though measured solo marked 'con moto' as a transition from

lento to the speed of the variation. The orchestration produces a
shimmering effect by the use of tremolando on the strings played
sul ponticello and the emergence of the decorative instruments,
vibraphone, xylophone, celesta, and harp. The first of the two
cadenza variations is marked 'risoluto' and 'brioso' and begins
gruffly with an obsession about the intervals G sharp and C sharp
on the one hand and G sharp and D sharp on the other, an oscillation which will be found centrally placed in the first chord Ex. 1
and in bars 6 to 8 of the theme Ex. 15. For his climax the soloist
falls back once more on the always effective double stop in sixths.
The next, orchestral variation is a toccata, again in compound (9/8)
time, a rumbustious affair with a good deal of percussion,
glissandi for horns and harps, use of the piccolo and such excitements. The connexion with the theme seems to be the sequence
of shifting tonalities implied in the descending arpeggios of bars
13 to 15 of the theme, Ex. 15.

In contrast to the first resolute cadenza variation the soloist now
has a licensed rhapsody to himself, in which between string-
sweeping arpeggios, double stops and the motif Ex. 14 wild
fluctuations of speed occur. The excitement culminates in trills
which provide a link with the final section. This is an epilogue
containing allusions to the first movement, notably the striding
phrase on the strings from the fourth section [at fig. 6]:

Ex. 16.   cantabile

and the double-stopped canonic cadence:

Ex. 17

which slides into the theme of the variations, literally quoted as to
its first five bars but thereafter in an alternating paraphrase. The
chords of the ambiguous semitone Ex. 1 recur at the end as the
cello climbs down to its bottom C.

The cellist's repertory of concertos is a small one—Boccherini,

Haydn (two), Schumann (one), Dvořák (one), Saint-Saëns (two) and Elgar (one). Elgar's received international currency to a greater extent than his Violin Concerto and symphonies—Casals played it, the Frenchmen Fournier and Tortelier have taken it up and Piatigorsky, who having commissioned this concerto from Walton remarked at the time of its first performance in London that the world in the twentieth century got its cello concertos from England—Elgar, Delius, and Walton all wrote cello concertos of English provenance. This one by Walton while lacking nothing in eloquence is the most intellectually challenging of them all.

CHAPTER IV

Smaller Orchestral Works

SCATTERED among the works of large scale discussed in the last chapter are a number of orchestral works of varied character, which show that Walton is a more versatile composer than the homogeneous character of his symphonic output, or the not very extensive range of mood portrayed in it, may lead one to think. Commissions, *pièces d'occasion*, and film music, have produced these smaller canvases.

The overture *Portsmouth Point* comes next to *Façade* in the list of his published works, since the intermediate compositions have been discarded. Its date is 1925. *Siesta* is a miniature for chamber orchestra which appeared in 1926. Arrangements for piano duet of both these works have been made by the composer himself. *Crown Imperial* was commissioned by the B.B.C.; it was first performed by its orchestra under Boult on 9 May 1937. It was written to celebrate the Coronation and is available in numerous arrangements for different instruments and combinations of instruments. *Scapino* bore the date 28 December 1940, at the end of the original score. It was written to commemorate the fiftieth anniversary of the foundation of the Chicago Symphony Orchestra and is dedicated to that body and its conductor, Dr F. A. Stock, who gave it its first performance in April 1941. It was first performed in England by the B.B.C. on 12 November 1941. A third concert overture, the *Johannesburg Festival Overture*, was another birthday commission—from the city of Johannesburg in 1956. A second Coronation March *Orb and Sceptre* was commissioned by the Arts Council for the Coronation of Queen Elizabeth II in 1953. Walton composed a ballet score for Frederick Ashton's *The Quest* in 1943, having previously arranged music by Bach for his *The Wise Virgins* in 1940. He began writing film music in 1934, with *Escape Me Never*, from which a ballet survives, and during the war wrote half a dozen scores of which *Henry V* was the chief. This was later followed by two other Shakespeare films, *Hamlet* (1947) and *Richard III* (1955). The *Spitfire Prelude and Fugue* was taken from the film *The First of the Few* (1942). *Music for Children* is an orchestral suite made from the piano duets he wrote for his nephew and niece in 1940.

It will be convenient to take these pieces out of chronological order and discuss them by categories, beginning with the three overtures.

Portsmouth Point

Portsmouth Point is correctly described as a comedy overture, and its inspiration was pictorial. *Portsmouth Point* was prompted by a print of Thomas Rowlandson, the English caricaturist who was a contemporary of Beethoven (1756–1827). The picture shows an animated scene on the water front at Portsmouth. There is roystering, fighting, kissing, street music, goods traffic, all preparatory to embarkation on the ships in the harbour, some of which have their sails already set.

Like the picture, the score is crowded with bustling figures. Bits break off like individuals and small groups from a seething crowd. Rhythmic irregularities induced by a perpetual change of time-signature impart tremendous animation to the music, and the element of vigorous caricature is reproduced by the deliberate exploitation of incongruities. Thus, a square opening theme in the robust style of Handel is dislocated in the first bar by a syncopation and subsequently by wilful cross-accents, phrases are repeated in sequence, a rare device in Walton's technique, but the sequence, whose normal function is to suggest a regular pattern, has its regularity clipped or is spread across different beats; the jostling of bars of 5/8 and 2/8 time implies that in a less erratic world they might all have been in a cheerfully commonplace 6/8; the melodic figures have a way of tumbling over with a bump. The scoring is both shrill and heavy. Indeed the piquancy of the viands is somewhat obscured by the extreme savouriness of the sauce.

The events in this eventful piece cannot be catalogued otherwise than as they appear in the score, one hard on the heels of the next. We may observe, however, the following detachable but not detached episodes. After the square introduction comes a tune:

Interjections of the opening anacrusis of a hornpipe let loose a sequential development of constituents of Ex. 1, with the square but syncopated introduction alternating with them. The second section of the overture goes from C to E flat, and there are several attempts to form another subject, of which these two are prominent:

Note the deliberate disturbance of symmetry between the first two phrases of Ex. 2, and observe that Ex. 3 develops into a solo for a boatswain's pipe. The two motifs are then amalgamated or transformed into something bearing the distinguishing mark of the four reiterated notes of Ex. 3. Two versions of it, one with semiquavers and the other with angular intervals, are then started off in a sort of canon, but the canon does not persist. Instead, we come to a section in B major founded ultimately but *longo intervallo* on Ex. 2 and its final bunch of semiquavers. A page or two of sequences and the recurrence of Ex. 3 in the bass leads to a recapitulation of Ex. 1 and its entourage. A flourish of the hornpipe finishes it sharply.

There is still a good deal of the *enfant terrible* about the work in its delight in prickly rhythms, the mockery of academic devices, and the revelling in enormous tonal masses from an orchestra with a specification of three each of the wind, trumpet included, and a copious battery. The composer has himself admitted the influence of Stravinsky. But it has the high spirits of youth and it asserted the arrival of a new personality in English music. It is dedicated to Siegfried Sassoon, and was first performed at the Zurich festival of the ISCM in 1926.

Scapino

The score of this comedy overture bears on its cover the portrait of its vagabond hero and its title page declares it to be 'after an etching from Jacques Callot's *Les Trois Pantalons*, 1619. Scapino appears from the portrait to be a proletarian Mephistopheles, but he has more style than his Germanic cousin, Till Eulenspiegel. Callot (1592–1635) was a French engraver born in Lorraine, who, after a training in Italy, achieved international fame and executed commissions for distinguished persons besides publishing sets of his own plates, as in the book which contains the picture under discussion. Scapino himself was the rascally servant of the Commedia dell' Arte, the confidential slave of the old Latin farces, who planned his master's escapades, especially amorous escapades. The erotic side of his character gets a section to itself in the middle of the overture. The revised score of 1950 bears this note:

Scapino is one of the less familiar characters of the Commedia dell'Arte, the hero of Molière's 'Les Fourberies de Scapin', who may figure in the complicated ancestry of Figaro. We owe him the word 'escapade', which is descriptive of the character's stock-in-trade. Callot's etching portrays him in his traditional costume.

The original score was laid out for large orchestra containing a full chorus of woodwind, three to each family, a couple of cornets to provide antiphony to the trumpets, harp, and a copious battery of percussion. The revised score, while retaining the percussion, is scored for normal orchestra. It begins molto vivace and fortissimo with a rushing figure from strings and wind and a clatter of percussion in Walton's old brittle style. A bold theme from the trumpet with a syncopated kink in it proclaims the hero at once. The smoother side of his tongue is indicated immediately after in an observation from the oboe and violas, a pert nonchalant little tune.

I

Here then is Scapino as he first presents himself:

Other melodic fragments and figures fly about and fill the air. There is, however, an important second subject in a new key:

These Scapino themes recur again and again among whirling scraps of melodic material, which coalesce into a continuous stream with firm outlines, just as moving pictures do in a cinematograph. The accents become irregular as the time signature shows the same sort of instability as in *Portsmouth Point*. Presently a new pattern is laid down with the direction 'giocoso'. It sounds familiar:

What is it? An echo of *Sheherazade* through a distorting medium—

There is no significance in the fortuitous resemblance, but as the phrase is repeated one's attention is diverted from what is going on by a puzzled search for its congener, and such distraction is bad for the apprehension of music so fleet as this. The similarity certainly never entered the head of the composer who considers it more like a phrase from the overture to *Tancredi* and certainly treats it more in the manner of Rossini than of Rimsky-Korsakov.

Its purpose is to provide a connecting counterpoint for the allusions to Exs. 1 and 3 which fly hither and thither. When the time comes for recapitulation it flowers into a major theme and dominates the last part of the work.

We now come to the half-way mark, which is an unaccompanied duet for side drum and tambourine. The time changes to a more languorous 3/4 'come una serenata,' the key to a sentimental A flat, the violins divide so as to imitate a guitar—they are directed to play pizzicato with the four finger-nails—and a solo violoncello starts a tune of 'exaggerated sentiment', which roams in a gallant and leisurely fashion through three clefs and a correspondingly wide range of the instrument's compass

Ex. 6

V'cello Solo

which is Ex. 3 in augmentation.

Presently a viola and a violin join in the serenade, but the woodwind poke out their tongues in mockery with fig. *a* of Ex. 4. The scoring becomes, if possible, more subtle and elaborate as counterpoints from Exs. 1 and 3 are added, and the key goes flatter still to D flat. But a quick change of mood supervenes, or rather the imitation love music is dropped and 'scherzevole' is the mark attached to a section in compound time, which is a free recapitulation of the first section. Compound time, however, is maintained till the end, so that the themes appear in rhythmic variants of their original form and we get occasional bars in 15/8 time. The details of the scoring—and Walton is always exceedingly particular about nuances, whether of accent or phrasing or tone-colour, and in this work the subtleties of percussion as well—are full of good touches, which are apt, however, to be lost in the congestion of the score and the forward impetus of the music. Emotionally and technically *Scapino* is a virtuoso work composed for a virtuoso orchestra, and it harks back to the mood and manner of *Portsmouth Point*. There are the same scintillating brilliance and brittle rhythms, a similar irony and tart-flavouring of what is essentially good-humoured toleration, but more poise and less assertion, less wit perhaps and more humour than in the older, which is to say the younger, overture.

Johannesburg Festival Overture

The concert overture is a form well adapted to Walton's concentrated style and tense delivery, since protracted bombardment may defeat its own ends—attention may snap and climaxes simply dissolve—whereas in the modest compass of an overture in a condensed or otherwise modified sonata form powerful ideas can be deployed, which do not call for extended development so much as terse juxtaposition, forcible statement and, if the subject is comic, as in *Portsmouth Point* and *Scapino*, high spirits. The *Johannesburg Festival Overture*, commissioned by that city for its seventieth birthday celebrations in 1956, makes a good third panel to a triptych of spirited overtures, for it has a sleek elegance, a nonchalance (really quite deceptive, for every effect is calculated with the composer's customary care) of manner in place of the youth of *Portsmouth Point* and the exuberant humour of *Scapino*.

Sir Malcolm Sargent gave the first performances both in South Africa on 25 September 1956, and in London, with the B.B.C. Symphony Orchestra, on 23 January 1957, though the first performance in Britain took place at Liverpool on 13 November 1956 under Efrem Kurz. It is noteworthy how many of Walton's orchestral works have been commissions—from places as well as people, Chicago and Cleveland, Johannesburg and Liverpool.

The *Johannesburg Festival Overture* is scored for large orchestra of triple woodwind, with harp and nine percussion instruments calling for three players. Among the battery are two loans from jazz, the maracas, a Cuban type of rattle made of a gourd containing dried seeds and rumba sticks which represent what in the original Cuban rumba was the rhythmic noise of knives and forks impinging on pots and pans. Lasting about seven minutes, it is fast all the way. Its first tempo marking is 'presto capriccio'; after a very small ritardando the tempo becomes vivacissimo, which accelerates into a prestissimo. The key is D, though the signature is neutral; the form is an elaborate rondo. One of the episodes consisting of bits of tune on horns accompanied by the more exotic percussion suggests actual African tunes.

The rondo tune, a full 16 bars in length, recurs five times, or six if its repetition a tone higher on the oboe immediately after its first statement is counted in:

Ex. 1

Rondos are notoriously unruly—it was Beethoven who tidied them up into simple rondos (ABACA) and sonata rondos (ABACABA). In the sonata rondo the first episode is also the second subject, duly recapitulated, whereas the second episode remains an isolated episode. Walton repeats all his episodes at a different, if not the classically conventionally different, pitch and key. The *Johannesburg Overture's* ground-plan would thus be ABACBAD—EACBA plus coda containing D and E. Rondo structure determines the character of the themes, which are more self-contained, less pregnant, than the first and second subjects of sonatas. No doubt about the rondo-like character of Ex. 1. The episodes also are clearly identifiable: they provide sufficient contrast without impeding the impetus of the movement, rather indeed accelerating it by contributing rhythmic variety. B and C, Exs. 2 and 3, are both horn tunes:

Ex. 2

D and E together form a central episode and are recapitulated in the coda. D consists of a semiquaver figure for woodwind in B flat—the signature is changed for it—lightly scored with various interjections of brass and timpani to decorate the antiphony of woodwind and strings:

Ex. 4

E might be called the African episode, since it brings the battery of side-drum without snares, timpani, maracas at two pitches, and rumba sticks, together with thrummings on the harp, into operation under a fragment of simple tune tossed between horns and trumpets:

Ex. 5

Closer examination would be both interesting and tedious—one may indeed wonder whether the above algebraic formula for the structure adds appreciably to the sum of human happiness. Tedious because words make heavy weather of describing thematic behaviour; interesting because such a feature, for instance as the three sharp chords with which Walton introduces his rondo tune, stand as punctuation marks later in the overture and, since all Walton's thematic procedures are fluid and protean, these landmarks are helpful in showing the way in which his mind works. Another such clue is provided by what he writes for his bass line which has figurative, rhythmic and harmonic significance and, of course, largely determines the tonality at any given moment. Thus at the fourth appearance of the rondo, Ex. 1, he writes as a bass counterpoint for harp a steadily descending scale. In the coda where he recalls D, Ex. 4, he puts under it a descending scale played by trombones and tuba, which having reached bottom A stands on it to form a dominant pedal point, over which the African material, Ex. 5 plus percussion, castanets this time, is played hell for leather, till the tempo changes to prestissimo and the time to three in a bar.

A surprise is in store for anyone who thinks that the change to 3/4 time is a gallop home. Eight bars from the end there is a check on repeated chords of D major, and the whole orchestra plunges down a major seventh to E flat, held and trilled. It resolves at once back on to D, and a curt unison is like a 'So long' with a toss of the head. Walton was always a wit.

Crown Imperial

The Coronation of 1937 produced from Walton a march that takes its place naturally by the side of Elgar's set of 'Pomp and Circumstances' marches, to which it no doubt owes something in the methods of uncomplicated rhythm and broad melody by which it secures popular allegiance. To the title *Crown Imperial: A Coronation March*, is subscribed a quotation from William Dunbar's poem 'In Honour of the City of London', which Walton had at that time been recently engaged in setting to music.

'In beawtie beryng the crone imperiall.'

Hence the name, apt to the occasion of its origin. It is scored for a large modern orchestra with three each of the woodwind and organ at the end. Its form is one commonly employed for marches, based on the Minuet and Trio; its key is C major. It is marked 'allegro reale': *reale*=royally, thus Walton goes one better with a king than Elgar did with the nobility (*nobilmente*)!

The first subject begins thus over a rhythmically articulated pedal point on the tonic C:

Ex. 1

The Trio contains a broad cantabile melody in A flat beginning

Ex. 2

All the matter is recapitulated, including the trio now transposed into C major, and the march broadens to a conclusion of great magnificence.

Orb and Sceptre

Sixteen years after the composition of *Crown Imperial* for the Coronation of King George VI and Queen Elizabeth, Walton composed another Coronation March for the crowning as Queen Regnant of their daughter, another Elizabeth, and the second to bear that name on the English throne. This march Walton called *Orb and Sceptre*, after the other emblems of royalty which the monarch bears at a coronation. It was commissioned by the Arts Council and was first performed before the ceremony, on 2 June 1953, in Westminster Abbey by the special orchestra under the direction of Sir Adrian Boult.

It follows the traditional form, but as far as its first section is concerned is more thematically complex than its predecessor. It opens with a fanfare in E major and proceeds thus:

Ex. 1

of which the first three beats are the germ of the principal material. The double dots in the treble and the quaver rest in the bass are typical of the means whereby Walton achieves his effect of forcible impact and electrical discharge of energy. The phrase is expanded to 8 bars and is followed first by 6 bars of more fluent antiphonal movement, then by 6 bars of C major after a drastic modulation, next by a new combination of short motifs that build up into a new idea, which in turn is rounded off by a return of Ex. 1.

The Trio section goes to C major and consists of this broad tune meno mosso:

There is an elaborate coda which includes a repetition of Ex. 2 largamente in the key of E. The speed is whipped up to make a brilliant conclusion out of various of the figures already employed, including a final fanfare.

OTHER CONCERT PIECES

Siesta

Siesta, which was first performed by Guy Warrack at one of his concerts with chamber orchestra at the Aeolian Hall in the autumn of 1926, retains some of the piquancy of *Façade* and *Portsmouth Point* but, as its title indicates, it is concerned with a quieter mood and is laid out for an orchestra without brass, except a couple of horns, and one each of the woodwind, except for an alternative piccolo to flute and a second clarinet.

There is room in this unhurried little piece for melody, and the word 'solo' appears from time to time in the score, as different instruments are told off one by one to deal with it. The first tune is an oboe solo:

Ex. 1

This is presented against a gently undulating figure that somehow makes clear the distinction between a siesta and a lullaby. The

next idea is a soft but quite awake dotted theme, or rather not a
theme so much as one of those extended melodic sentences that
are cast not in metre but in prose. It is muttered by the lower
strings. Soon, however, the woodwind start whistling an invitation to the wakeful sleeper to abandon all idea of a nap and join
his (or more probably her) playfellows in the street. For with a
change of key to E major the horns play this Italian street song:

Ex. 2

With the horns the violoncellos redouble the tune at their various
octaves, and this spacing of melodies in various octaves simultaneously is constantly being employed throughout the piece.
Over Ex. 2 dotted-note figures are maintained in motion. Ex. 1
reappears and brings back with it the key of A minor, which soon
makes way for A major, in which key Ex. 2 is recapitulated with
a light and fanciful accompaniment of chords on the second beat,
while solo instruments add as asides fragments of the dotted-
semiquaver idea. The siesta ends on a tonic chord which contains
an added second and an added fourth. Delius had regularly used
the chord of the added sixth as though it was a tonic triad. Walton
here uses a far more dissonant combination of notes as though it
was a perfect consonance, but, as a safeguard against misunder-
standing by less compliant ears, violas and oboes sustain an A after
the dissonant pizzicato chord has ceased to sound.

Music for Children

Like *Façade*, *Music for Children* exists in several different forms.
It first appeared as a suite of piano duets, not really too hard for
young pianists to play, though some of the pieces are tricky and
some require rather more skill in balance of tone than is to be
normally expected of four amateur hands in a medium that tends
to slogging. Composed in 1940, they were entitled *Duets for
Children* and were dedicated to 'Elisabeth and Michael', the com-

poser's niece and nephew. The change of title was caused by the orchestration of the ten pieces for ordinary symphony orchestra, of which the first performance was given by the London Philharmonic Orchestra in 1941. Separate titles to the pieces were attached when an arrangement for piano solo by Roy Douglas came out in 1949. In the orchestral version the order of the pieces is changed (though the score gives the references wrong) and further optional variation is allowed to a conductor who does not wish to play them all. As concert music the suite is insubstantial— how should it be otherwise?—but it is good and convenient material for broadcasting.

No. 1, 'The Music Lesson', is based on a five-finger exercise in the scale of C, but cheats in some bars by leaving out E and going up to A. Over this repetitious figure the woodwind (in the orchestral version) play little solos. No. 2, 'The Three-Legged Race' (vivo), has a nursery-rhyme sort of tune against which the bass-end player (or the trombone and cymbal) play on the off beats of the bar. Side drum and harp make a snappy finish on a chord of F plus 'added notes'. No. 3, 'The Silent Lake' (adagio), is in A minor throughout its brief course with a double pedal of tonic and dominant most of the time; somewhere in the middle a C sharp crunches with an F a ninth below. The tune of two bars' length is worth quoting because it repeats itself with small variations in its shape in the same way as Elgar's one-bar phrase repeats and remakes itself eight times over to form the theme of the finale of his Second Symphony.

So does the analyst break butterflies on his wheel. No. 4, 'Pony Trap', is a gay jog trot. It rather looks as though it had to pull up short at the end, though. Harp, tambourine and glockenspiel suggest that the pony had bells on its harness. No. 5 is 'Ghosts' in the Duet version but 'Swing Boats' in the Orchestral Suite, where 'Ghosts' comes last but one as No. 9. Here the ghosts walk up and down in the scale variously inflected of G minor so as to produce semitonal crunches to curdle young blood, B flat and B natural, F sharp and F natural—a mild form of typical Waltonian harmonic astringency. No. 6, 'Hop-Scotch', is throughout in 5/8 time, it is marked *leggiero* and goes at a good speed. A gap in the scale-passage five-finger exercise again helps the hop of the extra beat. In the orchestral suite where it is No. 8 there is a little semiquaver figure in the strings, where the rest comes in the piano version. Tambourine is the percussion employed. With No. 7, 'Swing Boats', Book 2 begins. It is No. 5 in the orchestral suite, where the tune, another variation on the five-finger exercise, is assigned to the tuba. The time is, of course, 6/8, the key D, and the direction 'giocoso deliberamente'. As in the previous piece the strings add a counterpoint not found in the original to add a touch of brilliance to the last appearance of the tune. No. 8, 'Song at Dusk', is No. 7 in the orchestral suite. Its structure is as simple as it is ingenious, one found incidentally in folk music, the repetition of a single strain with little variation except a change of pitch to mark the second section—'Nonesuch' is an English example. Walton shifts his two-bar tune up from B flat minor into its relative major. No. 9, 'Puppets' Dance' (No. 6 in the suite), is a little harder to play, the bass chords falling irregularly and the treble having some finger-work and jumps in and out of the key. In the suite these figures are bandied from one woodwind

Ex. 2
Alla marcia
(Horns)   (Tr. & Trb.)   (W.W.)

Ex. 3
Grazioso
p (Oboe)

instrument to another, and the puppets' attempts to keep time are marked by assignment to the bassoon or horn.

No. 10, 'Trumpet Tune', is a grand finale in all versions. Here are the Coronation marches in miniature. The key is C major, but it gives itself a glint by contagion with E. In Ex. 2 the A flat sounds like G sharp and is followed by a jump into E. The Trio section goes to A flat, and its tune, another bit of ingenious construction, is assigned to the oboe, Ex. 3.

BALLETS

The Quest

During the war Walton had been writing a number of film scores, which were in fact his only essays in dramatic music, since *Façade*, though it became a ballet and had some of the character of a number in an intimate revue, was not a stage work. *The Quest*, however, was a ballet composed during the war for the Sadler's Wells Ballet on its war-time strength under the musical direction of Constant Lambert, who was indefatigable in touring, conducting, and when necessary being himself a one-man orchestra at the piano. It was first presented at the New Theatre in London on 6 April 1943, with a strong cast in aid of Lady Cripps's Aid to China Fund. It won eulogy for its choreographer, Frederick Ashton, its designer John Piper, and for the composer who was commended for avoiding too thick a texture and too strenuous a tension for an allegorical piece and for his success in characterization. Yet it dropped from the repertory and indeed the score was lost for some eighteen years, until in 1962 Walton conducted a suite of four numbers from it at the opening night, 21 July, of the Promenade Concerts of 1962.

The reason for the lack of stamina in a ballet which, on these *a priori* grounds of such a combination of distinguished talents and its initial success, should have at least been revived from time to time, is given in Miss Mary Clarke's history of the Sadler's Wells Ballet:[1] it was too hastily compiled. Its patriotic theme—its hero is St George—which was an asset in the prevailing temper of

---

[1] *The Sadler's Wells Ballet* (Black), pp. 176–7.

1943, would do less to commend it when the country relapsed to its normal condition of mild self-depreciation and took its fundamental faith in itself for granted. According to Miss Clarke's account Frederick Ashton was given special leave from the Royal Air Force in the spring of 1943 in order to create a new ballet for the company to which he belonged. A subject had been provided by Doris Langley Moore in the shape of an episode from Spenser's *The Fairie Queen*, upon which Ashton worked during the company's spring tour to such effect that he was able to send to Walton a detailed scenario and some suggestions for the sort of music he had in mind for the characters and actions in his choreography. Time was limited: Walton took five weeks for a score lasting three quarters of an hour, a considerable achievement for a slow worker, and only finished it a week before the *première*, as the date at the end of the score shows, 29 March 1943. Ashton got his music piecemeal and had to sketch some of his dances without the music and to put the rest together as he got the separate sheets.

Not thus is strong inner coherence secured. Piper's scenery, the first designs he did for the theatre, were suitable and attractive— my own faded memory agrees with Miss Clarke's opinion—but the costumes were less pleasing and St George's white tunic and golden wig did not sit very comfortably on Mr Robert Helpmann, whose personality would normally drive him to poke fun at the stilted heroics of allegory. There were parts in the ballet for Margot Fonteyn, Beryl Grey, and Moira Shearer, and for Leslie Edwards, recently invalided out of the forces. My own notice in *The Times* remarked on the exciting pyrrhic dances and on the good effects of Ashton's grouping, but Miss Clarke says that Helpmann 'walked about with an air of patient resignation', depressed, she conjectures, by his costume. Her conclusion is that 'while it remained a patriotic novelty *The Quest* had a certain success, but it did not enjoy, and did not deserve, a long life'.

The plot of the ballet concerns the temporary delusion of St George of the Red Cross, who represents Holiness, by a magician, Archimago, who stands for Hypocrisy, and the consequent interruption in his search for Una, who is Truth. The obstacles put in his way are three Saracen knights and the Seven Deadly Sins, which he encounters in the Palace of Pride in the form, of course, of a series of *divertissements*. In due course he emerges to be united with Una and take her to the House of Holiness, where she abides with Faith, Hope and Charity, while the knight sallies forth once more on his chivalric quests. Margot Fonteyn (and subsequently Pauline Clayden) represented Truth (Una), Beryl Grey showed the nimbleness of Falsehood (Duessa), and Moira Shearer was Pride in her palace; Leslie Edwards was the magician (Archimago), and Robert Helpmann the Knight of the Red Cross. The pyrrhic dances were encounters with the three nicely named Saracen knights, Sansjoy, Sansfoy, and Sansloy. The hope was that the ballet would join those other English ballets in which moral issues are the subject of successful dramatic treatment, *Job*, *The Rake's Progress*, and *Checkmate*. In the event it was only a might-have-been.

Of the score there survive in the suite an Introduction, in which The Magician is presented and a Transformation scene to the Palace of Pride is depicted; a Siciliana which belongs to Una; a martial movement called the Challenge; and a final Passacaglia for St George and Una when they are united. This suite was selected and adapted by Mr Vilem Tausky from the complete ballet score with the composer's co-operation.

While this score has the recognizable ingredients of Walton's style, the rhythmic drive, the rich texture and the sharp sound on the ear, it is, as is fitting for a piece for the theatre, rather simpler in all these respects than the autonomous works for orchestra. The scoring itself is somewhat more modest in that the woodwind is only two a-piece, piccolo and cor anglais alternating with the second player of flute and oboe and not demanding a third player. The orchestral doublings are more conventional. The rhythms—see for instance Exs. 1 and 7—are uncomplicated and repeated with regularity so as not to trip the dancers' feet—this is specially true of The Challenge, No. 3. Nor is effort expended to avoid the normal language of the theatre for depicting the storm and the exercise of magic, such for instance as marking a turn of events by running down the scale to a unison and pivoting tremolando sul ponticello on it. The chief ingenuity, such as Walton normally devotes to details of orchestration, the bowing of string chords, varied doublings of wind, passing of figures from one instrument or group to another instrument or group and other refinements, is here expended on varying the bar lengths of the counterpoints over the three-bar ground on which he constructs his Passacaglia, No. 4.

The suite opens allegro con fuoco with a whirlwind such as magicians can step out of for the exercise of their art. Our magician, Archimago, does this in 10 bars and gets busy in an allegro malizioso—Walton is strong on malice, depicting it in *Belshazzar's Feast* and the First Symphony—in which his principal spell is

Ex. 1
Allegro malizioso

over a driving rhythm of

Ex. 2

decorated with interjections from harp glissandi, glockenspiel, and tambourine. Another of his wiles is for a scale containing the interval of the augmented second (this again is the conventional bogeyman doing his stuff) to descend and converge upon a rising chromatic scale, sinister as ever. Then with a familiar gesture, a harp playing a chord of the ninth, and an oboe in plain Tchaikovsky fashion waving its wand, the scene changes to a waltz:

Ex. 3
Tempo di valse

This tune, with its rather wry harmony is extended for 32 bars, then the horn and other wind take it up for another 16 bars. Whereupon Ex. 1 returns and a coda of muttering strings, as mentioned above and an allusion to Ex. 1 by bassoons and clarinets, closes what is an effective little piece. No doubt the film music he had been writing enabled Walton to avoid the temptation to put subtlety before effect, though there are plenty of nice touches for anyone who likes to look for them.

No. 2, the Siciliana, is called 'The Spell'. It is a protracted solo for flute with occasional counterpoints by oboe and cor anglais, lightly scored without brass, save for six notes from a solitary horn, and with harp and strings providing the main tonal environment. The flute's tune begins

Ex. 4

grows a little more florid, has a cadenza to itself and then stops, leaving a solo violin to pick up the rhythm and bring it all to a quiet conclusion.

No. 3, The Challenge, gets its martial character from the juxtaposition of a stamping and a running metre, which are alternated, combined, broken up, juxtaposed, and variously offset with interjections on different beats of the bar by harp, percussion, and celesta. The strong effect of men marking time is produced by the reiteration of a single note against a descending chromatic scale, all in rigid crotchets:

Ex. 5

while the running in circular motion is suggested by the simple dotted note *tum-te-tum*:

Ex. 6

K

The finale is a Passacaglia, which permits some quasi-religious counterpoint to symbolize the reunion of St George (Holiness) and Una (Truth). The ground is, unusually, a three-bar phrase:

It is varied (in pitch and contour) once (at fig. 3), has a crotchet kick inserted on the second beat of the second bar (at fig. 6) and picks up a few more crotchets (at fig. 7). Otherwise it is maintained with little deviation throughout. Over it flute and oboe first, then violins and others in turn draw lines of counterpoint of varying phrase-length until the reconciliation is effected and block harmony sets the seal on it maestoso, with bells pealing and the keyed glockenspiel joining in in octaves, and harps sweeping glissando on to high C, affirming that C major has emerged from the C mixolydian of the ground, Ex. 7.

The Wise Virgins

The importance in Walton's output of the transcriptions of Bach for Frederick Ashton's ballet, The Wise Virgins, which he undertook at Constant Lambert's request, is that it shows his taste in orchestral sonority and sheer skill in instrumentation more clearly than the original works, where they are involved in the stuff and substance of the music. Moreover, the suite of six numbers extracted from it makes agreeable concert music to fill an odd corner of a programme.

The re-scoring of Bach is an occupational disease of conductors and composers: Henry Wood did it, Elgar did it, Schoenberg did it, so did Respighi. But Bach is of such fibre that he survives the treatment. Himself an inveterate transcriber, he quite enjoys being dressed up in modern orchestral garments. In this case Ashton wanted to use Bach for a choreographic spring-board: he had running through his head the delicious tune of 'Sheep may safely graze' and persuaded Lambert to choose enough besides for a ballet on the Parable of the Ten Virgins.

The complete score consisted of nine numbers, beginning naturally enough with *Wachet auf* (Cantata No. 140), of which, however, the well-known figured version (described by Schweitzer as a dance processional) was passed over in favour of the concluding four-part chorale. No. 2 was a bass aria from Cantata No. 142, *Uns ist ein Kind geboren*, which is not included in the concert suite. No. 3, the opening chorus of Cantata No. 99, *Was Gott tut*, was used twice, once to begin the suite and again abbreviated and differently scored for No. 8 of the ballet.

Walton uses the ordinary full orchestra with harp, but uses it for the most part sparingly, though he lets fly with everything (except harp) in the last number, 'Praise be to God'. The chief points in his scoring are (*a*) alterations in the use of woodwind so that clarinets are not too obtrusive; (*b*) some doubling, e.g. of flute and bassoon (plus second violin) in octaves in No. 2; which is the transcription of the organ chorale prelude 'Herzlich tut mich verlangen' (BWV 727); (*c*) restriction of the solo line of the tenor aria from Cantata No. 85, *Seht was die Liebe tut*, to flute and oboe and the accompaniment to strings—the original scoring was for two oboes and the obsolete violino piccolo; (*d*) the use of harp in 'Sheep may safely graze' to suggest a continuo accompaniment in the recitative and the glint which a harpsichord imparts to a body of strings. Trumpets and trombones are used to carry the chorale tune in No. 6 (No. 4 of the suite), 'Ach wie flüchtig' (from Cantata No. 26); Bach's scoring of No. 9 (No. 6 in the suite), in the Cantata No. 129, *Gelobet sei der Herr*, is very full, one of his festival orchestras for which he requisitioned three trumpets, timpani, three oboes and oboe d'amore. Walton makes some use of brass in his interjectory manner but preserves the contrapuntal texture by careful underlining and produces a brilliant conclusion to both ballet and suite. It is the brilliance which bears the mark of Walton's handiwork.

The ballet did not remain long in the repertory of what was then the Sadler's Wells Ballet, which produced it on 24 April 1940. It had splendid sets by Rex Whistler, but was not a complete success. My own notice was luke-warm.

The ballet of five wise virgins . . . fortunately contains also the five foolish virgins, without whom it would be a slow-moving affair. Even for them Mr Frederick Ashton has devised no very eventful dancing, but they enter in their gay garments with obviously frivolous gestures at the right moment to relieve the tedium of the daughters of wisdom. [Then after a reference to Whistler's contribution I come to the thing that jarred.] Then also the music is by Bach. Ballet lays violent hands on whatever it would have nowadays and we steel ourselves not to be shocked even when Bach's lovely prelude on the Passion chorale is used to accompany the pirouettings of the languishing bride.

True, the chorale was once a love-song and sanctified itself by the familiar historical process of sacred parody, but as Bach uses it five times in the *St Matthew Passion* the associations for a modern man are too strong for him not to feel involuntarily some incongruity in its choice for this particular purpose. No such feelings need arise perhaps when it is part of an orchestral suite. The cor anglais imparts a dark tinge to the score of this number. Humphrey Searle's comment (in his book on ballet music) will be generally endorsed: 'this arrangement (of Bach's cantatas) was tasteful but effective, successfully avoiding both archaism and over-modernity'.

INCIDENTAL AND FILM MUSIC

The writing of music *ad hoc* for plays has over the centuries added up to a substantial gift from the theatre to the art of music. Shakespeare has never ceased to inspire new songs, and incidental music from Purcell to *Peer Gynt* has proved a source of pleasure in that it is good—the fact that it has survived differentiates it from ephemeral stuff—not so serious as to spoil its entertainment value and has the merit of superficial attraction. In the present century films and radio have extended the field of incidental music. Walton has provided scores for all three sorts: for the theatre incidental music to *Macbeth*, for the cinema several other Shakespeare settings, *As You Like It* (1936), *Henry V* (1944), *Hamlet* (1947) and *Richard III* (1955) as well as Shaw, *Major Barbara* (1941), and official propaganda films during the war. For radio he provided music for Louis MacNeice's *Christopher Columbus* (1942). Some of this music has survived the occasion and is available in score or on record. Thus *Henry V*, to which the music made a positive contribution acknowledged by devotees of the cinema, has left behind it a concert suite and two string pieces, of which scores are available, and records of the sound-track of the film which contain melodrama (with Sir Laurence Olivier speaking the verse), battle music, and two vocal pieces (a madrigal and a setting of the Agincourt Carol). The most substantial of these bequests from the cinema, however, is the Prelude and Fugue, called 'The Spitfire' after the name of the fighter aircraft which it depicted, from the film, *The First of the Few* (1942), about its development.

Escape Me Never

The first of Walton's films was *Escape Me Never* (1936), from which a ballet has survived in a reduction for piano solo. This is pleasant enough to play and would serve again for a dancer's solo in class or demonstration or recital, but its only distinction is the way in which the device for which we have revived the term *hemiola* is used to keep the perpetuum mobile rhythm from becoming mechanical: bars of 3/4 are interpolated without bothering to change the time signature into bars of 6/8 time. The six quavers to the bar are maintained throughout, and even push on to their climax with the old-fashioned repeated triplets. Good utility music.

Spitfire Prelude and Fugue

The 'Spitfire' Prelude and Fugue is more than that and has a continuing life of its own, though, like all these dramatic pieces in which the music is subservient to one of the other arts, Walton writes much more simply than in his independent compositions. The Prelude indeed is another Elgarian march like *Crown Imperial*, with opening fanfare, broad tune, tune restated and developed and then heaving itself into G (from C) for a final blazing statement. After a few bars of skirmishing trills, which being in F pull the tonality back to neutral, the fugue subject starts climbing like a plane in A minor:

The exposition contains three entries, an episode in which *a* and *b* from the subject are separately treated and then an additional entry in G (though it contains a persistent C sharp). In place of middle entries and developments a completely unrelated episode occurs, slower, more homophonic in character, with a soaring melody for a solo violin, doubtless illustrative of the aeronaut, if not in the stratosphere, at any rate in the blue empyrean alone. It modulates from D to F, and the fugue is resumed with the subject in the bass—it sounds quite like the 'revving' of the aeroplane engine. The fugal answer appears in the alto and breaks up, only to be restated in A major on the brass and developed from the ample material contained in the subject. Not a strict fugue nor one to exploit contrapuntal devices like stretto, but at once picturesque and fugal in temper and texture.

Hamlet, As You Like It, Macbeth

Walton's music for *Hamlet* is discussed in the article on 'Film Music' in Grove's *Dictionary*, where it is commended for its happy use of the leitmotif principle.

The Funeral March has been abstracted for concert use by Mr Muir Mathieson and separately published. It is not cast in march form with trio sections and recapitulations but is a short (60 bars) continuous Adagio lamentoso in E minor in which a persistent dotted-note fanfare is accompanied by flourishes of semi-quavers grouped in various rhythms and figures. The coda, however, has a pedal point to suggest the drone that was traditional in the trio sections of minuets and marches.

From *As You Like It*, the song 'Under the Greenwood Tree' survives, an excellent pastiche of the Jacobean period (see Songs, p. 154). The music composed for John Gielgud's stage production of *Macbeth* in 1941 has been praised by those who heard it but nothing has been extracted from it for further use.

Henry V

The *Henry V* music illustrates another aspect of Walton's film music: where he can he gives it a structural stiffening to elevate it above mere descriptive background noises—the Spitfire Fugue is a conspicuous case and so is the Passacaglia in which he describes the death of Falstaff. Scored for strings this beautiful, simple little elegy is founded on the four-bar phrase

Ex. 2   Molto lento

Its partner 'Touch her soft lips'—Pistol before the embarkation— is founded on a tune that might have been a slow country dance from Playford's *The English Dancing Master*.

The Suite consists of these two pieces and the concluding Agincourt Carol, prefaced by two preludes from the beginning of the film. Of these the first is called 'London 1600', a piece of pageant music in which an ostinato

Ex. 3

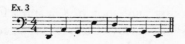

provides the foundation for a wordless chorus and instrumental flourish. The other is entitled 'The Globe Playhouse', is called an overture and is in fact a march. It too employs voices orchestrally, and to give a period flavour includes a tabor and a harpsichord in its scoring.

Richard III

In 1954 Sir Laurence Olivier made a film of Shakespeare's *Richard III*, for which Walton composed the music. From it Mr Muir Mathieson prepared with the composer's authorization a suite prefaced by the Prelude depicting the Coronation of Edward IV with which the film opened. The Suite contains a good deal of ceremonial and martial music, opening as it does with a Fanfare and concluding with 'Trumpets Sound' and between them enclosing 'With Drums and Colours'. This makes rather a lot of military music, which is relieved by 'Music Plays', No. 2, consisting of repetitions of a pleasant eight-bar tune ending in a semiquaver cadence, by 'The Princes in the Tower' for strings and harp, a little piece in ternary form marked 'andante doloroso', and by a quasi-pastiche of Tudor counterpoint called 'I would I knew thy heart'. At least it succeeds in suggesting a period flavour, though actually harmonically it does not conform to Tudor practice. Not the first time that Walton has worked this stylistic trick.

The same film score also yielded three short pieces for organ (published in 1963). Again all three are given a Tudor flavour, this time by means of false relations and hints of *musica ficta* inflection. 'Elegy', No. 2, goes further and uses the changing-note formula of the lutenists at cadences. Indeed, with its wayward time signatures and absence of pedal part it is a pastiche of Dowland—and very good Dowland too. The March, No. 1, begins in A but flattens most of its G sharps and finally ends on a chord of E. This, though faintly recalling the *Fitzwilliam Virginal Book* has more of the bite of Walton's numerous other marches. The Scherzetto, No. 3, marked to be played staccato on the choir organ with a baroquy suggestion of 8, 4 and 2 foot stops, is after the manner of Giles Farnaby. Genuine organ music, though of chamber not of church, the three pieces are deft and charming but so short as to perplex an organist for an occasion on which he could use them. They do, however, show Walton in lighter vein and go behind his public face to a more intimate mood.

Altogether over the years Walton has written music for fourteen films.

CHAPTER V

Chamber Music and Songs

CHAMBER music does not occupy a very large space in Walton's output, but it is important in that it was in this field that he began to handle instrumental forms and from which he launched himself at the Salzburg Festival in 1923 and in print with the Pianoforte Quartet in 1924. This chapter has an equal claim with Chapter II to the piano quartet and looks rather thin without it, but on the whole it seemed better to keep the early works together and to confine this chapter to the mature works of a quarter of a century later. Even the piano *Duets for Children* are treated elsewhere in their orchestral garb.

Songs, like piano duets, may be rated as domestic music, which is a sort of sub-species of chamber music. The two song-sequences, *Anon. in Love*, composed for the Aldeburgh Festival of 1960, and *A Song for the Lord Mayor's Table*, composed for the City of London Festival of 1962, are, however, public music, though certainly proper to a small hall, which is our equivalent of the baroque *camera*. They are in fact recital pieces, and the recital is a modern phenomenon which we now include in the category of chamber music. At any rate these two song-sequences can appropriately be discussed in this chapter on chamber music. The other principal chamber works are the String Quartet in A minor and the Sonata for Violin and Piano.

CHAMBER MUSIC

Quartet in A Minor

Walton's second essay in the form of the string quartet came more than twenty years after the first. Like the First Symphony it gave him some trouble to complete to his satisfaction, since its first performance was postponed from its announced date to 4 May 1947, when it was played by the Blech String Quartet on the B.B.C.'s Third Programme and repeated on the following day at a public concert at Broadcasting House. There is no sign of strain in it, for it is actually the most conventional in behaviour of all Walton's instrumental compositions. It belongs to the family of Beethoven rather than Bartók, though the medium is used forcefully. It is in the usual four movements, it professes to be in a key—A minor—and does not seek to obscure tonality or to assert it with pedal points; the first movement is cast in a pretty regular sonata form; the finale is a rondo. It is dedicated to Ernest Irving, the musical director of the Ealing Film Studios, with whom Walton had worked during the war.

The structure of the first movement then is that of a classical sonata with, however, a long development containing a fugato on a new subject, Ex. 4 below. The first subject, Ex. 1, is a melody for viola—it begins like a tune and is 16 bars long—in A minor:

Its counterpoint in the second violin supports its flowing character with an occasional swirl of semiquavers. This melody is restated by the second violin while the first violin gives it a slightly different articulation with octave doubling but always without the first beat of the bar—such minutiae are very characteristic of Walton. The second subject is different in character and tempo: the four strings suddenly snap like a terrier—and growl in turn—as the first violin ejaculates, Ex. 2:

which is the root idea from which much of an agitated character
develops, going from the locality of D minor to C minor for a
new theme, Ex. 3:

Ex. 3

which has the advantage of providing a quintuple pulse for a
change of rhythm and thematic distraction.

The development begins with the first subject in C minor: it
continues, as in the exposition, with a change to a more tart
dialogue, this time in fugato with Ex. 4 as subject:

Ex. 4   Più mosso

When the fugal exposition is completed, each voice having duly
had its entry, there is an additional entry not quite so punctilious
in behaviour but turning itself into a development of motifs from
Ex. 1. The signature is still three flats, but a codetta cancels them
and leads formally to the recapitulation, which is somewhat
shortened. It is enough to restate Ex. 1 once only, but characteristically it begins in an augmented form—nothing with Walton is
ever twice identical—so that the first three bars of the theme take
six to declare themselves but thereafter get in step. The sections
signalized by Exs. 2 and 3 are fully repeated with key adjustment
to put Ex. 3 in A minor. The brief coda is an allusion *sotto voce*
and not very literally to the opening of the second subject Ex. 3:
it is marked 'a tempo secundo' and is only a dozen bars long.

The second movement is not labelled, but is, a scherzo, marked
'presto'. But all it keeps of the conventional design is a repeat of
the first section, a balancing second section starting off with a new

or newish tune on the cello and a trio—if one may take a drone bass as a determinant of what constitutes a trio. What Walton does not do is to repeat the first minuet after the trio or indeed the second section of it at its first and only statement. He has a brief coda which by a few reminiscences, the strong pizzicato chords on violas and cellos and a single statement, three bars in all, of his initial idea, serves in place of the second-time-through of the minuet of the classical quartet.

His first section which is in a kind of E tonality (very near but not quite the Locrian mode—it has a diminished fourth as well as a diminished fifth) starts after a preliminary bar or two to make the engine fire:

Ex. 5

which is the gist of the whole matter. He heaps up a moto perpetuo of regular quavers in the lower strings save for an occasional hiatus deliberately engineered to enable him to snap with a sforzando, a sudden brief octave doubling, a pizzicato chord, four bars of cross rhythm in the cello and a trill on top and other such devices for securing his characteristic dynamism. After the double bar the cello give out the following extended melody:

Ex. 6

which the violas take up but modify, starting it with a bit of theme off the same roll:

Ex. 7.

This fragment is augmented and played pizzicato on the first violin and it is heard at the end though, Walton being Walton, not exactly so.

The trio, so called on the strength of its persistent pedal point, develops a late Beethovenian tune, which when you come to look at it is related to Ex. 6:

Ex. 8

The drone in the trio sections of minuet is accounted for historically, according to Eric Blom's plausible hypothesis, by the social custom in the aristocratic society of the eighteenth century of all classes dancing together—since everyone knew his proper station it would be easier than in our own democratic society—at occasions like weddings. Mozart provides two instances in the Haffner Serenade and in *Don Giovanni*, where three different sets of people dance their own dances simultaneously at the same party. The gentry danced their minuet and then the villagers danced theirs, but theirs was a simpler minuet and they had only an unskilful bass player who found it prudent to stick to one note in the small rural band—three players only, one of whom was a drone. Hence Trio. The traditon persisted, though it weakened, but it can be seen at work in Beethoven's middle symphonies and in full vigour in the five-four movement of Tchaikovsky's Pathetic Symphony, though not in Brahms, who anyhow avoided minuets. It is not suggested that Walton consciously followed precedent—he did not even mark off the section or call it a trio, and those who do not like the idea or feel the change of character after [49] can retort that the scherzo itself begins with 12 bars of pedal point on E. Still . . .

The slow movement is cast in a clear sonata form in F major and it begins and ends on a chord of F. Its first subject is a

long-drawn melody, beginning

Ex. 9

Viola con sord.

which when it comes to its balancing phrase veers into A major
with a D sharp in it for more distinctive flavour. The second
subject at a slightly quicker tempo bears the signature of three
flats but sounds like A flat. It too is another long-drawn
melody, also on viola, and being accompanied by pizzicato
chords suggests that the movement though pensive and emotional is a serenade:

Ex. 10

Viola

A middle section develops a little more semiquaver motion, becomes sharper in tonality and more fluid thematically: indeed, in
the middle of it some imitational entries are marked 'fluente'. A
definite allusion is made to the second subject, Ex. 10, before a solo
viola leads into the recapitulation in F. The first subject, hardly
recognizable as Ex. 9, is now given to the cello. Nor is the second
subject recognizable as Ex. 10, though the tempo più mosso,
triplet figuration and the general character of the arabesque
identify it as filling its place in the design—a literal repetition
would be inept after the appearance in the middle section. The key
for this equivalent passage is F minor.

The finale is a rondo, containing two episodes in addition to a
second subject, which in a Beethovenian sonata rondo counts as
a first episode even though it is subsequently and duly repeated.
The sections are in round numbers of bars if one discounts the
links—32 for the spitting rondo theme itself, 21 for the second
subject, 27 for the first episode, 29 for the second episode, with
changes of key signature—the main tonality is A minor all right—
to mark the changes.

The elements of the rondo are (*a*) one of Walton's crackling ejaculations compounded of strong accents, rests and staccato marks:

Ex. 11 Allegro molto

(*b*) a sequential bit of tune:

Ex. 12

1st-2nd Vlns. *p*

cresc.

f

and (*c*) a section, all semiquavers in imitational counterpoint. (*a*) and (*b*) form the first paragraph. (*a*) now transposes to E minor (with a B flat inflection), and a delayed appearance of F sharp introduces (*c*) and concludes the second paragraph. Now follows the second subject in C major-minor—this is based on the same sort of figuration as Ex. 11 but develops a melody in quavers:

Ex. 13

p cresc.   etc.

Next comes the first recapitulation of the rondo complete.

The first episode provides a strong contrast: the signature goes to six flats and semiquavers disappear. The second violin has an expressive melody against triplet accompaniments by the first

Ex. 14 Vln. II

espress.

violin and viola—the cello joins in later pizzicato. Instead of the reappearance of the rondo we have the second subject in C as before, complete with Ex. 13 which is extended by 4 bars before the rondo, (a) and (b) but not (c), comes round again. The third episode in A major consists of a viola solo over an oscillating figure in the cello and tremolando quavers in the violins:

Ex. 15

The solo passes to the second violin, cello, and first violin in turn. The rondo is due to finish off the pattern, but something actually different which progressively approximates to Ex. 11, restores the chordal, brusque, forceful character of the initial idea of the rondo. Nothing but the notes E and A are heard during the last 10 bars, a stark sort of A minor.[1]

Violin Sonata

Having turned to chamber music again after a diversion of some twenty years in the String Quartet (1947) Walton continued a little longer in that field and produced during 1949 a Sonata for violin and piano, which had its first performance at Drury Lane Theatre (of all strange and inappropriate places) at a Sunday night concert on 5 February 1950. It was written for Yehudi Menuhin and Louis Kentner, who played it on that occasion, and it is dedicated to their wives, who are sisters, Diana and Griselda Gould, daughters of Evelyn Suart who was until her marriage a pianist of distinction, and as Lady Harcourt, one of London's musical hostesses. It was played at the Edinburgh Festival of that year by Max Rostal and Franz Osborn. On both occasions it was noted that it was a highly concentrated work, typical of its composer yet containing something new in it that would reward further acquaintance. The score bears the legend that 'the composer is indebted to Mr Yehudi Menuhin and Mr Louis Kentner for the many valuable suggestions they have made in preparing this work for performance and publication'. On the

[1] For the rescored version of the quartet, see page 232

violin part Mr Menuhin has inscribed a note about his editing of the bowing. 'Whenever I have marked bowings in brackets, they indicate a practical violinist's solution of the ideal phrasing set down by the composer. Thus (V) in the middle of a ⌒ indicates one change of bow at that point. I firmly believe the composer's markings should always remain available to all interpreters.' His editing also includes specific indications of the string preferred, G, D, A or E, for particular passages.

The sonata is of great executive difficulty and has thereby some affinity with the violin concerto in its writing for the violin. Passages sweep through the whole compass of the instrument and octaves, harmonics, and double stops are called for. There are only two movements, Allegro tranquillo and Variazioni. But the work plays twenty-four minutes and is formally satisfactory, since a set of variations can deploy the character of slow movement, scherzo and rondo if it is well designed. The first movement is a large sonata movement, regular but rich in material. It is in B flat. The theme of the variations is in B flat minor but the sonata ends in the major. It has been pointed out that in a little codetta to the statement of the theme for variation Walton has set out in octaves on the piano the sort of twelve-note series that serialists use, spelled in equal quavers so:

Ex. 1

But he makes no rigorous use of it as a proper serialist would—it may even be a sardonic quip on his part—quite characteristic, if it is. A similar but more serious gesture is made in the Second Symphony. The series does, however, appear in bits and in transpositions in the codas of the variations. Some of its characteristic shapes and intervals are strongly hinted. The interval of the fourth, both rising and falling with semitones, is the distinguishing characteristic of the series and it is these features which colour the endings of the various sections, mostly in the piano but also in the unaccompanied cadenza to the fourth variation.

This is not a very serious flirtation with the Viennese daughter

of Arnold Schoenberg and it occurs in a context wherein the
composer has proclaimed his fidelity to traditional tonality with
more than the usual clarity and emphasis. For a composer who
will on occasion put a sixth or a seventh into a tonic triad the
opening is as firm and uncomplicated as Brahms's G major Sonata:

The violin gruppetto *a* is germinal, thematically and rhythmically,
and the melody, of which the beginning only is shown in Ex. 2,
expands into a long paragraph of 15 bars, after which the piano
takes up the violin tune as shown above but at different pitches,
so that the bridge passage shows a measure of thematic development. The key signature has been changed to one sharp but there
are enharmonic changes of harmony which are suspended by
sleight of hand from a whole-tone scale running through the
violinist's play with the semiquaver gruppetto so:

The second subject is introduced by the piano in a sharpened form
of G major (the C is sharpened):

which is soon taken up by the violin. Triplets have now taken

the place of the four-note gruppetto though they fail wholly to
extrude it. A new idea of a more brittle kind in a restless tonality
constitutes the rest of the second subject, a sort of sparring match
between the two performers, in which the violin asserts the
gruppetto:

Ex. 5

against the piano's sextuplet arpeggios. Note Walton's favourite
interval of the rising seventh in Ex. 5 and note the use of sevenths
and ninths as substitutes for octaves in the subsequent piano writing.

Ex. 6

However, it all comes nicely to rest on a comfortable reassuring
chord of F, from which a modulation leads into a development
section signalized by Ex. 2 in D major. All the hinges at development, recapitulation, and coda turn on Ex. 2 in appropriate keys.
This development is the longest section of the work: it numbers
105 bars against an exposition of 66 and a recapitulation of 54.
The coda, which in an opera would be called an apotheosis—for
both violin and piano soar into a sonorous haze—is 42 bars long.

At the beginning of the development Walton, who professes
to be nothing much of a pianist and had written little for the
instrument, tries some experiments in the sonority of chords—it
is noteworthy that he employs the extremes of the keyboard—
with which he is sufficiently satisfied to use without much else
throughout his coda. An example of its figuration and sonority
is given from the beginning of the development section:

Ex. 7

Most of this writing is marked to be played quietly—the coda is
marked 'una corda'—so that the pianist will require a jolly good
piano with a bell-like treble. The violinist begins a cantilena
punctuated by some insistent murmurs of the gruppetto (*b* not *a*
from Ex. 2) and both instruments become romantic and flowing—
this sort of thing over murmuring semiquavers:

Ex. 8

This is derived from the first subject and becomes more and
more lyrical on the violin and more and more ethereal on the
piano right up in the top octaves, from which a descent is
made to the deep bass—there is a five-bar trill on bottom E—
and a page or two of sequential development leading into the
recapitulation.

The spelling of Ex. 2 is considerably altered: the triad contains
added notes; there is a sort of horn tune in minims for the thumb of
the right hand; the violin part is more fluid and is higher. The
second subject is again introduced by the piano a third higher in
pitch (with a signature of two flats). The conspiratorial mutterings
of Ex. 6, with its violin part of appoggiature, formally recur and
subside on to a chord of D flat in the rhythm of Ex. 2. The remarkable coda has been described already as the elements of which it
is composed make their first appearance in the movement, in so
far as ingredients can suggest the confection which emerges from
them. This confection touches the sublime and serves the purpose
of the deeply felt slow movement that Beethoven required in his
chamber music.

The theme and variations which constitute the second and last
movement of the sonata show in an extreme form that combination of wayward improvisatory melody and harmony with great
care over *facture*, meticulous attention to small details of expression and sheer ingenuity in the exercise of the craft of composition. The ingenuity is the element most easily exposed in
analysis.

Take the theme

or rather the essence of it, with its gruppetto, dotted note figures and its ambiguous seventh in the key of E flat minor. But this is only half the theme, and, to complete it in the regular binary shape of 16 bars proper to variations, Ex. 9 is repeated half a tone higher, i.e. in E minor, though the six flats in the signature are merely cancelled and not replaced by an F sharp. Such is a structural feature of some East European folk-songs, notably Slovakian and Hungarian, though the amount of the shift in pitch varies and is often a fifth—the English tune 'Nonesuch' goes through a similar manoeuvre to complete itself. But Walton is constant only in his inconstancy, and the last part (extended from 4 to 5 bars) introduces some new, though congruent, rhythmic features:

Nor is this all: the piano has an extended coda to the violin's theme, amounting to another 8 bars, in which the left hand echoes the disjointed accents of Ex. 10 (penultimate bar) and the right hand has a rather intense descending melody:

almost a ten-note series in itself, to which is attached the twelve-note series already mentioned, Ex. 1.

So there is plenty of material for variation.

Variation 1 smooths the contours by putting the tune into 6/8 time and by the left hand of the piano putting against it a single chromatic counterpoint, derived actually from the accompaniment to the theme at the beginning. The piano's postscript consists of Ex. 11 and the series, both up a tone.

Variation 2 is marked 'quasi improvisando' and consists of a decorated version of the theme, while the piano plays chords in the manner of the coda of the first movement, i.e. an exploration, though less elaborate, of the sonority of the piano's higher octaves. The coda transposes the series up a tone.

Variation 3 was described (by Herbert Murrill) as 'an amusing vivacious and march-like variation, designed perhaps to fulfil the function of a scherzo'. The piano plays 'una corda' chords of C major with a drum tap of dissonance on the second beat of each bar. The violin plays double-stop and false relations. At the half-way double bar the signature which had been one of four flats to signify this rum sort of C major now professes C major but sounds more like E. The piano coda continues the march rhythm but the series is only present in influence not in literal notation—Walton's passion for variation would never brook the quasi-logarithmic exactitude of serialism.

Variation 4 brings piano and violin together in unison and octaves. It is marked 'allegro molto strepitoso'. The outlines of the theme are by this time blurred and even the half-way bar line has disappeared. Perhaps the connection of thought is an inaccurate recollection of the angular shape of the series but considerable use is made of the figure found in bar two of the theme.

Variation 5 is all pizzicato for the violin and all arabesque for the piano with the hands coming together in octaves half-way through as in Schubert's 'Trout' quintet. The arabesque bears recognizable resemblances to the theme and the violin's continuous quaver arpeggios could well derive *longo intervallo* from the series in rhythm and interval. The key is roughly A minor. The variation ends with a short cadenza for the violin.

Variation 6 is marked 'scherzando' and resumes formal behaviour in that the figuration is consistent, the sections are marked, though the violin plays through what had hitherto been the piano's solo. The key is an Aeolian E flat, changing up at the B section to E minor. No trace of the series, Ex. 1.

Variation 7 is the last and at andante tranquillo the longest. It is cast in a 9/8, changing with 6/8, rhythm. The violin muted plays 'sempre ma dolce espressivo' and a version of the theme as wide-ranging over its compass as the original was compact. A section comes to a clear chord of E major, B section to an equally clear chord of B flat and C to F. The piano writing is based on semitonal clashes and resolutions so:

The series turns up in disguise. In the C or coda section in the bar after the violin stops the last six notes are heard, transposed up a fifth and not in their level rhythm but shaped into a melodic arabesque which grows more fluid for a moment before the violin makes an extra entry echoing a rocking figure that is gently being coaxed by the piano. What should then be heard in the tenor register but the first six notes of the series untransposed!

Movement having been reduced nearly to a standstill as the last variation feels down for its bottom F, the coda bursts away molto vivace, soon to become presto. The coda pretends it is going to be a fugue and firmly enunciates this:

The violin imitates it but is not prepared to play at fugue by providing an Answer; it merely imitates at the octave, and again an octave higher. The rest is fireworks in B flat.

Two Pieces for Violin and Piano

A postscript should be added at this point on the two pieces for violin and piano, Canzonetta and Scherzetto, which came out in 1951. The piano writing is less elaborate than in the sonata, but shows the composer's characteristic attitude to the instrument.

During the neo-classical reaction against the romantic movement of the nineteenth century, in which the piano's capacity for swooning arpeggios and melodic illusion was exploited to the full, composers of the first half of the twentieth century begged to remind you that the piano was an instrument of percussion, that its simulated singing melody was a form of dishonesty and that *toccata* was the sort of thing it was really good at. There is a certain amount of martellato chord playing by the hands alternately in both the Sonata and the Scherzetto, but Walton does not carry the dry style as far as the dog-biscuit manner of Prokofiev. Rather he suggests that the piano is a string instrument which may be plucked as well as hit. It is not quite the sonority of the gamelan orchestra of the East that he has at the back of his mind, but rather the guitarist of the Mediterranean who lightly sweeps his lower strings. And so we find him gracing a substantial chord, often in the bass, with a light well-splayed arpeggio of which the keys are only just touched, gracing that is before not after the main notes. Light touch in the higher octaves is another device employed, in this case to reinforce the high harmonics of a chord. Nimbleness of finger is required in both these pieces, which are of the character of the *morceaux* which Kreisler knew how to turn with a graceful air. Indeed Canzonetta has some superficial resemblances to Dvořák's famous 'Humoresque', not only in rhythmic figuration but in its aim of wooing you in order to give you pleasure.

The dotted-note rhythm is in the piano part; the violin has a smooth tune:

which is based on a troubadour melody.

There is also a taking little tune in the Scherzetto:

The violin plays it in several forms and the piano quotes 6 bars of it. There are a good many open fifths in the accompaniment, which is nimble and well aerated.

The two trifles together play for five minutes and show the composer in, for him, an unusually relaxed and light-hearted mood.

SONGS

Three Songs

Solo song is the strongest tradition in English music. Church music, its only rival for the title, suffered a jolt at the Reformation (though it is the smoothness of the transition rather than its difficulty that is remarkable—difficulties affected composers more than composition) and a more serious jar during the Commonwealth. But the song has had a continuous descent from the Agincourt carol to Berkeley and Britten, the line running through Byrd, Morley, Dowland, Purcell, Arne, Dibdin, Bishop, Sterndale Bennett, Sullivan, Parry, Ireland, and Vaughan Williams. One of the features of the modern renaissance is that the field of symphonic music was explored for the first time successfully by English composers, and that as concomitant rather than consequence song-writing was put on one side by Elgar, Bliss, Walton, Rawsthorne, and Fricker. The generalization must not be pushed too far: Elgar wrote songs but not very good ones, and Walton wrote a very few before the composition of *Troilus and Cressida* turned his attention to words as a source of inspiration for music as never before, though of course in their unique way Edith Sitwell's poems had prompted *Façade*, which, whatever else it may be, is not a match of voice and verse as understood by Campian and Milton in the seventeenth century or by the lieder composers of the nineteenth century.

Three of Edith Sitwell's poems appeared as songs in 1932, two of which had been utilized in *Façade*, 'Through gilded trellises' and 'Old Sir Faulk', but the first, 'Daphne', is an independent composition. Of the two in *Façade* a true vocal line replaced the monotone and a true piano accompaniment was fashioned out of the substance of the score of the sextet. 'Daphne' was originally marked 'Nello stile Inglese', the other two of the set being respectively Spanish and American in style. 'Daphne' is indeed English-sounding—but why? The airy texture of the accompaniment is of the sort that Stanford used to urge upon his pupils, the tune

Ex. 1 Songs
Andante

When green as a riv - er— was the bar - ley, Green as a riv - er the rye.—

is of the kind that one has to call English pastoral—or 'blithe' if the word had not an archaic ring—something less perfumed than French, less sumptuous than German, less exuberant than Italian. The last three notes of Ex. 1, which are matched at other cadences, put it into the twentieth century. If confronted with the song out of the blue and asked to guess the composer one might put forward the names of John Ireland or Armstrong Gibbs, but of course it is like nothing but itself. The setting of 'Under the Greenwood Tree', which Walton wrote for a film in 1936, is pastiche of Morley or Dowland, but none the worse for that, a syllabic setting in three-part harmony not imitating but suggesting a lute.

Of the three early songs 'The Winds' (1918) is a simple setting of verses by Swinburne, with a murmuring accompaniment, 'Tritons' (1920) of a poem by William Drummond, and 'Bucolic Comedies' (1924) of poems by Edith Sitwell, of which 'Old Sir Faulk' is actually one, the fox-trot so named in the Suite derived from *Façade*.

Anon. in Love

Walton had no interest in the folk-song revival nor in the Tudor revival, though no English musician could be unaware of them, and the song, 'Under the Greenwood Tree', as already mentioned, betrayed his familiarity with the lutenists. In 1959, however, when the guitar had begun to do for our century what

the lute did for the seventeenth, Walton composed for Peter Pears
and Julian Bream a sequence of six love songs, which he called
Anon. in Love. The poems were chosen for him by Christopher
Hassall from Gerald Bullett's *The English Galaxy of Shorter Poems*
and were all anonymous lyrics of the sixteenth and seventeenth
centuries. The first performance was given by the two artists at
the Aldeburgh Festival of 1960.

The words of the first three songs of the set are familiar from
their use by the madrigal and lute composers. They are 'conceits'
in which similes and word-play throw up a pretty idea and opportunity for word-painting and rhythmic point-making. The other
three are more overtly salacious, so that their flavour is of nearly
a century later, when Purcell had begun to turn this sort of verse
into catches and D'Urfey still later to print it in *Pills to Purge
Melancholy*.

'Fain would I change that note' is a lutenist's ayre from Hume's
Musicall Humors of 1605 and well known to modern singers from
its inclusion by Frederick Keel in his first set of *Elizabethan Love
Songs*, with which he reopened for the twentieth century the
treasures of the seventeenth in 1901. In this song Walton indulges
his propensity for wide-intervalled melody and big compass, an
octave and a half from D to high A. The guitar too covers a wide
range and employs harmonics. Ex. 2 is really an instrumentally
conceived tune

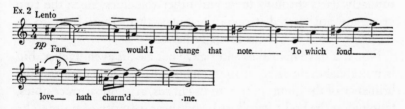

and can be paralleled in the orchestral works, though the minor
ninth on 'change' might perhaps be regarded as a bit of verbal
illustration. Compare it with Ex. 1 for a vocally conceived
line.

No. 2, 'O, stay, sweet love', gives a more compact and conjunct
line of melody, of which the chief feature is a recurring group of

four semiquavers. The guitar part is mainly chordal but includes also some downward arpeggios. The strings on which they should be played are denoted by the composer, and variable tunings of the sixth string to D or E are prescribed. The words come from John Farmer's first set of madrigals of 1599.

Still more compact is the beginning of the vocal melody of No. 3, 'Lady, when I behold the roses sprouting', but it expands at every occurrence of a semiquaver gruppetto, which extrudes a leap of a fourth or fifth, so that in the end the voice spans a compass of a twelfth. The accompaniment is a rocking arpeggio figure; the resources of the guitar are continually explored and exploited as the sequence of arpeggios progresses. The words are from Wilbye's first book of madrigals of 1598, in which he sets them twice over.

There is a change of mood to a franker sauciness but still in the mode of a conceit in 'My love in her attire', short and to the point, as wit should be. This is a syllabic quasi-patter song to an accompaniment in C which flirts with the mixolydian mode, the tonic minor and the relative minor. The vocal line which begins

Ex. 3

similarly darts through these and other tonalities, since the two verses are not treated strophically but with mercurial zip, to an A minor chord as bare as the lady herself.

No. 5, 'I gave her cakes and I gave her ale', is even livelier, but is more elaborate alike in the gracing of the voice part and the brilliance of the guitar part with its chords, arpeggios, grace notes, tapping on the body (tamburo), and sheer quantity of notes to be got in. The basic rhythm is a lilting 6/8, the key a cross between E minor and G major. Like the next song, only less so, it is a strophic setting of roistering erotics, in which the enumeration of the gifts causes a cumulative elaboration and drives the voice up to high B flat in verse 3.

'To couple is a custom', No. 6, expresses the sentiments of

Shelley's 'Love's Philosophy' but in a more nimble quatrain, which is marked by the guitar with our old friend and never-failing pace-maker, oom-pah rhythm. Since the fourth and last verse invokes the fiddler—'Come fiddler scrape thy crowd' (i.e. crwth, the forerunner of the viol and played with a bow)—we have some open fifths of the violin's tuning up in the guitar part. This is the most diatonic song of the set, clearly in A minor and only allowing the chromatic shifts to which Walton is partial for flavouring his melodies in the last verse, which ends both the song and the set brilliantly with the repetition of 'Peggy and I' to produce the climax in the very last bar, by means of an octave swoop of the voice on 'agree' and an emphatic chord of A minor spread sharply over the whole of the guitar's compass.

A Song for the Lord Mayor's Table

Another set of songs followed fairly soon and was also composed for a festival. Its dedication is 'In Honour of the City of London'. Strange how this Lancastrian with an Oxford education is again associated with a city in which he has spent comparatively little of his working life. The occasion was the festival organized in 1962 to save London from the reproach that almost alone of great cities it boasted no festival that it could call its own, as Edinburgh and Vienna, not to mention Amsterdam, had their famous festivals. The singer of the cycle on 18 July 1962 was Elisabeth Schwarzkopf, accompanied on the piano by Gerald Moore at a recital in the hall of the Worshipful Company of Goldsmiths, who had commissioned it. Again the choice of texts was Christopher Hassall's. The title of the set, *A Song for the Lord Mayor's Table*, is taken from the title of the first single song, No. 1: a ceremonious setting of a rumbustious poem by Thomas Jordan,

> Let all the Nine Muses lay by their abuses
> Their railing and drolling on tricks of the Strand,
> To pen us a ditty in praise of the City
> Their treasure and pleasure, their power and command.

It might almost be a Coronation instead of a banquet, Ex. 4 being quite in the vein of *Orb and Sceptre*:

This is a longish song of four verses, the fourth being a repetition of the first extended into a coda. The second verse leaves A flat, cancelling the signature and showing marked mobility of key, and adopts 6/8 time. A figure of repeated notes in the piano part suggests the use of corkscrew and the popping of corks from bottles of Claret, Canary, and Rhenish—except that the same figure (but with seconds instead of thirds) depicts in the next verse wallowing in milk and honey:

Repetitions and sequences build up excitement for the recall of the first stanza, which is not, it need hardly be said, an exact repetition.

No. 2, as is right, invokes the Thames and provides every sort of contrast. 'Adagio tranquillo, ppp, una corde, sost.espress.' are the directions to the artists. The words are Wordsworth's 'Glide softly'. The time signatures are as fluid as the river itself, 5, 7, 6, 5, 9, 8 and 4 quavers to the bar—one might not unreasonably suppose that Walton is playing a new sort of serial game were it not that the pace of the quaver is constant. The fundamental bass lies deep in the bottom octave, and the sustaining pedal (carefully marked) gives a kind of depth to the stream of sound, which is anyhow muted. There are few wide intervals in the vocal line, but a long slow scale-wise descent from top F to low A and back up again to G carry the lines.

> Till all our minds for ever flow
> As thy deep waters now are flowing.

This is a deeply felt and deeply imaginative song. 'Deep' is indeed the word for it.

'Wapping Old Stairs' is one of Anon.'s sea-songs of the inconstant sailor, which was well described at its first performance as 'a wry half-teasing complaint of the jilted girl' from Wapping. The time signature is unusual, one minim per bar. The accompaniment is a strumming of chords rich in crushed seconds:

Ex. 6

The voice part, mezza voce not quite parlando, runs easily on alternations of two and three crotchets to the bar.

'Holy Thursday', No. 4, takes us from the East End to St Paul's. Blake's picture describes one of the Charity Children's services, such as impressed Berlioz during his visit to London in 1851. For each of the three stanzas the composer employs a different figuration. The interval of the major second is again in evidence. Chords accompany the first verse in 6/4 against the voice's 2/2 time, grace notes and arpeggios, still marking the processional pulse regularly, are used for the second verse, and runs, passing from left to right hand, for the third. The song ends as it began on a chord of E containing a second (and no third).

No. 5, 'The Contrast', is a setting of a poem by Charles Morris about a Londoner who cannot bear the boredom of the country with nothing but natural phenomena to look at—'an ass on a common, a goose on a green'. This quick (scherzando) patter employs a device composers normally avoid in writing for the voice but which Walton uses in all his songs for emphasis, frequent short rests in the middle of a phrase or between two words that really go together—thus:

Ex. 7

En-rap - tured   with this

The accompaniment to the London thesis is all staccato, sometimes in octaves, sometimes one hand passing a splayed chord to

the other an octave higher; the country antithesis on the other
hand has sustained chords, with a sort of bell tintinabulating on an
E flat. At the first ironical reference to the restorative effects of
rural peace the singer is to assume an exaggeratedly soulful
expression 'noiosamente' and with portamento. Amusement is
unrestrained when the little devil love finds that in London
there's always a new devil to drive an old devil out.

No. 6 is discreetly called 'Rhyme', and is, in fact, after an
introductory verse over a bell ostinato:

with some small bells tinkling over it, none other than our old
nursery rhyme 'Oranges and Lemons', but without the chopper
of the child's singing game. For this is a longer version from
Gammer Gurton's Garland (1810), in which there are many more
bell towers than in the nursery rhyme version. They are St
Clement's, St Margaret's, St Giles's, St Martin's, St Peter's, White-
chapel, St John's, St Ann's, Aldgate, St Helen's, Old Bailey, Shore-
ditch, Stepney, and Bow. So the singer has to repeat the tune more
frequently and does so through many keys by pivot modulation.
A gay conclusion to what started so ceremoniously at the Lord
Mayor's Table!

CHAPTER VI

Choral Works

Belshazzar's Feast

WALTON had already established himself as an orchestral composer even more decisively, for instance, than Elgar had done,
though at a younger age, when he turned to the oratorio form,
which sooner or later engages the attention of all British composers. The viola concerto bears the date 1929; *Belshazzar's Feast*
was first performed at the Leeds Festival of 1931 under Dr Malcolm
Sargent and was heard shortly afterwards in London at a B.B.C.
concert. After this it went the rounds of all the big choral societies
of the country and was performed at the International Contemporary Festival at Amsterdam in 1933. Twenty years later its great
technical difficulty had so far been assimilated by choralists that
performances were no longer limited to crack choirs with virtuoso
conductors, but had come within the capacities of more modest
pretensions, such as could master *The Dream of Gerontius* which
of course is not an easy work, but does not present the difficulties
of intonation and time-keeping of its successor. Before the composition of this cantata, which is dedicated to Lord Berners,
Walton had only flirted with words at a distance in *Façade*. Now,
relying perhaps on his choral experience as a boy at Oxford
Cathedral, he boldly essays a big subject and produces a work
whose sheer striking power was something quite new in English
choral music.

The text of *Belshazzar's Feast* was put together by Osbert Sitwell and is an abridged and dramatized form of the narrative of
the fall of Babylon in Daniel v., written therefore from the Jewish
point of view and incorporating parts of two Psalms, 137 and 81,
and also Revelation xviii. The work is continuous, and the divisions made in this note are solely for convenience of commentary.

M   161

The composer, however, uses long pauses to mark the abrupt and dramatic changes in the narration of the story.

The vocal score gives but a pale reflection of the full score; the piano reduction cannot show the powerful and distinctive character of the instrumentation. The early part of the work is not merely dark but bitter, and contrives to match the ferocious hate which lies just beneath the mournful surface of the text. The exact flavour of Jewish nationalism is caught alike in the harsh substance of the music and in the instrumental dress which it wears. The passion and the sorrow break through in the long stretches of beautiful writing for unaccompanied voices. This indeed is one of the most remarkable features of the work: voices alone, orchestra alone, and voices and orchestra together form three distinct forces each of which is capable of gradation and climax in its own sort: they are set over against one another and reinforce each other's effect by their contrast. The orchestra employed is a very large one, and its full resources are unleashed in a crescendo of barbaric splendour in the chorus of praise to the heathen gods. It includes over and above the usual instruments of the full modern symphony orchestra an alto saxophone, an E flat clarinet (a military band instrument), and a pianoforte which is treated purely orchestrally; the composer desires when possible to have separate brass bands to the right and left, in the manner prescribed by Berlioz for his Requiem. For the 'kitchen' department a large equipment of furniture is required: side drum, bass drum, cymbals, triangle, tambourine, glockenspiel, xylophone, gong, anvil, slapstick, and Chinese block. The score, however, is so arranged that performance of the work is possible without certain optional instruments. The cantata takes about forty minutes in performance.

Leading themes are exceptionally plastic. Their main outlines are clear enough, but no one form belongs more authentically to the idea it signifies than another. The composer has made a brilliant use of this plasticity in the chorus of Babylonian praise of the heathen deities (see Exs. 8–16), but the same principle is observed throughout the work, whose great vitality may be largely attributed to this constant adaptation of the theme to its environment. Thus a practice to which the composer had become increasingly prone was established in this cantata as a permanent feature of his style.

The opening bars may be quoted in their entirety, as they show Walton's characteristic use of dissonance, whether to give bite to his harmony or for the more specific purpose, as here, of illustrating the harshness of Isaiah's prophecy:

Ex. 1

Psalm 137 follows, prefaced by seven bars of orchestral prelude, in which an important theme is heard in the bass:

Ex. 2

The smoother beginning of this chorus, which almost immediately opens out into eight parts, may also be quoted:

Ex. 3

Phrases based on figure (*a*), which has some kinship with Ex. 2, recur in all parts of the score. The violoncellos and the woodwind especially make much of its distinctive curve. The dark colours of these opening pages are applied with bass clarinet, saxophone, bassoon, double bassoon and trombones; the violins are not heard at all until the word 'song'; the piano is used to make the edge of the striding bass more incisive. When the destruction of Babylon is contemplated in the last sentence of the chorus, not only the percussion but the brass is used to jab the texture with baleful rhythms.

A new figure, terse and sturdy, is heard before the indignant question is asked 'How shall we sing the Lord's song in a strange land?' (which is afterwards repeated unaccompanied *meno mosso* more in sorrowful despair than in rage):

Ex. 4

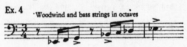

This is accompanied by insistent and angry protest from the brass:

Ex. 4a

It does not persist for long but it is heard again when the destruction of Babylon is so ardently desired at the end of the Psalm. The baritone soloist now joins in antiphony with the chorus against an urgent accompaniment made of the figure:

Ex. 5

and a new version of figure (*a*) of Ex. 3 is heard, first on the flute and oboe and then from the sopranos of the chorus:

Ex. 6

The opening music of Ex. 3 returns again, followed by the vicious figures of Ex. 4a with additional rhythmic punctuation from percussion, additional counterpoints from the brass, and other changes to increase its intensity. Finally Ex. 2 returns and completes the first section of the cantata.

The baritone soloist now embarks on a piece of unaccompanied declamation (quasi recit. ad lib. robusto).

> Babylon was a great city,
> Her merchandise was of gold and silver,
> Of precious stones, of pearls, of fine linen,
> Of purple, silk, and scarlet,
> All manner vessels of ivory,
> All manner vessels of most precious wood,
> Of brass, iron, and marble,
> Cinnamon, odours, and ointments,
> Of frankincense, wine, and oil,
> Fine flour, wheat, and beasts,
> Sheep, horses, chariots, slaves,
> And the souls of men.

The chorus takes up the narrative, heralded by a furious arpeggio, tearing down through the score like a flash of forked lightning:

Ex. 7
Allegro molto

Wood-wind, Trumpet
Xylophone, Piano, and Strings

The mere mention of the feast lets loose this angry phrase and the story of the sacrilege of drinking out of the Temple vessels gives a savage movement of quavers to the bass of the accompaniment. Constant changes of time signature—2/4, 3/4, 3/8—increase the agitation. At the King's command for music the choir divides into two choruses, but reunites after tremendous fanfares on the brass in a passage of tight and angry homophony of great force.

In Babylon
Belshazzar the King
Made a great feast,
Made a feast to a thousand of his lords,
And drank wine before the thousand.

Belshazzar, whiles he tasted the wine,
Commanded us to bring the gold and silver vessels:
Yea! the golden vessels, which his father, Nebuchadnezzar,
Had taken out of the temple that was in Jerusalem.

He commanded us to bring the golden vessels
Of the temple of the house of God,
That the King, his princes, his wives,
And his concubines might drink therein.

Then the King commanded us:
Bring ye the cornet, flute, sackbut, psaltery,
And all kinds of music: they drank wine again
Yea! drank from the sacred vessels.
And then spake the King:

The baritone soloist begins the heathen hymn, but the chorus
takes the words out of his mouth.

Praise ye the God of Gold,
Praise ye the God of Silver,
Praise ye the God of Iron,
Praise ye the God of Wood,
Praise ye the God of Stone,
Praise ye the God of Brass.
Praise ye the gods.

Into the orchestra a figure is now introduced which is repeated
in different guises after each salutation to the gods of gold, silver,
iron, wood and the rest of them:

Ex. 8

Another 'praise' figure that is extensively used is:

Before this is heard, however, there has been a priestly march in procession before the god of gold:

The swaying motif of these quotations, with or without its appendage of dotted notes, is used as a melisma at each 'praise'. For the god of silver, who is addressed by female voices only, it is given appropriately to flute and piccolo in this form:

with a glockenspiel and a triangle picking out in silver tones its rhythmic outline. The iron god is hymned by male voices only, and for him the salutation has become a fanfare of trumpets:

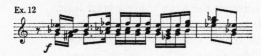

which is immediately followed by a reply from the brass band situated away from the main body:

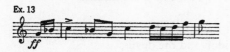

The god of wood is greeted with fiddles playing col legno and with the xylophone:

For the god of stone a slapstick is introduced, which accompanies the following:

The god of brass is rightly praised by brass bands:

After their several announcements these phrases, especially Exs. 9 and 16, are incorporated in the final pæan of praise. Ex. 10, the march tune, also adds splendour to the general musical scene.

There is a long pause and the choral narrative is resumed. Before the words 'Thus in Babylon' Ex. 7 is heard again and the story of the feast retold. A good deal of the music is the same, notably the opening and the passage about the instruments of music. Between them is a new and derisive allusion to false gods, devils and idols. The texture now becomes clearer, and the heathen climax is upon us at 'O King, live for ever'.

> Thus in Babylon, the mighty city,
> Belshazzar the King made a great feast,
> Made a feast to a thousand of his lords
> And drank wine before the thousand.
> Belshazzar whiles he tasted the wine
> Commanded us to bring the gold and silver vessels
> That his Princes, his wives and his concubines
> Might rejoice and drink therein.
>
> After they praised their strange gods,
> The idols and the devils,
> False gods who can neither see nor hear,
> Called they for the timbrel and the pleasant harp
> To extol the glory of the King.
> Then they pledged the king before the people,
> Crying 'Thou, O King, art King of Kings:
> O King, live for ever. . . .'

But the words have not been uttered before the 'thunderbolt' motif, Ex. 7, is heard in the orchestra. There is a pause. The baritone soloist tells the story of the writing on the wall to an accompaniment of cymbals, drums and gong:

And in that same hour, as they feasted,
Came forth the fingers of a man's hand.
And the King saw
The part of the hand that wrote.
And this was the writing that was written:
'Mene, mene, tekel upharsin'.

'Thou art weighed in the balance and found wanting.' (*Male chorus*)

In that night was Belshazzar the King slain
And his kingdom divided.

The word 'slain' is snatched from the soloist's mouth by the chorus in a great shout.

The ironical hymn of praise to heathen deities is now balanced by a fanatical chorus of genuine thanksgiving to the God of Israel. The rejoicings of the Jews in the words of the first four verses of Psalm 81 are set to a vigorous 'allegro giocoso', in which justice is done to the blowing up of the trumpet in the new moon. The opening words of the Psalm are repeated to different music in a staccato style. A semichorus undertakes the 'molto espressivo' section dealing with the wailing of the kings and merchants. The semichorus is divided into two four-part choirs which sing of the silence of the trumpeters and pipers without accompaniment.

At the resumption of 'Sing aloud' the orchestra breaks in with an animated toccata-like movement:

This rhythm and this kind of figuration are maintained while the chorus sings *Alleluia* in antiphony. Soon the voice parts are marked 4/2 and become sweepingly diatonic, while the accompaniment has the strange time-signature 4/9/8, which means that each pulse of the 4/2 bar is accompanied by a whole bar of 9/8 time. The enormous impetus of the music may be imagined from the mere look of the opening measure:

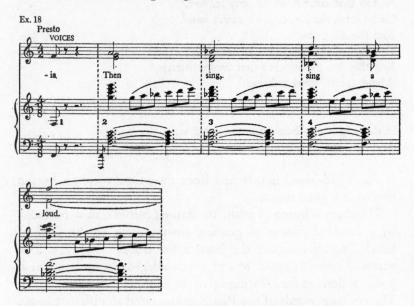

Ex. 18

Enough of the libretto has been quoted to show the skill in construction for musical setting. A touch or two of archaism in the words maintains the atmosphere of the Old Testament. And there is no suggestion of Christian sentiment anywhere, or indeed of edification which has always been a defining element in oratorios, to weaken the homogeneity of the story. The work, therefore, in spite of its Biblical origin, is more truly a secular cantata than a descendant in the English oratorio tradition of *Elijah*. It thus escaped performance at a Three Choirs Festival or in cathedrals, until 1957, when it was given at Worcester. Deans and Chapters are more broad-minded in these matters than formerly—thus *A Sea Symphony* of Vaughan Williams was sung at the Gloucester Festival of 1962—but a sense of what is fitting does indicate that its place is not in church.

In Honour of the City of London

The success of *Belshazzar's Feast* at the Leeds Festival of 1931 was such that it was inevitable that Walton should be asked for another cantata. Yorkshire indeed has been faithful to the Lancastrian composer, for it included *Façade* in the programme of the 1928 Festival, followed with *Belshazzar's Feast* three years later, and put into the 1937 Festival not only the cantata *In Honour of the City of London* but also the Coronation March, which derives its title, *Crown Imperial*, from the poem of this very cantata. Years later *Gloria* was written at the request of the Huddersfield Choral Society.

The vocal writing of *In Honour of the City of London* is bold—its choral counterpoint has been called 'rough' and the parts do clash sharply at times—the orchestration is exuberant, and the whole proceeds with tremendous vigour and buoyancy. The cantata, however, has not made the same widespread appeal to choral singers as did *Belshazzar's Feast*. It is difficult to sing, no doubt; difficult not only to get some of the discordant harmony in tune, but also vocally difficult, as when at the beginning the sopranos have to jump from high G to the F sharp a ninth below and again at the end when they have to snatch at their high B's:

Ex. 1

Lon - don!   Lon - don!   Lon - - - don.

On the other hand here is a vocal line very much in Walton's restless melodic vein yet entirely grateful to sing:

Ex. 2

pp   *rubato*

Pryn - cesse of town - és— of   plea - - - sure and of joy

The harmonic asperity or ferocity—it is both by turns—is accounted for sometimes by Walton's palate for pungency—compare the taste for tonic sevenths in the later Violin Concerto.

Sometimes it is the outcome of a piece of logic, thus:

Ex. 3

Here is a cadence in B flat. On the strong beat, however, we have in the orchestra a tonic ninth. This makes a pungent tonic chord, but it is also part of an ascending sequence of chords of the diatonic seventh which the orchestra is bent on establishing in a series of consecutives. Even so the chord of G in the bass of the orchestral part seems a deliberate darkening of the harmony, making the complete chord opaque instead of piercingly bright, but its logic is established at the fourth beat of the bar in the progression of the bass down from B through G to F, each note bearing on it the notes of an open triad.

This kind of thing makes the music very strong in flavour, very energetic in movement and keeps up an excitement that becomes a little tiring until it is eased by the tranquil section describing the River Thames, which affords a welcome relief. On the whole the impression from the first performance was that so much strenuousness, which was an inheritance from *Belshazzar's Feast*, here overreached itself and defeated its own end, an impression confirmed many years later (see below, p. 175). These vivid strokes, this exuberant movement, though in keeping with the vitality of the poem, were apt to be overlaid in their own plenitude and to leave only an impression of bustling cheerfulness. If, however, the cantata did not make its way as might have been expected, it may have been due to the fact that Sir George Dyson's setting of the same words had a nine-years start and had found favour with choral societies, which would hardly be likely to undertake two settings of the same poem together. Perhaps, too, provincial sing-

ers are unwilling to pay such unqualified compliments to a metro-
polis which in their view already gets far too much attention!

The poem 'In Honour of the City of London', is the work of the
Scottish poet, William Dunbar (c. 1460—c. 1520), who being a
Lowlander, wrote not in Gaelic but in Chaucerian English, which
has been retained unmodernized in the present setting by Walton.
How a Scot came to be so fulsome about the Sassenach capital is
not clear unless he really was impressed by London. Or was it
rather due to the official necessity of pulling off the royal marriage
between King James IV and Margaret Tudor in 1501, which was
the occasion of his visit to London? In any case his handsome compliments make a fine piece of occasional verse which has survived
by reason of its other, more intrinsic merits.

> London, thou art of townes A per se.
> Soveraigne of cities, seemliest in sight,
> Of high renown, riches and royaltie;
> Of lordis, barons, and many a goodly knyght;
> Of most delectable lusty ladies bright;
> Of famous prelatis in habitis clericall;
> Of merchauntis full of substaunce and of myght:
> London, thou are the flour of Cities all.

—and so on for five more complimentary verses praising its
riches. Its beauty 'beryng the crone imperiall', its river, its
Bridge, its Tower, and its people.

These verses are set for chorus in four parts, expanding to five
six, seven or eight at pleasure, with accompaniment for the ordinary large orchestra, including piccolo and harp, but without
double bassoon or bass clarinet. No soloists are employed. The
main tonality is a kind of E. The several verses are differentiated in
their setting mainly by differences of musical rhythm. Thus the
first verse is set in 3/2 time, the second and third in 9/8 and 6/8,
verse 4, which pictures the River Thames, in a broad and sustained
4/2, the Bridge in verse 5 is built on 'pylers' of four alternating
with three crotchets in a bar, and the last verse returns in the main
to triple measure, sometimes simple (3/2) and sometimes compound (9/4).

The cantata opens with an invocation to London in solid chords,

but a figure is soon introduced into the orchestra and is thereafter
worked with some persistence:

The 'famous prelates' are introduced appropriately in plainsong
with a counterpoint in third species (though played unecclesi-
astically on strings pizzicato). The rich merchants are accompanied
by Ex. 4, which therefore must be the symbol of 'substance and
myght'. There is a short interlude between the first and second
verses of an energy that recalls passages in *Belshazzar's Feast* and
scored with Walton's characteristically crackling orchestration.
Verse 2 is marked 'con agilità e molto ritmico' and two new short
figures are introduced into the accompaniment—a group of oscillating semiquavers and a brief undulating arpeggio:

The chorus is content to sing in four parts lightened occasionally
by taking turns two by two; in the third verse there is a good deal
of homophonic singing which culminates in a passage of exultant
thirds in contrary motion. There is a change of mood as well as
rhythm at the fourth verse; female voices in four parts are employed to sing the praises of the river in long flowing lines of melody, accompanied by a murmur of triplets in the orchestra. The
men enter for the last two lines of invocation to the 'towne of
townes' and the verse finishes in unaccompanied eight-part harmony. Another interlude (brioso) intervenes before London
Bridge and the Tower are described. This verse is the men's turn.
The basses lead off:

The tenors follow:

Ex. 7 Tenors

Up - on thy stre - tis goth ma - ny a seme - - ly knyght

Comparison of the two leads, Exs. 6 and 7, shows a typical example of Walton's transformation of themes. This is the cause of the music's bubbling energy and also of the feeling that somehow it all hangs together just as much as if the imitation was strict and the recapitulation exact. Another example is provided in the next verse by the ground bass that is no repetitive ground, upon which the strong walls are raised in unison (i.e., strictly speaking in octaves). There is a touch of illustration by means of rhythmic chords on the brass at the reference to 'artillary', followed by runs in thirds by way of contrast for the refrain. The sturdy bass already laid down for the massive walls is continued for the strong tide of the river with triplets again playing on its surface; there is a suggestion of bells in the part writing; the wives are described thus:

Ex. 8 Sopranos mp

Fair be their wives,____ right love - som, white____ and small;

which is the theme in augmented time-values that has already been heard in the third verse at the words 'Swete paradise precelling'. Here in the later context the trend towards E major is confirmed and in that key, with all the bells ringing, the final apostrophe of the city is made in eight parts over a busily humming bass.

After a long interval the cantata was taken out again for performance in London in 1962. The occasion was the Festival of the City of London, when it was sung in St Paul's Cathedral by the Goldsmiths Choral Union under the composer's direction, though this in fact had been narrowly anticipated shortly before by a performance at the Royal Academy of Music. The view that the setting was too strenuous for the character of the poem, which calls for something more spacious if no less exuberant, was confirmed. There is too little variety and even the Thames has too much movement in its waters. It needed stronger singing than it got at this revival, but an element of miscalculation has flawed what is none the less an entirely characteristic product of the composer's idiom.

Coronation Te Deum

For the Coronation of Queen Elizabeth II in Westminster Abbey on 2 June 1953, Sir William Walton composed a setting to the English text of the ancient hymn of the Church, *Te Deum Laudamus*. He has thus to his credit three pieces of occasional music, all ceremonious, connected with coronations, and over the years many of his works have been commissions in celebration of some occasion of rejoicing and thus up to a point wear an official air. True, the *Johannesburg Overture* (1956) and the *Partita for Orchestra* (1958) were composed respectively for African and American anniversaries so that they do not count towards a laureate status in Britain, but they do emphasize the brilliant extraverted side of the composer's genius, just as the Huddersfield *Gloria* of 1961 does, at the expense of the romantic and witty sides. He is himself a retiring person, quiet in manner, slightly sardonic in conversation and not apparently devoted to or influenced by the brave shows of things. The psychologist can therefore speculate whether it is because of, or in spite of, his quiet demeanour in the ordinary affairs of life that he can come out with these shatteringly apt displays of pomp and circumstance.

It is safe to declare that the *Te Deum* is the best of them all and, *Belshazzar's Feast* apart, the best of the choral works, 'best' meaning that it combines in a maximum degree the aptitude to the passing occasion and the permanent qualities of a work of art independent of an occasion. In firmness of structure, strength of harmony, and imaginative fire this *Te Deum* is among the best things Walton has done. Length, weight, brilliance are right. Perfectly adapted to its first use in the Abbey it transfers to other occasions, such as the opening service of an Edinburgh Festival or to nothing more than a choral concert.

Walton took immense pains to make it right for its ceremonial first purpose, visiting the Abbey frequently beforehand and listening from various parts of the building to the effects of organ

Plate 5   Scapino. From an etching by J. Callot of 1622

Plate 6 A page of the original manuscript of Walton's Second Symphony

and choir. Attention to detail is a mark of all his scores and in this case acoustic effect was specially considered. It determined the major principle of the structure of the work, namely antiphony. In the Coronation service it came immediately after the Archbishop's benediction, to which the choir sang an Amen in D major by Orlando Gibbons. 'The solemnity of the Queen's Coronation being ended the people shall stand and the choir shall sing: *Te Deum Laudamus.*' It was the last music of the service except the National Anthem, which was sung as the Queen left the Abbey. An adaptation to the Latin text was subsequently published.

The antiphony was not just a matter of Cantoris and Decani but a deployment of all the available forces, which consisted of two choirs, two semi-choruses, boys' voices, organ, orchestra, and military brass. The choir consisted of the full complement from the Abbey, the Chapels Royal, St George's Chapel, Windsor, and St Paul's Cathedral, augmented by representatives of Canterbury, York, Oxford, Cambridge, Edinburgh, Dublin, and Llandaff collegiate foundations. The only women's voices were 19 representatives of the Dominions, an awkward constitutional anomaly, which caused some feeling among English and Scottish singers who were excluded, but could not be circumvented without offence to the Dominions. The orchestra was made up of representatives of all the leading symphony orchestras. The organ was played by Dr Osborne Peasgood, assistant organist of the Abbey. The conductor was Sir William McKie, the Organist of the Abbey, who was in charge of all the musical arrangements for the Coronation. The first antiphony was between orchestra and organ—the organ echoing the opening praise motif which dominates the first section and recurs at 'O Lord save the people':

Ex. 1

The next antiphony was between Choir I and Choir II, which was a matter of response from north and south triforia where the

N

largest number of singers was placed. Next came antiphony
between semi-chorus and full choir, followed by sopranos of
Cantoris and Decani answering each other. Now in place of these
as it were vertical divisions the composer employed a horizontal
antiphony between high and low voices, which passed doctrinal
theses to each other. The orchestra-organ antiphony is resumed at
'O Lord save thy people', but gradually the disparate forces are
brought together into six-part harmony at low pitch and pianissimo for the final 'Non confundar in aeternum'.

The key scheme and the use of common chords often in juxtaposition without modulation are singularly direct in their effect,
and Walton uses fewer added dissonances to his chords than elsewhere in his choral writing. The composition is in fact in traditional style to suit the acoustic conditions of a high vaulted church.
The key of D is firmly established at once. The first move out of it
is up a semi-tone to E flat for the Angels and the Seraphim. The
harmony pivots to a 6/4 chord with a flattened sixth which gives
A flat minor in due course for 'Holy, Holy, Holy!'. Enharmonic-
ally a return is made *via* chords of F sharp minor and E major to C
for 'Lord God of Sabaoth'. This sequence is repeated more or less
until it is the turn of Apostles and Prophets to sing praises. Here
we come to what in a sonata would be the second subject, and it is
in the orthodox key of A major. This is a piece of quasi-recitative
in block harmony for the tenors and basses specifying the various
choruses of praise, while the praise itself is a melismatic swaying
theme sung by the upper parts:

Ex. 2

The key goes to G major and minor for the next section of the hymn which opens with fanfares. Just before the return to Ex. 1 for 'O Lord save thy people' there are a few bars of quiet evensong sort of music that might have come from the pen of S. S. Wesley:

Ex. 3

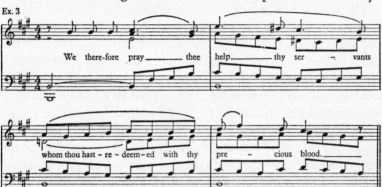

A throw-back to Christ Church days? Perhaps. Incongruous? Not in the least; the moment of repose is welcome and reminds us where we are—in church and the heirs to a thousand years of polyphony. First and second subjects (Exs. 1 and 2) are recapitulated, and a coda based on triads for 'Lord, let thy mercy lighten upon us' leads to the wonderful final cadence, 'Let me never be confounded'. Ex. 4 shows the triadic juxta-positions mentioned above in their simplest and most cogent form. The voices sing these chords in quasi-recitative and the organ supports them thus:

Ex. 4

col 8

Gloria

During the years that elapsed between the Coronation *Te Deum* and the next substantial choral work, the *Gloria* composed for a double celebration by the Huddersfield Choral Society in 1961, Walton had been engaged on finishing his opera, *Troilus and Cressida*, and on a number of commissions, the Johannesburg

Festival Overture of 1956, the Cello Concerto for Piatigorsky of 1957, the Partita for Orchestra for Cleveland, U.S.A., of 1958, and the Second Symphony for the Royal Liverpool Philharmonic Society.

The trouble about festive commissions is that from the nature of the case they call for something jubilant, and it may well be that these products of the fifties, with the exception of the opera and the concerto, have overdrawn on the strenuous emotions and the tense ejaculatory vein of Walton's style to the detriment of his more lyrical and reflective vein. The choice of text was probably determined by the success of the *Te Deum* and the need for something brilliant which the famous Huddersfield choir could get its teeth into and fling off triumphantly. In the event the *Gloria* served its purposes—the celebration of the choir's 125th birthday and of Sir Malcolm Sargent's 30 years' association with it as its conductor, the provision of a difficult modern work for the choir, and of a successor to *Belshazzar's Feast* after an interval of 30 years.

But it does not wholly escape the suspicion that so much celebration, jubilation, and acclamation have sometimes forced the composer's invention. The *Gloria* has not the liturgical purpose to serve that the *Te Deum* had, though it is conceived on the same sort of dramatic lines. Nor is it part of a larger whole, of a complete mass, as a setting of the *Gloria* normally is, so it has not the advantage of providing contrast and variety to the adjacent sections of the Ordinary of the Mass as it would have even in a non-liturgical oratorio. This consideration represents the defect of its quality as an occasional work, but it is more serious that the word setting is more conspicuous for its accentuation than for its symbolism, except for 'Miserere nobis', it need hardly be said, which is almost too clamant in its plea, and that the text, having no liturgical function or religious significance, becomes not much more than a vehicle for a good Yorkshire choral jamboree. It follows that it requires superlative singing if this hollow at the heart of it is not to be exposed.

The choral writing is more dissonant than in *Belshazzar's Feast* in so far as there is more block harmony in which chords containing clashes of a second and a semitone, or scrunches such as F sharp

and E, C and B juxtaposed in the same chord, or cases where as at
'Qui sedes' a repeated reciting chord, consisting of minor third,
diminished fourth and fifth, major seventh, and ninth is hammered
and sustained and not resolved, are treated as consonances, albeit
consonances flavoured with a dose of quinine. The acuity of such
dissonance is modified by voices compared with their sound on
the piano or orchestral wind: it becomes a curdle and sets up a
jangle of overtones that colours but does not conceal, still less up-
set, the basic harmony. It can sound muddy; it can tire the ear; it is
difficult to sing in tune and especially to strike it as a chord; but it
effectually banishes the ghost of Mendelssohn and memories of
the hymn-book.

If in *Gloria* there is so much of it as to make different harmonies
sound much of a muchness, or if, as suggested, the invention is not
running in spate, a look at the score quickly reveals that the composer has bestowed all his usual care on detail. Much of it cannot
be identified by the ear in performance: it is designed to modify
the total effect, not to be recognized for its own significance. A
few instances can be assembled to show Walton's way of work.
The very first word uttered by the choir, 'Gloria', contains a propulsive (but hardly audible) two-against-three:

Similarly 'gratias' has a slight displacement to give it bite.

At 'miserere' the composer has added a vocative 'O' to the text (as
Beethoven did) to provide an anacrusis and lengthen the phrase
for which he needs a melisma. At 'pax' he contrives a double
effect of nucleus and particle by making his tenors hold a pianissimo chord quasi inaudibile while sopranos and basses explode
on a brief quaver fortissimo. There is no need to give further instances of these nicely calculated effects. The only doubtful point
about them is whether some of them at least are not totally lost in
the mass of sound and the prevalent density of texture. Walton

certainly feels his music as something to be forcibly propelled and makes every provision that it shall be.

The oratorio, for that is what it is, falls into eleven sections that correspond to the clauses, the changes of emphasis, of idea and address, in the text, and they are marked in the score by changes of signature—of key, time, and tempo.

There are 14 bars of orchestral summons to attention before the voices enter with their ardent and repeated glorias. Trumpets and trombones announce a strong upward thrusting motto, which is alluded to, though not actually cited in so many notes, at the beginning of the penultimate section, 'Quoniam,' and indeed sung unaccompanied to 'Cum sancto spirita':

While this G sharp is held, a fat chord containing two acute dissonances comes down heavily and lets off an upward triplet run which ends in a screaming trill. Ex. 3 is repeated a tone lower, though ending in a trill a third higher, and again at other pitches and yet again in diminution. The first section is laid out in eight parts, is ejaculatory in manner and is comfortably in D major. It picks up sufficient animation to end in a swirling tutti for orchestra stiff with contrary motion and cascading chords.

Calm and C major, with a strong infusion of E major, for 'in terra pax' so:

The descending figure on flute and oboe answers a similar rising figure in the bass, and together they give some horizontal movement to add to the suave effect of consecutive thirds to express the goodwill for humanity. 'Pax' is passed in antiphony between women's voices and men's and finally settles on a unison without orchestra. There is here some suggestion of tonal symbolism.

The change to 'Laudamus te' is instantaneous with a reversion to D major and 6/8 time, to the mood and animation of the opening. 'Be-ne-di-ci-mus te' is used to introduce some dotted-note impetus. At 'Glorificamus' the signature changes to five sharps but the key is certainly not B; it is more like F sharp major-minor. The basses start a promising subject for a fugato:

but though the writing is now contrapuntal no fugue emerges from the points of imitation. Still, it is the nearest we get to a fugue. At 'gratias' we come back to the ejaculatory style, and the voices throw the figure noted above, Ex. 2, from one to the other over an oscillating pedal—at least that is the effect of the very deliberate movement of the bass, A sharp, A natural, then a long dwelling on G, followed after a break by A flat. 'Domine Deus' builds up to an elaborate climax. The voices settle for a phrase characterized by a triplet figure—the orchestra is increasingly pervaded by triplets, the tempo is sempre più mosso, the key is more G minor than B flat, but the chord upon which the voices arrive consists of all seven notes of the scale of B flat. The chord is held and then repeated unaccompanied marcato. It is resolved, if that is the word for the release after a grand pause, on a unison thus:

Ex. 6

De - us Pa - ter__ om - ni - (i)' - po - tens__

still another version of Ex. 3.

This melodic idea is now transposed into B minor and given to the basses, while the altos reiterate 'gloria!' in a fanfare figure in thirds and the orchestra sets up a moto perpetuo in triplets over heavy pedal basses. The section is rounded off with an explicit reference to Ex. 3.

There is a sudden change and contrast. The markings are 'lento, sotto voce, pianissimo' and unaccompanied—in the full score there are parts for clarinets in brackets and labelled 'only if necessary for pitch'. The reason for the change of mood is the introduction of the Second Person of the Trinity, the name of Jesus Christ, the Lamb of God. The orchestra is silent at first but it accompanies the semi-chorus when it is their turn to sing 'Domine Deus', and echoes the complete choir's ejaculation of 'Agnus Dei, Filius Patris' in eight agitated chords.

'Miserere' brings in the solo voices. It is unusually conceived as a cry of anguish and despair. It begins loudly with an octave leap to a high B flat for the sopranos while the other voices interject a figure of this shape.

Ex. 7

mi - se - re - re

The orchestra is all trills, tremolandos and drum rolls, signifying alarm. The tenor soloist begins an unaccompanied melisma with a prefixed 'O' for anacrusis and urgency. Before he embarks on the second part of his clause, 'qui tollis peccata mundi', the orchestra establishes an accompanimental figure with percussion:

He is joined by the alto and the bass soloists, who sing similar long-drawn lines that are neither identical nor canons nor inversions but contrive to sound like all three, while the chorus mutters 'miserere nobis' on A flats and B flats. The expression mark 'quasi bisbigliando' (Italian for 'whispering') is borrowed from the harp technique of soft thrumming. This section, though encompassing two ideas, 'suscipe deprecationem' and 'Qui sedes ad dexteram', is held together as one, a kind of slow movement, by the repeated prayer for mercy. It ends quietly.

Trombones open the introduction to the 'Quoniam' section with something like the opening pages of the work. The chorus begins 'quoniam tu solus sanctus' in eight-part interjections which are gradually integrated, gather momentum and end in a blaze of quavers followed by block-chord assertion 'Tu solus altissimus Jesu Christe' unaccompanied.

The Third Person of the Trinity is in most settings of the mass treated with brilliance to make up for the theological brevity which merges him in the glory of the Father. Walton's treatment is to broaden the tempo to maestoso, begin with a unison phrase derived from Ex. 3 and then set in motion three different figurations, fast tremolando on strings, moderate chords falling in even crotchets and a great swinging bass like a tenor bell so:

though the bass line represented above is only an approximation giving the main rhythm; timpani and bells reinforce it and the harp adds its chords every half bar. The organ joins in and the woodwind trills in a counterpoint of rhythm.

For coda 'Gloria' returns unliturgically, for the choir, besides its ejaculation of the single word 'gloria', adds 'Gloria in excelsis Deo, Amen'. All this is done in D—except for a typically Waltonian harmonic progression pivoting on B flat—D unison, D mixolydian and in the final chord D tetratonic. D is the main key of the work, but for Walton's use of tonality one needs a new set of labels besides major and minor.

Such then in arid detail is the way Walton has composed (the Latin con-ponere means literally 'put together') his *Gloria*. The completed work would not yield to thematic analysis more readily than it does to structural analysis, for his themes are unstable elements, varying their intervals and rhythm at every appearance, an instability which ought to cost them their identity but somehow does not do so. They are fused in the high-powered discharge of his fundamental rhythm. The harmony, though complicated with added notes till one ought to be dizzy with seeking the key or the root or the pivot or the tonic, is usually pretty firm under the feet as we are marched forward on it. There is nothing doctrinaire about his composing—not for him twelve-note serialism with its charts and numbers—and its elasticity conceals the internal mechanics, such as recapitulation and key relationships, on which the unity of a piece of music can be seen to rely. But his terseness at any rate relieves the auditor of the risk of losing his way among discursive, repetitive and redundant material. You do in fact know where you are, even if he plays hide-and-seek with analysts.

Part-Songs

Four short pieces for unaccompanied voices, which are all that have come from his pen in nearly fifty years outside the cantatas, hardly call for extended comment. The most substantial is 'Where does the uttered music go?', an elaborate part-song composed for the unveiling of the memorial window to Henry Wood in St Sepulchre's Church, Holborn, on 26 April 1946. The sentiment of a not too dexterous poem by John Masefield, in which the idea of the transience of musical performance is transfigured into the music of the spheres—'the planetary tune of sun-directed influence' is apt enough and poetical, but the rather obscure working-out of this in itself appropriate tribute to a great conductor, who had served his fellows with diligence and imagination, led the composer to match it with equally complicated part-writing, expanding into parts for six sopranos, six altos, two tenors and two basses. The harmony is difficult to sing and inclined, as dissonant harmony on voices is apt to do, to sound acrid rather than refulgent. It sounds like a *tour de force* rather than a spontaneous tribute or a ceremonial elegy.

On the other hand the earliest, 'A Litany', composed as long ago as 1917, has a direct appeal arising out of such a treatment as Stanford might have brought to Phineas Fletcher's poem. Stanford would probably not have established his key of E minor like this:

nor his final cadence like this:

But the handling of the part-writing and the underlaying of the words has a touch of mastery remarkable for a boy and comparable with the older composer's.

'Set me as a seal upon thine heart' is an anthem—the words from the Song of Solomon—composed for the wedding of the Hon. Ivor Guest and Lady Mabel Fox-Strangways on 22 November 1938. This too has a clear four-part texture, but the harmony contains some of those enharmonic switches that produce the instability of key which Walton exploits without ever relinquishing his hold on a fundamental tonality. Two Christmas carols,

'Make we joy now in this fest' and 'What cheer', of which the text is taken from Richard Hill's *Commonplace Book* of the sixteenth century, are harmonized with mild progressive dissonance that would not have been written by Stanford nor yet by a serialist composer.

CHAPTER VII

Troilus and Cressida

'IF ever you prove false one to another, since I have taken such pains to bring you together, let all pitiful goers-between be called to the world's end after my name; call them all Pandars; let all constant men be Troiluses, all false women Cressids, and all brokers-between Pandars.'

So Pandarus in Shakespeare's play when he brings the lovers together. How false then is Cressida? Shakespeare portrays her as an incarnation of the sex instinct, her vital function is to react to men and though she loves Troilus she cannot resist other men. She kisses all the leaders of the Greeks when she is exchanged for Antenor except Ulysses who, being not 'wily' in Homer but both wise and shrewd (πολύμητις), refuses her offer, and she is quick to respond to the blandishments of Diomedes, who is at first kindly disposed not to press his suit unduly. According to Chaucer she is not that sort of girl, but, poor thing, an unfortunate dumped down in her father's tent among the Greeks with nothing to do and no one to play with, incapable of executing any plan of escape or temporary return to Troy to see Troilus, as she would like to do, and indeed has promised Troilus she will do, both when they parted and subsequently in letters which apparently were easily smuggled. Christopher Hassall, who in his libretto follows Chaucer and not Shakespeare, quotes a comment by C. S. Lewis as the key to her character, as he conceives her. 'Fortunately Chaucer has so emphasized the ruling passion of his heroine that we cannot mistake it. It is Fear—fear of loneliness, of old age, of death, of love and of hostility—— And from this Fear springs the only positive passion which can be permanent in such a nature, the pitiable longing, more childlike than womanly, for *protection*.' This is the Cressida of the first act of the opera, who has to be thawed by Troilus before she can be wooed; and she is the more vulnerable as she has just lost the protection of her father, Calkas, who has gone over to the Greeks. Hassall adds two other elements, 'a grave, sober, considerate personage, who has an alternate eye to her character, her interest and her pleasure' (Hazlitt), and a touch of Cassandra who foresees trouble. Troilus is less subtly drawn. He is not shown as in Chaucer as a young man who scoffed at love before being caught in its snares. He is merely a spirited Prince of the Blood Royal, though Pandarus remarks when he surprises Troilus in his soliloquy in Act I, 'What do I hear, plain chance, but my prince, my friend, easing his load in accents dulcet and honeyed, *quite out of character*, if without offence I may say so.'

The story is not Homeric but medieval and romantic. Troilus is mentioned once only in the *Iliad*: at the end when Priam laments the ruin of Troy: 'Now all of them are gone, the godlike Mestor, Troilus that happy charioteer and Hector who walked among us like a god' (Rieu's translation), and as for Chryseis she has nothing to do with him but was a prisoner given to Agamemnon. The story evolved in the age of chivalry and is traced by Hassall from a Latin work of the fourth century A.D. in which Troilus the lover appears; his juxtaposition to Diomedes occurs in a troubadour *chanson de geste*, while Pandarus was an invention of Boccaccio in the fourteenth century. It was from *Il Filostrato* that Chaucer took his theme. But Hassall has really paid little regard to Chaucer, still less to Shakespeare—whose play is after all a mixture of two themes with two light women, Helen as well as Cressida, and not a rounded tragedy—for his *dénouement*, which incidentally does much to reconcile the story with its Homeric setting. He boldly explains the failure of the two lovers to communicate with each other in his third act by inventing Evadne and fixing bad faith firmly on her. The result is a tragedy—*force majeure*, politics, war, a conflict of loyalties, as well as the person of Diomedes, break all the efforts of true love to retrieve something from the ruin of all the hopes of Troy. This un-Homeric episode therefore is now a part of the ruin of Troy.

Shakespeare and Chaucer both cause discomfort to anyone who takes seriously their setting of the story in the centre of the Trojan War, for one of the things that emerges in all Greek thought about war, notably in *The Trojan Women* of Euripides, and Electra is always bewailing it, is the complete helplessness of women when men go to war. They are taken prisoner and used as concubines of their conquerors. There is no question of falsity; they have no options, no freedom of choice. It is true of course that the Trojan War, dreadful as it is shown to be by Homer with all its consequences in the horrors of the house of Atreus and the ten-year-long odyssey of Odysseus, is not like our modern wars *à outrance*. Truces were arranged, captives exchanged or redeemed, and though 'atrocities' occur as in every war, the conduct of the war is chivalrous and according to rule; normal daily life in the Greek camp and in Troy is not extinguished by hostilities, as it is in our modern wars. The aim of the war was not total war but the capture of Troy, and in Troy there does not seem to have been any rationing, so that Pandarus's soft living is not beyond probability, unless he was a Black Marketeer, which would indeed be in keeping. Hassall's libretto thus has the unexpected advantage of being more Homeric than Chaucer or Shakespeare. He explains in the Preface to the printed libretto that the code of chivalric love is implicit in Chaucer and unintelligible to a modern audience. 'As I lifted the story out of the Middle Ages and retold it in a setting of legendary Troy, all that was essentially Chaucerian fell away.' Chaucer's *Troylus and Criseid* may be a masterpiece in its own right but it would not make a drama. By condensing and altering his story the librettist has made a strongly knit three-act drama for music.

The comparison that forces itself on me is *Tristan and Isolde*. It is a music drama of the consummation of love in death, a *Liebestod*, played out with a few characters in clear, tragic situations. I do not say it is the universal masterpiece that *Tristan* is, nor that it has the seminal force, but it has all the same ingredients—situation, symphonic structure, two splendid singing parts, and the fulfilment of the Aristotelian criterion of purging by pity and fearsome awe. It is not a seminal force because it comes at the end instead of the beginning of romantic music-drama. But those critics who complained after the first performance at Covent Garden on 3 December 1954, that it marked 'no advance', as they said, in Walton's development were wrong on two counts; it did; and if it didn't must every new work be an advance on its predecessors? This is surely to push the doctrine of evolution in music further than Parry or any historian who agrees with him would expect. Can one imagine a citizen of Prague meeting a fellow music-lover in the street on the morrow of the première of *Don Giovanni* and saying to him, 'Ah, poor little Mr Mozart, his latest piece shows no advance on *Figaro*'? Works of art exist in their own right, and while it is true that in some composers development can be traced, Verdi for instance, there is very little in Puccini, nor would most people say that Britten has shown any advance on *Peter Grimes*.

But it is possible to see in *Troilus and Cressida* a development of Walton's art in that the words and the situations have extended his emotional range. I have found in the process of writing this book that the orchestral works cover a rather narrow range of feeling and experience, as compared for instance with Vaughan Williams. There is the characteristic tension in all of them, a peculiarly bitter-sweet lyricism in some of them, and the element of sardonic wit here and there, but not a world, as Mahler significantly if unwisely prescribed. It is a personal and circumscribed experience that is communicated, but presented with one of the great love stories of the world the composer has extended his sympathies. And he has written a great opera in the romantic tradition, which may be out of fashion. But romance is not dead in our century even if it is recessive rather than dominant. Here then is Walton's only opera.

Christopher Hassall's libretto is very skilful in the use of dramatic irony. Antenor must be redeemed at any price, says Troilus, *at any price*, and then the price is named, the bartering of Cressida. In the third act Pandarus says, 'Now watch how negotiations should be conducted. I will show you', and, the words no sooner out of his mouth than Diomedes appears and produces that fatal bargain sealed with the seal of Priam. Likewise Evadne's premature relief that her deceit will cause Cressida 'to live to bless me', which is shattered by the next turn of the wheel of events. The conclusion of the opera, in which the action hurries to its climax

through events happening at the wrong time, the mistaken deceit of Evadne, the silence of Troilus, the submission of Cressida, the gift of the red scarf to Diomede, the arrival of Pandarus and Troilus too late, is dramatically telling but yet permits the situation to be poised stationary for the great sextet.

This situation comes near to the Greek conception of tragedy. As Hassall portrays her and her circumstances Cressida had no real choice: Fate, as the Greeks would say, is too much for her. Yet, like Oedipus, she is held responsible for her decision and her action and must suffer the consequences of them. The chorus brands her 'False Cressida' when she keeps faith with Troilus only to break faith with Diomede. She thus pays a double price to free will and to necessity. This gives to the opera the height and depth of tragedy. Perhaps Mr Hassall uses too easy a device to kill off Troilus, the stab in the back which recalls Hagen's dispatch of Siegfried. Yet it is consistent with such characterization as has been bestowed on Calkas. He too is the victim of Fate: he knows—the oracle has told him and we know by hindsight—that Troy is doomed, so his treachery is almost imposed on him from without, and having made his decision, to go over to the Greeks, he abides by it and the consequences that flow from it. His honour in dishonour stands and faith unfaithful keeps him falsely true. But it is his daughter who pays, just as she did when he deserted her in Troy. So Cressida is doomed by the Trojan War itself, as much as, or more than Hecuba and Andromache. She is a widow (in Hassall's version); she is twice betrayed by her father, she is tricked and betrayed by Evadne—but in this version she is true to Troilus at the end. Hence *Liebestod*.

In setting the libretto the composer has been liberal with repetitions of key words and phrases of the text, so that the sense will come over the heavy orchestral environment. This method may be contrasted with Britten's in *Peter Grimes*, where it is essential that Balstrode's injunction to Peter to go and sink himself at sea be heard. Britten resorts to the spoken word unaccompanied. Walton uses repetitions of the sung phrases, which are open to an equal and opposite objection, for the same purpose. This strain on the aesthetics of music-drama is part of the price to be paid for the

o

integration of the ingredients. Furthermore libretti are not for
fire-side reading. Not much of the text of *Troilus and Cressida* is
lost in performance, and the text conveys the action in a sufficiently compressed form to make it quite clear to the spectator
what the situation is, from which the music arises.

The composer follows the method of Straussian rather than
Wagnerian music-drama: there are some recurrent themes but
they are not used conceptually as by Wagner to determine the
counterpoint. Thus Cressida, or perhaps the love of Cressida is
variously presented in

where the curve is fairly constant and a falling fourth is the vital
feature. Walton is too incurably fluid in his salient intervals and
themes to use them identically and consistently like Wagner, so
that Cressida's theme at the end of the opera when she makes her

decision to return to Troilus and repudiate Diomede has become

Ex. 2

Cressida's fear tends to recur as a quintuplet beginning with an appogiatura:

Ex. 3

Pandarus has a couple of themes, a rising scale of major thirds and a fluted roulade:

Ex. 4

Ex. 5

which stand for his irresponsibility, for they are never twice alike, and do not accompany him when in the last act he comes with Troilus into the Greek camp to do serious business. Finally Cressida has in the third act a motif of suspense, simply the interval of a major second:

Ex. 6

Her aria in Act I 'Morning and evening' contains it in a good many of the chords, but as Walton's harmony throughout the opera is full of added notes, which inevitably produce seconds somewhere in the harmony, it does not stand out as of special significance as it does in the third act.

Walton's added-note harmony is more often of sevenths than sixths for the sake of pungency: he often writes diminished octaves and there is much dissonance which adds movement as well as flavour. Every now and again in this kaleidoscopic flow of dissonant harmony a passage of triads stands out, or a figure of unisons and octaves. As an illustration of triads perhaps the C major assigned to the oracle at Delphi is ironical, for Apollo was a master of double-talk, but here it is, Calkas speaking:

(The F sharp marks a return to normal from the supernatural!)

The unison figures correspond to the *pas d'action* of a ballet, i.e. they are not significant but pieces of musical fabric used at joins when the action changes. Another harmonic feature that is very noticeable is the use of pedals, internal or more usually in the bass. As in the first symphony they are determinants of key, and dramatically they pile up great tension. The first act opens with a pedal E persisting for 40 bars—not so long as *Rheingold's* E flat to be sure—but a powerful agent for conveying the urgency of the people's prayer. Similarly the third act begins with 32 bars of pedal C—and it ends on a chord of C minor. Many instances will be noticed where the pedal serves a triple purpose of tonality, structure and expression.

The story of the opera has been told by the author of the libretto in a synopsis of the action. The music follows and fits the action, so that it can best be expounded by the interposition of musical examples and verbal descriptions. Hassall's words are printed in italic, mine in roman type.

Act I. Troy: the citadel. The people of Troy are praying before the Temple.

Ex. 8 shows the seven-pulse measure of the invocation *Virgin of Troas* transgressing the bar rhythm, the cross rhythm, the pedal point and the motif of anxiety (Ex. 6) which creates at once the atmosphere of strain in Troy.

Calkas, High Priest of Pallas, Cressida's father, convinced that further resistance to the besieging Greeks is useless, makes an impressive but vain attempt to awe the people into believing that the Delphic Oracle has advised surrender. Calkas is a bass. He begins a recitative, in which he announces that the oracle has spoken. This is where Ex. 7 occurs, to which the crowd immediately hurls questions at him. It is also the cue for an aria in which he describes—we are not sure whether the story is true or whether he is making it up—the mission sent by sea to Delphi. He begins in a monotone (on C), but with a B flat crushed against it to convey the anxiety of Ex. 6, and a rocking figure underneath to suggest the sea journey, until the messenger steps ashore (presumably at Itea) on a clear chord of B minor. He continues over a long pedal on B, rising presently to A, over a new figure embodying a technical harmony of clash and false relation that goes back to Byrd:

Ex. 9

Perhaps after all the Oracle is running true to form in giving deliberately ambiguous advice, which the enquirer will interpret according to his own desires. Calkas describes the usual ritual, and when thunder is heard off-stage the crowd breaks in again in prayer. A priestess of the temple announces, with megaphone in a monotonous intonation that is half-speech, 'Beat flat the sword, let the arrow rust; Troy or the spear must come to dust', which sounds unambiguous enough. A downward unison, spiced only with the interval of anxiety, the major second, urges them to 'Go parley with the Greeks'.

The populace is divided, but the first to challenge him openly is Antenor (baritone), a young captain of spears and friend of Troilus. He is accusing Calkas of being in the pay of the Greeks when Troilus (tenor) appears, rebukes his friend and gives assurance of the High Priest's good faith. It is during the colloquy of Antenor and Troilus that Cressida's name is first mentioned—Ex. 1(*a*): Antenor has observed Troilus's attention to the new novice who attends the altar. Antenor goes off and Troilus then gives vent to his feeling for Cressida in an aria 'Is Cressida a slave?' At his invocation to Aphrodite something like the essence of Ex. 1 with its falling fourth is heard both in the voice and in the orchestra:

God-dess of Love

Troilus has at this point something like a recitative and aria, as detachable as the big set love solos in the operas of the past, 'Celeste Aida', for instance, as the first that comes to mind. The accompaniment to the recitative goes in for a little word-painting to describe the guttering candles. The aria is in G flat and ternary form. The melody is worth quoting to show how Walton in a conventional operatic situation can write the appropriate music of romantic chords and arpeggios and still by an admixture of a few chromatic notes inject his own mercurial essence into an essentially diatonic tune.

Child of the wine – dark wave Mant-led in beau – ty
Spi – rit of mor – tal love, 'Tall Aph-ro -. .di – – te.

The middle section, continuing to translate into song the vision of Botticelli's goddess, goes to F major with triads, harps and Neapolitan sixths, though the tonality grows restless. Ex. 11 recurs (though the notation is different) and ends in a great peroration dominated by still another variant of Ex. 1.

Cressida replies in an aria, of which the recurrent motif is

p Morning and eve-ning· I have felt your glance

Her fears, Ex. 3, interrupt this simple strain, and Troilus takes her tune, Ex. 12, out of her mouth to reassure her. Cressida goes on, Ex. 3 and other disturbed figures accompanying, to tell him the story of her life's bitterness, her widowhood and her father's desertion. Troilus again tries reassurance, reverting to G flat in the attempt. The appearance on the scene of Pandarus (brother of Calkas) brings about a sharp change of mood—and of key, to E, and to Exs. 4 and 5.

Pandarus undertakes to plead Troilus's cause for him. While still in the offing Pandarus overhears Calkas bidding Cressida farewell and to his dismay discovers that his brother is deserting to the Greeks. Pandarus tries to console Cressida with the thought that a powerful Prince is in love with her. Comic relief is perhaps a crude way of describing Pandarus's function in the opera—his function in the plot is serious enough—but the part, which was taken by Peter Pears in the first performances at Covent Garden, gives rich opportunities for character acting. Have we met this epicene dandy in real life in our wars? He is a caricature, but there were people off whose back the strains and restraints of war rolled like the water from the duck. People despised them yet tolerated them from amusement and reluctantly recognized that they were not so despicable as they seemed, since they were good-hearted and were doing their bit in keeping up standards and civilized ideals. At any rate Pandarus provides the foil of comedy to tragedy. His first appearance is only long enough for him to speak to each of his protegés in turn and he withdraws to one side as the doors of the temple of Pallas open and priests enter chanting prayers of entreaty to the goddess.

Calkas's farewell to Cressida is accompanied by a reiterated figure of grinding chords which begin

Pandarus is alarmed and Cressida embarks on an aria in which she describes how even when she was a child her father seemed to her as inconstant as a wavering shadow. The motif pervading the aria 'Slowly it all comes back' is

Ex. 14

This, however, is no formal aria but *durchkomponiert*.

He (Pandarus) has barely reached the crucial point of his case when the return of Troilus, anxious to hear how he has fared, coincides with the reappearance of the soldiers who went off under the leadership of Antenor. They show their leader's shield as evidence that they were ambushed and their commander himself made captive. Troilus swears that if he fails to win back his friend by force he will persuade King Priam, his father, to negotiate for an exchange of prisoners. Whatever the Greeks demand in exchange it shall be granted them. He begs a blessing on his expedition, but a priest confesses that Calkas has mysteriously vanished. Pandarus still bent on his intrigue (with the rising chords of Ex. 4 against a bass in contrary motion) *invites Cressida to a supper party at his house to-morrow evening and at the last moment prevails on her to let him deliver her scarf to Troilus as a 'favour'. Troilus, banishing from his mind the realization that Cressida is the daughter of a traitor, exalts in this his first token of her goodwill.*

The music of this invocation, immediately before the fall of the curtain, is a modification of Ex. 11. The key is really C major, built up through shifting harmonies on a bass of subdominant and dominant, but the orchestra breaks off without finally resolving that dominant thrust, and its last chord is not a triad but a chord containing fourth and fifth on G.

Act II. Scene I, in the house of Pandarus on the evening of the next day. Supper is over. Cressida and her fellow guests are playing chess.

The curtain goes up on an extended passage based on Pandarus's Ex. 5 theme, with off-beat pizzicato chords underneath it. The chess is played over a light accompaniment of triplet semiquavers.

The character Horaste, a baritone, is Cressida's opponent. Pandarus minces around, singing sometimes quasi parlando and sometimes falsetto on high notes (if that is what the composer means by marking them with a violinist's indication to touch a harmonic).

Bad weather has been blowing up, to the satisfaction of Pandarus who has conceived a plan. He secretly dispatches a messenger to fetch Troilus, then begs his niece not to risk going home.

All Pandarus's hospitality is expressed in the incessant triplets and his main theme Ex. 5. The storm breaks with thunder off-stage (by tenor drum and side drum prescribed in the score). Slave women of the house enter and Cressida's ladies prepare her for the night in a three-part serenade over a swaying figure:

They continue to sing as they go off-stage. *Alone at last Cressida has to admit to herself that she who had renounced the world has fallen in love again.* This she does in what is really a short recitative and aria. 'How can I sleep?' she asks, and immediately there is orchestral agitation in 5/8 time. The aria is again in an AABA form with a cadenza coda. The feature of the harmony is that since sevenths and ninths and their inversions are so much part of the normal texture and give it its astringency, an even sharper dissonance is needed to express the heightened emotion and so we have semitonal clashes, an E natural and an F and a C natural and a D flat in a chord of B flat minor:

an asperity which recurs. The melody may be quoted for comparison with Ex. 11 as examples of a diatonic tune still within the
composer's vocabulary. The repeats are not identical though.

Ex. 17

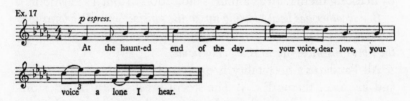

At the haunt-ed end of the day___ your voice, dear love, your

voice a lone I hear.

Pandarus comes back with the startling news that Troilus is in the house.
The Prince has called at this unlikely hour, so Pandarus falsely makes
out, because he is racked with jealousy. Troilus has overheard the climax
of this baseless rigmarole. He bursts in, eager to comfort a by now per-
plexed and tearful Cressida. Troilus denounces the conspirator. Pandarus
takes this as the moment for a quick exit.

Not, however, before he has explained his technique for bring-
ing young lovers together in the midst of the trio which develops.
The convolutions of Ex. 5 particularly the descending triplet
arpeggio, pervade the score. *When he returns he is delighted to dis-*
cover how things have gone in his absence. Just as he had planned, the
happy relief of reconciliation has led to the breakdown of all reserve.

Which means a long impassioned solo from Troilus, followed
by a great love duet which bears the lovers into the curtained alcove that had been given to Cressida for the night. The storm continues and the shutters are blown open only to be shut by someone while the entracte is played.

This big scene begins with something like Ex. 1(*d*) in the
orchestra, followed by the motif of fear, i.e. Cressida's shadowy
fears, Ex. 3, to which Troilus pours out his words of comfort and
reassurance. The figure stretches itself out in augmentation as it
dies away in intensity, and a second section of the aria begins with
a shift of tonality that pivots on B flat and is established by a tolling
figure in the bass, tonic and dominant, as it might be a double
pedal if it remained in one place, as it does not. There is a link to a
third section which has a chordal accompaniment over a pedal on
F, which pounds away in even crotchets. As they embrace the

orchestra plays something with a strong likeness to Ex. 2 in its melodic line:

Ex. 18

The way in which the progressions, containing semi-tonal clashes, resolve and repeat themselves in the curtailed rhythm of quintuple time is typical of Walton's extreme care for nicety of detail even in the broadest effects and suggests the catch in the breath of the lovers as they physically touch each other. Cressida now gives voice to her ecstatic release and relief 'New life, new love!' over an accompaniment of tremolando strings. The duet sweeps majestically forward over chords and points of melodic imitation between the two voices and between the voices and the orchestra. There is an apostrophe to Aphrodite. Even Pandarus, whose music is heard between the two last of their impassioned utterances, is shamed enough, though equally delighted, at the success of his plan, as to have the decency to blow out the candles and tiptoe away.

The words that lovers sing in operatic duets do not matter greatly. They cannot be love poetry, for there is not the distancing of the emotion that is necessary for art, rather it is the immediacy of the emotion that is shown. They cannot be realistic for words falter into silence in such a context of real life. But they must sing something. Hassall's lines set out the main currents of feeling which the composer is to swell into a flood. Troilus has to revive Cressida, to give her the will to love. Then the two of them, with dramatic irony, thank the Gods for relenting, and as they close their arms about each other congratulate themselves that they are out of the storm—a sign for a flash of lightning from heaven.

The music turns into an entracte 'a tempo tempestuoso'. It is not a representation of physical passion like the orgasms in the Introduction to *Der Rosenkavalier*, but the translation into music of the rising tides, the ecstasies so acute as to verge on pain, the subsidence into tenderness and rapture of love's consummation, and as Cressida calls them, the glories. Everyone knew, even before Deryck Cooke (in *The Language of Music*) demonstrated it with chapter and verse, that chromatics mean agitated, as opposed to serene, emotions. So we have, with drums thundering, in shrill trills of acute, suspended sensibility:

Rising above the agitation snatches are heard of Ex. 1 with its falling curve and falling fourth. Presently it becomes more diatonic, though suspensions and added notes proclaim that emotion is still warm, even if the dulcet tones of the harp declare it to be more beatific. Then passion and Ex. 19 return and issue in a variant of Ex. 1 as a soaring and extended melody:

Thereafter the music dies down and as the lights come up Cressida appears in a shimmer of tremolando strings—'molto lento' is the marking. This is the morning after, not of disillusionment but of fulfilment: three horns play triads and chords of the sixth, signifying content and those tranquil emotions that consonance represents in the vocabulary of music:

Ex. 21
Lento

Though there is a strain of heartbreak in the words they sing to
these horn chords—that there is an end to all mortal joys if not to
mortal ills. These, alas! are not slow to be made manifest. There is
a noise of drums behind the scenes which brings Pandarus rushing
on. The synopsis reads.

*Scene II. The same. Next morning. The storm has blown over.
Cressida, with Troilus at her side, stands at the window watching the
dawn break over the roofs of Troy. They are disturbed by the sound of
an approaching drum. Pandarus enters, deeply concerned for the good
name of his family. A military deputation has come to the door. Troilus
must on no account be discovered here. The lovers must conceal themselves in the alcove while he deals with the situation. Diomede, commander of the Greeks, strides in on an urgent mission of state—an exchange of prisoners. He explains that Calkas has done the Greeks good
service. He will, however, accept no other reward other than that his
only child be restored to his care. By happy accident this request has coincided with a similar plea from King Priam for the return of Antenor, the
friend whom Troilus had failed to redeem in battle. When Diomede produces the seals of Troy and of Greece as authority for the exchange
Pandarus realizes the trap has closed.*

This is the περιπέτεια, the turning point of the tragedy: the
action has moved fast. No opera composer expends imagination,
or writes detachable nuggets of melody or composes a symphonic
poem on a situation which such treatment can only impede. Skill,
choice of apt figuration, something to convey rhythmic urgency
and speed is what is needed, the sort of thing he may have to write
in recitativo stromentato or, if he is composing a ballet, for the
pas d' action. A couple of bars will show Pandarus trying to cope
with the situation:

Ex. 22

and four more serve to present the entry of Diomede:

Ex. 23

Diomede searches the room, draws back the curtain of the alcove, and discovers Cressida standing alone. He cannot conceal his wonder at her beauty. He bids Evadne make her ready for travel and then join him in the yard. Troilus enters from the balcony in a frenzy of frustration and despair. He promises to smuggle messages through the enemy lines. Meanwhile, as a symbol of their vows of fidelity, he gives back to Cressida the red scarf that she had given him the day before. The escort arrives. Cressida, accompanied by Evadne, goes out under guard.

The anguish of the situation is presented in harmonies that contain still more clashes. Chords shaped like triads contain major and minor sevenths and grinding passing notes. The following passage expressive of Cressida's poignant horror shows how the bitterness expressed in the opening strains of *Belshazzar's Feast* is conjured up and intensified by the same harmonic means:

Ex. 24

The red scarf is a fatal token. As he hands it back Troilus pro-
nounces the name of Cressida in the form shown above Ex. 1(*f*).

*Act III. The Greek encampment. Before the pavilion of Calkas.
Evening. Ten weeks later.*

A long pedal point on C, a resounding boom on drum and gong,
the key C minor, a figure of a rising major second periodically
uttering a questioning sigh. The scene and the mood are set and
they match through the agency of that perfect pathetic fallacy
which music can convey without seeming fallacious. A cor anglais
adds to the melancholy—the parallel with *Tristan* is exact—with
a wailing tune:

Ex. 25

Then in the tenor a slow chromatic scale descends bar by bar on
the first beat on horns and cellos only to climb back again and stir
the strings to a murmured tremolando, over which the watchman's call rises faint from the near distance. Walton sets the mono-
syllables 'All's well' as though they were dissyllables and so gives
them melodic contour and a double impact, just as he often makes
his violins use a double bow on a single marcato chord to increase
the attack. Trumpets are heard echoing round the camp—that
simple military music that evokes the isolation and camaraderie of
the soldier's life. Cressida appears at the entrance of Calkas's tent
and Evadne enters. Immediately Ex. 6, the motif of doubt and
despair, sounds and Cressida asks, 'Is there no word no message
yet from Troilus?' The synopsis reads. *Cressida has received no word
from Troilus. She persuades Evadne to go and for the last time keep
watch at the frontier-line for a messenger.*

Evadne thus for the first time becomes an important person in
the drama and a new, mezzo-soprano, strand in the texture.
Evadne is practical, obviously of Calkas's way of thinking, and as
events are to show, disloyal to her mistress with the best intentions. She even blurts out that if she had the strength of mind she
would destroy any message that Troilus might put into her hands.
Cressida rages at her for this but quickly remembers that she has

no one else to whom she could look for any help. She gives vent to her heart-break in an extended solo, in which she imagines Troilus calling her name. This time Ex. 1 appears in the form Ex. 1(g).

Then the opening music returns with its moaning—'Only the watchman's cry and a wind in the long grass blowing' but without Ex. 25.

Calkas, finding Cressida alone, seizes the opportunity of reproaching her for her ill-advised coldness towards Diomede. He leaves her shaken, then the intrusion of Diomede takes her by surprise. Calkas's expostulation is treated in arioso accompanied by various figurations, punctuated by occasional chords like those of recitativo secco, as he points out the doom of Troy, the fate of captives and the chance of a change of fortune with Diomede. Cressida in anguish calls on Pallas for guidance in her frightful dilemma—against a toccata-like accompaniment of chords. One piece of characterization besides the traditional pride of Diomede is added in a passage of rising parallel thirds:

This is a psychological stroke and it is repeated to Cressida's words 'All goad me on one headlong way', just before the entry of Diomede, who like the good soldier he is, sings in march time. He is no villain but patient and courteous. We, too, in spite of our sympathies for Troilus are shaken, as Cressida is. Then the fatal scarf. *Already not untouched by his personal charms and mindful of her father's warnings, she yields completely and allows him to take her red scarf as a token of her favour. Diomede bids her make ready to be ac-*

claimed that very night as Queen of Argos. As they embrace various versions of Ex. 1, Cressida's love, are heard ironically in the orchestra. *Evadne, who has overheard this, secretly destroys the last of several messages from Troilus, all of which in obedience to Calkas she has concealed from Cressida.* She congratulates herself thankfully if cynically that she has acted for the best, and to underline her words the watchman's cry 'All's well' is heard from the ramparts. Then *Troilus and Pandarus, admitted through the Greek lines in an hour of truce, come upon Evadne and urge her to fetch Cressida, whose ransom is being arranged. While Cressida is trying to convince Troilus that he has come too late, the Greeks begin to converge from all sides to pay her homage, among them Diomede wearing her favour.*

The plunge to disaster is precipitated by Ex. 1(*f*). Cressida hears Troilus calling her name. There is during the lovers' exchanges and explanations a moment when Cressida has a rapt strain in F minor over swaying chords of a fairly simple and diatonic character, of which

Ex. 27

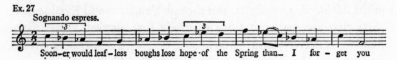

Soon-er would leaf-less boughs lose hope-of the Spring than_ I for - get you

is the first four bars.

This is transformed and glorified by the orchestra just before the practical business of ransom is mentioned—to clashing major seconds, it need hardly be said:

There is a moment of pageantry in the wedding march, all very diatonic and enriched with added sixths or sevenths. *Troilus in horror recognizes the favour and claims Cressida as his own. Diomede orders her to renounce the Trojan but she cannot do it.* The stage direction says, 'She faces her moment of decision and walks over to

P

Troilus'. Her theme reappears in one more of its Protean shapes, something like Ex. 1(d).

Ex. 29

Whereupon the great ensemble develops for all six characters, soprano, mezzosoprano, two tenors, baritone and bass, over massive and reiterated chords in the orchestra, in B minor. Each character speaks in character: into each mouth Hassall has put the appropriate comment—Diomede on the falsity of Troy and the affront to Argos, Troilus on the inconstancy of woman, Cressida on the doom of their love, Pandarus on the futility of trying to oppose anything to man's pugnacity, Calkas repenting his default and Evadne unrepentant and shallow-hearted. To which the chorus adds 'False Cressida!'

The musical texture is woven of successive entries, very much as in the *Meistersinger* quintet, and though Pandarus and Evadne have parts that are not imitations on their first entries, most of the material is derived from two themes, one with descending curves, first uttered by Diomede and taken up by Calkas and later by Evadne:

Ex. 30

(Troy, false of heart yet fair)

and one first enunciated by Troilus in which the movement is mostly ascending, which in an elongated version is taken up by Cressida:

Ex. 31

These are extended in time values corresponding to the words of the person from whose mouth they proceed; underneath the orchestra expands its sharply articulated chords into a sustained and slow progression.

Enraged by the public humiliation, Diomede tramples on the token. Troilus assaults him with drawn sword but is mortally wounded from behind by Calkas. Diomede sends Calkas back to Troy, but declares that Cressida must stay behind as a prisoner without privilege. She cheats her captors by taking her own life.

Diomede's comment on Troilus is, 'Would I had never seen such valour squandered in a cause so base.' There is no one to say, with Brynhilde, 'Alles weiss ich', since there is no resolution of the catastrophe, no deeper comprehension of its nature, no further enlightenment for them or for us. But Cressida, before she dies, addresses a plea to Troilus on 'that cold river's brim beyond the sun's far setting'—and how cold it is:

Then with a sudden change, as she pulls the sword out of the scarf in which she had concealed it after it fell from Troilus's grasp, she has a vision of them riding together triumphantly into Troy. Her last words and the last statement of her love theme is *in hoc signo*:

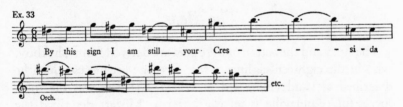

CHAPTER VIII

Compositions 1965–1972

OF the eight works composed and published between 1965, when this book of commentary was published, and Sir William's seventieth birthday (on 29 March 1972) which he came home to celebrate, four were church music and two were orchestral pieces, but the most substantial by far was the one-act comic opera *The Bear*. This is rightly described as an Extravaganza and as such allows the composer to return to work the veins of parody and allusion, high comedy and wit, that he had tapped years before in *Façade* and *Scapino*. His librettist, Paul Dehn, has described the circumstances of the composition of the work—on the sleeve of the gramophone record—and a commentator who failed to raid him for the copious and interesting information he has provided would be failing in his duty to his readers.

The Bear

The story and the action of the opera are derived from Chekhov, who in the eighteen-eighties wrote five one-act pieces which he described as vaudevilles, and of which *The Bear* was the most successful. Vaudeville is an elastic term: Mozart described the finale of *Die Entführung aus dem Serail* as a vaudeville and provided it with a catchy tune. Originally in France it had stood for a farcical entertainment mounted at a street fair and garnished with some popular song to which new and topical words could be fitted. Chekhov's vaudeville had no music but the possibility of it would occur to any musician with a sense of theatrical history—and actually did so occur, according to Mr Dehn, to Mr Peter Pears, who promptly fired Dehn and Walton with the idea of adapting it for music. So they set to work, on what they were to call not a vaudeville nor even a 'jest' or 'tra-la', as Chekhov himself did, but, most aptly, 'an extravaganza'. For that is what it is: the three participating characters are caricatures and their acts are farcical, but the situation is a real-life possibility, if an improbability, and the emotions are real, if exaggerated and absurd.

Walton himself made a prose version of the plot and Dehn began to provide verses for the arias. Together they made their text and Walton started to compose the music in October 1965, but was interrupted by an operation and only completed the work a year later, which left time for the opera to be performed at the Aldeburgh Festival of 1967, when it had its first presentation on 3 June by the English Opera Group with Colin Graham as producer and James Lockhart as conductor. The cast consisted of

Popova	*mezzo-soprano*	Monica Sinclair
Smirnov	*baritone*	John Shaw
Luka	*bass*	Norman Lumsden

The same musicians made the record of *The Bear* (EMI SAN 192).

Since much of the dialogue is accompanied recitative and arioso with few extended passages, and those often of a parlando or patter character—for example there is the caricature of a French song in even quavers—the accompaniment must of necessity be light to allow the words to get through. In this respect Walton is very careful and has scored the piece for a quintet of strings (single players or a small number of desks) with piano and one each of woodwind, horn, trumpet, trombone, and harp, though he has allowed himself an ample assortment of percussion. Even so, he often repeats key phrases of the libretto, as he did in *Troilus and Cressida*, to ensure that the sense gets through his harmony, which is amply spiced with major, minor, and augmented seconds that may not coagulate but still affect the transparency of the texture.

The opera opens with some chromatic wailings of wind and descending portamento of strings and the curtain goes up to reveal Madam Popova (*in deep mourning gazing disconsolately at a photograph of her late husband*)[1] and Luka, her old manservant.

[1] Italics signify actual stage directions throughout.

Luka reproaches his mistress for being so obstinately miserable. It is time she came out of mourning for her dear departed; the cook and the housemaid are out in the wood picking strawberries, and after all she is not yet so old that life has no more in it to offer. On the contrary, she answers, life is finished as far as she is concerned, and please, would he not take the liberty of talking to her like this; she had made a vow to wear mourning always and not go out. Luka is not to be repressed: he reminds her that her late husband had not showed a like devotion to her, had indeed not always been faithful to her. Why does she not have the horse Toby put into harness and go and call on the neighbours? This is too much; Toby—and we hear the clip-clop of his hooves for a moment in the bass—brings back his master's visits to the neighbours, so he must have an extra bag of oats today, a vicarious indulgence of her own grief, which makes her feel just sufficiently better to turn on her husband for his deceptions and desertions of her. At which moment a knocking is heard and Luka, who had gone off to see about the oats, returns and says there is someone to see her and his business is urgent. He will not accept Luka's statement that she is not at home. She goes off again into sentimental reveries:

Ex. 1

Enter Luka and Smirnov fighting. But catching sight of Madam Popova the visitor becomes all courtesy, bowing, clicking his heels, and announcing himself as Grigory Stephanovitch Smirnov, landowner. He has come to ask repayment of a debt incurred by the dead husband for oats for the horse, 1,300 roubles. The debt, the money, the interest on the loan from the bank raised for the purchase of the oats, have something like a leit-motif, a rising scale over a pedal point:

Ex. 2

which is repeated in an augmented form while Smirnov talks about the money, which he must have at once; the end of the week when Madam Popova's bailiff returns will not do. Madam sweeps out and leaves him; he changes his tune to one of lament at the way of things: 'creditors appear and debtors vanish' in a fairly substantial aria, during which he works himself up into a fine state of frenzy. Various devices are used for working up this lather. One of them used throughout the opera is schoolboy mockery, i.e., the instrumental repetition of the tail-end of a sentence with some sort of exaggeration or change of tone—followed in the case of schoolboys with 'Yah!' or sticking out the tongue—primitive it is true but effective, as in Exx. 3 and 4.

Ex. 3

Ex. 4

Or the composer may run a wind instrument in unison or octave with the voice in the same time values. Or use a short bit of figuration as in Ex. 5:

Ex. 5

When Madam Popova returns and asks him not to shout but to behave like a gentleman Smirnov changes his tactics and parodying a French singer begins to address the lady in French like any Russian aristocrat:

Ex. 6   *capriccioso e rubato*   *elegante*

Ma - da - me, je vous pri — e, Sor - tez d'i - ci with me — er, And

This is a parody both on Chekhov's part and on Walton's. The even stress of the French language often produces in the accompaniment of French songs chords of even crotchets or quavers. It may be that Walton is parodying some specific composition in Ex. 6, but he has refused to divulge the sources of his many parodies in this extravaganza, so that it is open to anyone to guess or spot where the idea came from. But of the style in general one will find examples in Fauré (e.g. in 'Adieu'), Reynaldo Hahn (e.g. 'Mai'), or Debussy (e.g. in several passages of *Pélléas et Mélisande*) and the cadence might have come out of Massenet or Gounod:

Ex. 7

the   mo - ney —   that——   you   owe——   me.

col canto

French makes Smirnov fanciful: he begs her put off these widow's weeds and unveil like—like, if you please, Salome. This would seem to be the moment for an allusion to Strauss's opera. If there is, it is no more than this Ex. 8 (from the Dance of the Seven Veils) in this phrase Ex. 9:

Ex. 8

Ex. 9

They fall to altercation again. He doesn't know how to behave in the company of ladies, doesn't he? He knows all about women. In that case, then, would he be good enough to say whether men are more faithful than women in love? But she gives him no chance, embarking instead on a tirade about constancy à la Rossini, and finally telling Luka to show him the door—the back door. They are now calling each other names, Boor, Bore, Bear. Whence the title of the piece. From abuse it is but a step, in these days of the equality of the sexes, to a duel. 'Yes,' says Madam Popova, 'my husband had some pistols, I'll get them.' This is the peripeteia, the sudden change: such spirit, such flashing eyes! Too much for Smirnov. The further they go with the duel—and Smirnov has to show Popova how to hold and fire a pistol—the more does he like her. He will fire into the air. 'Get out,' she says scornfully, but he pauses at the door and their eyes meet and hold each other for as much as seventy-five seconds while *con molto*

sentimento falso Ex. 10, the leitmotif of sentiment, and itself a parody of Puccini, is heard.

Ex. 10

He clutches the back of a chair which breaks with a loud crack. They continue to shout at one another, she threatening him, he offering her marriage, to the accompaniment of a figure of demisemi-quavers. At last she capitulates and again spills on to Toby the vicarious indulgence of her own feeling: no oats at all for Toby today.

One of opera's dramatic difficulties is that music and speech move at different speeds, but, as we know from Mozart's *secco* recitatives, the difference is not absolute nor its resolution insuper-able. Walton's crackling music, embracing, that is, note values and figural ejaculations as well as his piquant instrumentation, does not hold up the dramatic pace of this squib. He has used parody and mockery to increase the dramatic force of the stage action, of which the chief single element is Chekhov's use of caricature. 'Caricature,' says Walton according to Mr Dehn, 'is so accurate an exaggeration of the real thing as to be funny,' and Chekhov's caricature is, in Mr Dehn's words which cannot be improved upon, 'the exaggeration of three real Russian nineteenth-century types: the outwardly genteel but inwardly passionate Popova; the outwardly brutish but inwardly sentimental Smirnov; the out-wardly servile but inwardly seething old manservant'.

Capriccio Burlesco

André Kostelanetz, the Russian-born conductor, went to the United States in 1922, became conductor of the Columbia Broadcasting System in 1930, founded his own orchestra, made a reputation as an exponent of the lighter forms of music, even with the New York Philharmonic in a famous series of concerts. Walton was commissioned by the New York Philharmonic to write a piece for it in celebration of its 125th season. He wrote the Capriccio Burlesco and dedicated it to Kostelanetz, who conducted its first performance in New York on 7 December 1968. Its first European performance was at a Royal Philharmonic concert on 5 February 1969, by the B.B.C. Symphony Orchestra under Colin Davis.

'Burlesco' in the title indicates that whatever else it is, it will be light-hearted, high-spirited, suited both to the man and the occasion. It is not so much the elements of parody and caricature exploited in *The Bear* that are conspicuous here as the sheer brilliance of the orchestration—there is hardly another epithet that will go with 'orchestration' yet Berlioz, Rimsky-Korsakov, Elgar, are all 'brilliant' but do not sound alike, are difficult to differentiate and describe in words, or to account for in technical terms. Blend and doublings are only the beginning of orchestration. Modern percussion has added new colours to the sound spectrum. To the numerous string effects, *divisi con sordine, sul ponticello*, Walton has added *glissando* chords, but he has obtained colour effects by the kind of edge he gives to the sound, and this is in part determined by the angularity of his motifs and their speed of discharge. Indeed the themes are not so much there for their thematic interest as for their colouristic possibilities, and the same applies to individual chords and arpeggios, especially on the harp. The very opening of this Capriccio makes a noise like tearing the paper off the packet, a sonorous kind of paper but a tear nevertheless, revealing a smooth surface (a chord of C on trombones pianissimo) which yet has a shimmer produced by violins doing this:

Ex. 1
Vivace

Much use in many varieties of pitch and colour is made of this bit of thematic tissue:

Similarly in the second half of the movement one such motif, first enunciated so as to sound of some thematic significance, makes a protean use of the semiquaver figure and its inversion:

Thematic polymorphism was ever a conspicuous feature of Walton's style. So too was a discriminating taste in refinements of percussion. In this glittering piece he prescribes the following instruments, which require three players to attend to them: timpani, sometimes *col bacchete di legno*, sometimes *coperti* (i.e. muted with a cloth cover); side-drum, bass drum, tenor drum, bongo (Cuban hand-drum), and tambourine; cymbals, castanets, block, whip; xylophone but no glockenspiel.

In such high-pressure music as Walton writes for orchestra one may well wonder how effective all these subtleties are. Sound waves naturally combine, 'so that the whole sound of an orchestra reaches the ear in a single wave'. We appreciate blend of tone. Yet equally we can and often do analyse this single wave and hear in it its constituent contributions of strings, wind, brass, and percussion. But what seems to happen in a scintillating score like this is that even when we are not aurally aware of all that is going on—too much going on to take it all in at once even with a score in hand—the total sound varies with the constituent ingredients, like a cake or pudding, and we may in consequence hear this score as characterized by a particular sheen, glitter, or coruscation. Also we have some amount of subliminal perception. At any rate Walton is immensely particular about these niceties, and in Capriccio Burlesco they are responsible for the individual character of the work.

Formally its organization is not complex. It is a sort of scherzo and trio without formal repeats. Instead of repeating the scherzo after the trio, as in minuet form, a coda recapitulates briefly the material of the first (or scherzo) section. For the listener there are two gaps in the texture which define the shape of the piece. In the first of them the run-down is from three-part strings to a single mutter, so that there is no mistaking where this 'trio' begins, though the key change (to four flats) occurs after the second gap. There are no double bar-lines, for this is not a minuet-scherzo but a Capriccio, though the Burlesco of the title guarantees its scherzo character.

And now in spite of what has been said about the substitution of motivic for thematic interest we are confronted at the very beginning with a plain unmistakable melody:

Thirteen bars of it all told. This is balanced by a passage of equal length consisting of figures like Ex. 2, derived in the last resort from Ex. 4. There follows another section made up of another string derivative from Ex. 4 and some other ideas, such as one for harp arpeggios, another for some percussion (and trumpet) solos, and still another to impart some syncopation to the rhythm. After the first gap, i.e. at the beginning of the 'trio', there is a melodic line made out of repetitions of Ex. 5

Ex. 5

over an oom-pah bass accompaniment, followed as in the previous section by a number of explosive thematic fragments which lead to a climax before the second gap and the change of key. A return to the precariously balanced C major of Ex. 4 rounds off something which being capricious is recalcitrant to thematic analysis, which indeed it hardly needs.

Improvisations on an Impromptu of Benjamin Britten

Musicians have never been scrupulous in their use of the nomenclature of their art. 'Symphony', 'concerto', and 'motet' are all fairly stable now but were not always so. Sometimes in despair a composer calls his composition simply Music for Strings (as Bliss did) or Music for Orchestra (as Lambert did). But surely the above is the most mendacious title ever conferred on a work of musical art. There is never anything improvised about a Walton score: it is always finished *ad unguem*, to the last expressive dot, hairpin, and slur. Also Britten's tune is not an impromptu but a second thought. However, there is nothing we can do about it except register the facts.

Which are these. Britten's first piano concerto, Op. 13 in D, is an early work, which had its first performance at a Promenade Concert in 1938. Seven years and a whole war later Britten substituted for the Recitative and Aria, which had been the third of its four movements, an Impromptu. In its revised form the con-

certo was heard at the Cheltenham Festival in 1946. The impromptu was in fact a passacaglia on this theme:

Britten decorates seven successive orchestral statements of this
theme with florid elaborations from the solo piano. Walton found
this theme, which one might suppose to be too repetitive to stand
so much further reiteration, sufficiently stimulating to inspire a
further set of variations, albeit a very different kind of variation,
on it when he came to take it up as a gesture of friendship from
one composer to another.

Walton is partial to the writing of variations. They may be just
plain variations as in the fianales of the Cello Concerto and the
Violin Sonata. They may be of the ground bass kind, as in the
dramatic scores of the film *Henry V* for the death of Falstaff and
the ballet *The Quest* for the reunion of St George and Una. They
may be serial as in the finale of the Second Symphony and in the
Hindemith Variations. But variations seem to have a peculiar
suitability as tributes of friendship. Elgar's Enigma Variations,
though on an original and not a borrowed theme, were dedicated
'to my friends pictured within'. Britten himself used the variation
form in his acknowledgement of his debt to his old teacher, Frank
Bridge, and of course Walton did the same in repayment of his
debt incurred to Paul Hindemith many years before in rescuing
his Viola Concerto. So when a commission came from Dr Ralph
Dorfman of San Francisco to write a work and dedicate it to the

San Francisco Symphony Orchestra Walton seized the opportunity to associate Britten with it in this graceful way.

The first performance of the Improvisations was given by the San Francisco Orchestra under Josef Krips on 14 January 1970; the first European performance was, appropriately, at the Aldeburgh Festival of 1970, when it was played by the Royal Liverpool Philharmonic Orchestra under Charles Groves.

In the course of its nine bars the theme, Ex. 1, repeats a descending phrase made up of augmented seconds, minor thirds, and semitones no less than four times. To achieve these parachute descents it climbs back on intervals of thirds, major and minor, and semitones. It accomplishes these feats on a firm tonal basis of E, either major or minor, while inducing a series of harmonic false relations. These features naturally determine the nature of Walton's procedures.

After a preliminary statement (lento) of the theme, Ex. 1, on the clarinet with Britten's chordal harmonies transferred from the solo piano to the harp, five substantial Improvisations on it follow. It now becomes clear why they are called Improvisations instead of Variations—they are of their nature motivic rather than thematic. Walton expends his invention and ingenuity on converting the six-note melodic and the four-note bass motifs into the most varied figurations. The first Improvisation is characterized by fluctuating compound-time rhythms. The second is marked 'vivo and martellato' with Walton's characteristically snappy presentation touched up with the xylophone. Number 3 is marked 'pochissimo meno mosso' and begins lightly, though it ends massively, and it exploits the false relations and the downhill elements of the theme. Number 4 marks the biggest change of mood: the tempo goes to moderato, the time-signature to four-two; the sound texture takes on an extraordinary shimmer produced by clashing seconds, which are disposed on the strings with one desk only of violins and cellos playing with mutes, the rest something different without mutes. For number five quick compound time is resumed (scherzando) and the movement is extended to make a brilliant, animated climax with a code marked 'risoluto'.

CHURCH MUSIC

Four pieces of church music in seven years hardly amount to a new trend and it would be straining at a non-existent significance to deduce any sort of throw-back to the cathedral service after half a century, yet in view of Walton's very small output of music in the smaller vocal forms it is natural to look for any stylistic features or changes of feature in the anthem composed for Christ Church in 1965, the *Missa Brevis* for Coventry Cathedral in 1966, the little carol 'All this time', and the *Jubilate Deo* of 1972 for the English Bach Festival, since no previous septennium has anything similar to show.

One feature of the choral writing is the use of dissonant harmony as a form of pungent consonance. When the passage about the waters of Babylon in *Belshazzar's Feast* was new choirs did not find it easy to strike and hold in tune a seventh or a second in place of an octave or a third—they had only just got used to Delius's added sixths—but in a very short time provincial choral societies without pretensions to the status of crack choirs were confidently singing these acrid progressions, and when it came to crack choirs like Huddersfield Walton could, and did, ask of them, as in his *Gloria*, a good deal of difficult (from the point of view of intonation) chording. In these new liturgical pieces the dissonances are dissolved in some almost Schubertian modulations, in some parallel consecutive six-four chords which ease the tension and some occasional triads in root position, which serve the same purpose by comforting the ear with a momentary feeling of tonality. This last is a device used extensively by Herbert Howells in his numerous settings of the Anglican canticles, which thus sound ecclesiastical without sounding old-fashioned; it is in fact a modern kind of harmony by key. The refrain of the carol shows the way in which tonality, dissonance, and triad are combined to give the feeling that tradition is not being flouted in church nor yet jellified (à la Barnby) nor ossified. We have a chord of A establishing at start and finish the feeling of key base,

Q

but a chord of A saved from softness by the inclusion of a fourth instead of a third. We have progressions of sevenths, which retain some of, but not their full, propulsive force as dissonances and which are eased by the intrusion, if that is a word to be applied to a triad, of simple honest-to-God common chords:

In the anthem *The Twelve* the organ is used; though subsequent orchestration allows the published version to be described as for mixed voices and orchestra, so that concert or festival use is not precluded. In the *Missa Brevis* the organ is required only in the Gloria, the rest is *a cappella*. In the *Jubilate Deo* the organ is essential throughout. 'All this time' is for unaccompanied SATB.

The Twelve

Described as 'an Anthem for the Feast of any Apostle' *The Twelve* is the setting of a text by W. H. Auden derived, but not culled, from Scripture, a text in three sections, the first of which describes the mission of the Twelve to the world and its immediate consequences, the second a prayer for support in verse, and the third a poetical reflection upon their work and praise for its fruits. Auden is, like Walton, a Christ Church man, and their joint composition is dedicated to Christ Church and to its Dean, who was Dr Cuthbert Simpson at the time of its first performance on 16 May 1965, when it was sung at evensong in the cathedral with Dr Sydney Watson at the organ.

The opening page reveals an unconventional-looking organ part, chords of the second and the fourth and little splurges of demisemiquavers; later on even when it has chords to play they are arpeggioed and played staccato, but in the second and third parts the writing is more linear; everywhere a thick texture is avoided. A bass solo begins with some declamatory recitative which leads to the phrase 'to bring it joy'. This is set to a rising phrase which is taken up in imitation by the eight-part choir and brings a sudden climax in Walton's exclamatory style. Next is a descriptive passage for two antiphonal choirs, 'some mocked, some were shocked, some were stirred', over a figured accompaniment with staccato pedal notes. The next section of the text dealing with the reaction of the Dark Lord is homophonic, but rough-edged.

Auden's Part II is a conflation of echoes from Bach's Passion chorale 'If I should e'er forsake thee', the twenty-third Psalm, and God's promise to Moses. The texture of the music changes to a smooth mezzo-soprano solo accompanied by flowing quavers on the organ. Part III, which leads to a poetic fancy of the Twelve being as the winds and months, has its text distributed among soloists with choral interjections. The glory of the Twelve is unfolded in a fugal exposition of a twelve-bar subject:

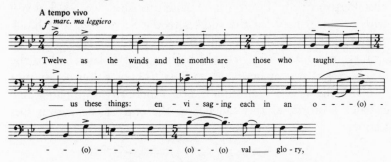

Thus a great deal of the technical interest, as well as the musical effect, of this big anthem is textural.

Missa Brevis

The *Missa Brevis* was commissioned in 1966 by the Friends of Coventry Cathedral for liturgical use by the Cathedral choir. It retains the Greek words for Kyrie but elsewhere it is in English and puts the Gloria after Agnus Dei at the end according to Anglican usage. Its musical design is one of expansion from a simple beginning in two parts by the addition of counterpoints of various kinds, with the organ entering in the Gloria (and nowhere else) and, in the final cadence, drawing its Tuba stop. The setting is for double choir, though the harmony does not often contain more than five real parts. It is easy from the look of the page to underestimate the variety of texture and colour obtainable from the antiphony of plainsong-like lines and chordal passages. These include some of those consecutive six-four chords that Walton uses for vocal euphony.

The Kyrie, in a qualified E major, achieves four-part harmony. Sanctus and Benedictus (for which alternative dispositions are provided according to which version of the modern Communion service is used) begin in five parts which increase to seven in Hosanna. Agnus Dei is based on an antiphony of two soloists (soprano and tenor) and four-part choir. The entry of the organ, a glorified anacrusis of five bars on D, adds another dimension for the expression of praise, blessing, worship, glorification of the First Person of the Trinity; a reversion to single voices, but still with organ, is used for the address to the Second Person; block harmony and a quickening of pace complete the address to the Trinity in a blaze of tone, which though it is launched in the bright key of A somehow ends in E flat. There is thus no attempt to make this service Walton in E, nor is there any dominant-tonic cadence business, as this cadence at the end of the Agnus Dei testifies:

but there is enough feeling of key to add both strength and colour to a closely wrought piece of church music.

Jubilate Deo

The setting of the morning canticle *Jubilate Deo*, which Walton made in 1972, is much more direct, simpler in execution, less abrasive in harmony, than the two other pieces. Its basic principle of construction is ostinato. It is set out vocally for two choirs, which are no more than the regular Cantoris and Decani of any cathedral choir, and it requires of them the ability to undertake solos, as in a verse anthem. It is thus much more nearly in line with traditional settings, which befits the unsubtle sentiment of the words.

The first ostinato is a bell-like figure of one bar's length, repeated over a rising bass, which moves up sometimes a bar, sometimes a beat at a time:

Ex. 1

The voices, after a rising phrase of adjuration to rejoice, employ the same figure and its harmonies, a device making for strength and none the worse for being less sophisticated than those subtleties employed by Walton in his more elaborate scores, and indeed in the other substantial liturgical works. A change of key from G minor to F sharp minor introduces the verse 'Be ye sure that the Lord he is God', which may however be sung either as solo or as tutti. A new ostinato figure, which proceeds over a bass that moves conjunctly a bar at a time, is introduced at 'O go your way into his gates with thanksgiving':

Ex. 2

et sim.

There is a slight change to an even smoother figuration at 'And his truth endureth'. For the Gloria there is a recapitulation of the first section and Ex. 1.

It is almost a relief to find that Walton can and will write a good sound academic miniature, which is jubilant without being restless or over-subtle!

Five Bagatelles for Guitar

After the success of the song-cycle *Anon in Love*, composed for Peter Pears and Julian Bream and first performed by them at the Aldeburgh Festival of 1960, Julian Bream hoped that some day he might obtain from Walton a work for solo guitar. It took more than ten years to do so, but at the Bath Festival on 29 May and at the Cheltenham Festival on 12 July 1972 he was able to present a suite of five pieces, aptly described as Bagatelles. Walton dedicated them to Malcolm Arnold on the occasion of his fiftieth birthday, another gesture of friendship from one composer to another.

The score assigns no titles to them though it would not be difficult to invent such for them. It does, however, say 'Edited by Julian Bream', and one has to expect that a composer may require some guidance on the technical possibilities and impossibilities of so idiosyncratic an instrument as the classical guitar. But when one hears the first of these Bagatelles, so far from it sounding as though Walton was feeling his way in an unfamiliar medium, the reverse is the case: he is exploiting its resources, wide-ranging melody over wide-spread chords, its line rejoicing in arpeggios and repeated notes, fluctuating time signatures, harmonics, and every sort of piquancy natural to it—true guitar music and true Walton, as an early comment recognized.

No. 2 is a slow valse. No. 3 is marked 'alla Cubana', which is to say in this rhythm:

a thematic idea that is in itself a piquancy like an oxymoron. No. 4, the slow movement, exploits rapid thrumming: indeed, it carries the injunction 'trem. più presto possib.'. No. 5 is marked 'con slancio', a term previously used by Walton and meaning 'impetuously'.[1] Sure enough the figuration leads off fortissimo and builds up with runs moto perpetuo and suitable moments of contrast to a final climax of chords struck off the instrument marcatissimo.

Postscript

In the spring of 1972 Sir William celebrated the seventieth anniversary of his birth (on 29 March) with a visit to England and the occasion was marked not only by a number of special performances and revivals but also by the publication of an edition de luxe of *Façade*.

So long as the ballet was in the repertory of the Sadler's Wells Ballet and the Royal Ballet the *Façade* Suites in both forms were much played, while the Entertainment version with reciter relied on occasional performances, often with *Pierrot Lunaire* in the same programme. But now to acknowledge the revived interest in the melodrama form the composer excavated from among his rejected numbers *Herodiade's Flea* and published it along with a recorded performance of *Façade* in this special birthday edition. It is only twenty-seven bars long, is based on rhythmic ostinatos and

---

[1] In the Second Symphony and the Hindemith Variations.

is bedecked with flecks of tone from the woodwind. It had not been previously produced and has only been performed once.

A further innovation, however, marking the birthday celebrations was the use of the Entertainment version as an accompaniment to the ballet. This was done at the Aldeburgh Festival on 28 and 29 July 1972. Two evenings were devoted to Walton's dramatic music by the English Opera Group with its Orchestra and the Royal Ballet, at which the composer was present. The programme consisted of a revival of *The Bear*, a new *pas de deux* danced by Vyvyan Lorrayne and Barry McGrath to *Siesta* with choreography by Sir Frederick Ashton, and *Façade*, in which Peter Pears was the reciter. In this festival performance of *Façade* at the Maltings at Snape only a few minor adjustments had to be made to the choreography and one section of the Tango had to be repeated to fit the dance.

The scenario of *Siesta* is simple: a girl wakes up from sleep on a hot afternoon, is joined by her lover and after a brief amorous interlude falls asleep again, an idyll of tender affection.

By a curious coincidence in this same year (1972) when the ballet *Façade* was revived—it was also put on at Sadler's Wells in February by a visiting American company—and *Siesta* used for a ballet, the First Symphony and the Viola Concerto were also requisitioned for use by choreographers: André Leclair composed a ballet *Salome* to the First Symphony for the Flanders Ballet at Antwerp in January, and Layton's American company during its Sadler's Wells season introduced a ballet about Oscar Wilde, *O.W.*, to the Viola Concerto.

Also in 1972 Walton extended his field of operations into the medium of the string orchestra, which had been restored to currency in the present century by Elgar, Vaughan Williams, and Bliss, when he transcribed his String Quartet for string orchestra. The music itself is virtually unchanged but its name in this form is Sonata for String Orchestra. The transcription was suggested by Neville Marriner with a view to its inclusion in the repertory of his Academy of St Martin-in-the-Fields, who gave its first performance at Perth, Australia, and at the Bath Festival of that year.

CHAPTER IX

Style

IF one surveys Walton's total output one is struck by three facts about it: it is not very large; it is predominantly instrumental; it contains few miniatures, consisting in the main, as it does, of extended works, most of them symphonic.

The two symphonies, the four concertos, the Hindemith Variations, *Belshazzar's Feast*, and *Troilus and Cressida*, which have been examined in these pages, do in fact constitute a substantial corpus and are in sum a great achievement, but they are not the product of a fertile mind oozing music incessantly, as for instance was Arnold Bax's, nor do they amount quantitatively to what Britten turns out or what Vaughan Williams, who originally seemed to be inarticulate, composed so copiously for all sorts and kinds of media. Walton takes time over each work and pains with its details, so that *premières* are infrequent. Yet each work as it comes takes its place in the world—there are no failures. Each work is tightly wrought, contains no adipose tissue, speaks to the point. Again the comparison with Bax is instructive, for Bax had great talent, but his fecundity, his very facility, proved a drawback in the end, for since his death in 1953 his seven symphonies, his tone-poems and his concertos have suffered a worse eclipse than the normal reaction with which a cruel public is wont to reward its artists at their deaths.

For a time it looked as though Walton was to be a César Franck with one of each in the categories attempted, each more than a success, a unique specimen of its kind, one *Façade*—there could only be one of that—one concerto, one oratorio, one symphony, one quartet, one duet sonata, and ultimately one opera, but the four concertos soon spoiled that too facile generalization and a second symphony wrecked the pattern for good, but the fact that the comparison suggested itself does tell us something about the

R   233

working of his mind, namely that he is not a fast worker nor a copious producer, that he likes to concentrate on one thing at a time, that he polishes each work to the last slur and accent, and that nevertheless he steadily extends his range round the whole art.

A glance at the film scores is almost reassuring in that it shows that he can be superficial, that he could turn out more if he wanted to, so that it is readily deducible that he works as he does because he thinks that is the right way (for him at least) to work. The craftsman will not let the artefact out of his hand until he has wrought it to the perfect realization of the conception he has of it. He is thus a dedicated artist, dedicated not to music in general but to the work in hand. That he works largely to commissions reinforces this attitude of mind. He does not seek, as Vaughan Williams and Britten, towards a way of life, an outlook on life, or the fulfilment of some purpose, proximate, ulterior or overriding. We do not know from his work what he thinks about things, or except within certain limits what sort of a man he is. He might be compared in this respect with Hindemith, another predominantly instrumental composer, had not Hindemith revealed his mind in *A Composer's World*. Walton is reserved and does not give vent to subjective emotion in his music. He is, in so far as that old aesthetic distinction between absolute and programme music is valid, an absolutist.

It is strange that an English composer with Walton's first-hand contact in early life with vocal music should have worked that vein so much less consistently than the symphonic. The balance between the two categories is not of course wholly out of proportion, for *Belshazzar's Feast* and *Troilus and Cressida* are too big to be obscured by the purely orchestral works, but words do not offer to him the same sort of ready stimulus to the imagination as they do to Britten. He thinks in themes, textures, and structures rather than in transcripts of visual and verbal images and concepts. He pays words the greatest respect, as his collaboration with the Sitwells testify, but does not fall in love with them or even rely on them. He creates large structures without them and relies on thematic processes for their skeletal coherence.

The two song sequences *Anon. in Love* and *For the Lord Mayor's*

Table do however tilt the balance nearer to an equilibrium with the instrumental music, and this late adoption of the song sequence as a congenial medium shows a disposition to develop the more lyrical and the more humorous sides of his personality which have not been much in evidence since *Façade*. But they too are extended compositions, not the sort of trifle such as Stanford for instance threw off in profusion (and which in retrospect look like his finest achievement).

The miniatures in his output are almost negligible, a couple of violin pieces, bits from the films, a few, very few part-songs. *Music for Children*, either in its original piano-duet, or in its orchestral version as a kind of latter-day *Wand of Youth Suite* is not negligible and does reveal what results when his ingenuity is warmed with a touch of avuncular feeling. It is modest in scope and is in fact a series of miniatures, which assures that he can trifle with trifles if he wishes, as the film music also does, but there is no overflow of small things, such as keep Stanford's memory green, no Brahms *Walzer*, no Mendelssohn vocal duets, no Grieg *Lyric Pieces*. This means that his output is all of a piece with few divagations of style, a singularly consistent *œuvre*.

A birds-eye view of it shows certain characteristics of his musical thought, though not any immediately obvious mannerisms of personal vocabulary or idiom, such, for instance, as makes any note of Vaughan Williams or phrase of Dvořák immediately recognizable. The most conspicuous feature of his style is what must be called, in a horrific mouthful of description, his thematic polymorphism; plain repetition is so antipathetic to him that he cannot bring himself to give a definitive form to his themes for their various appearances; they must have new heads or new tails or must vary their intervals, but they retain their identity nevertheless. This feature can be seen in an extreme form in *Belshazzar's Feast*, where, however, it is consciously used for a dramatic purpose, but it occurs as early as in the piano quartet and is found in all the orchestral works. His harmony gets its sharp flavour from a deliberate confusion of modality: shall it be sharp or flat, natural or inflected? His answer is generally 'Either or both'. The false relations of the consecutive sixths in the Viola Concerto are the most conspicuous example of a hesitation that has in it no element of indecision. The Sinfonia Concertante shows examples of a similar oscillation, such as Schubert used to indulge in between major and minor thirds, but without limiting the inflected notes to the third degree of the scale. And there are even cases where the music seems to be poised between two keys. Indeed it is often impossible to determine the key of a particular passage, though certainly it is not atonal—only fluid in tonality. The general contrapuntal texture is conducive to the practice of different inflection in different voices, which is a modern resumption and extension of a common Elizabethan procedure.

In symphonic writing it is Walton's method to condense his recapitulations, and he has a way of recalling his themes for simultaneous presentation in mutual counterpoint. Indeed his whole symphonic style is contrapuntal rather than harmonic in its mode of progression. A conspicuous instance of simultaneous statement of themes, not merely in recapitulation but in exposition, is at the opening of the Violin Concerto where the bassoon states a countersubject to the soloist's main theme in order to provide material for subsequent development. Augmentation is another contrapuntal device that is frequently employed.

Some works make extensive use of some particular technical feature. Thus in the early piano quartet he favours a modal kind of tonality, in the symphony the elaborate development of the pedal-point. Rhythmic caprice is to the fore in Façade and the two comedy overtures. Antiphony is exploited in the Te Deum. Variation has increasingly engaged his attention, in the Violin Sonata, the Cello Concerto, the Second Symphony and the Hindemith Variations. And there is a discreet flirtation—it hardly gets beyond holding hands—with serialism in the Violin Sonata and the Second Symphony and a quite new application of the principle, to determine tonality, in the Hindemith Variations.

The range of mood was not perhaps very wide, though even in the thirties, which were also his thirties, he had brought the unusual emotions of ferocity and malice (in Belshazzar's Feast and the First Symphony) within it. He had also tapped a vein of public sentiment in his ceremonial music. Behind the wit on the one hand

and the forcefulness on the other, which are the most obvious characteristics of his style, is a vein of somewhat wistful romanticism. In one hand he carries a rapier, in the other a bludgeon, but behind this formidable armament beats a heart not devoid of gentleness, and in control is a very clear head. It is from the romantic vein that Walton draws his sustained melodies and his lyrical utterance. This side of his musical personality was dragged from its modest abode behind the bold front of high temper and tension in *Troilus and Cressida* and exposed as the central dynamic of the opera alongside of the wit (of Pandarus) and the tragedy. The acerbity and the piquancy, which at first blush one is inclined to attribute to his instrumentation, is really the product of his harmony and his stringent use of dissonant, thematic counterpoint. For his use of the orchestral palette as such, the ballet, *The Wise Virgins*, which consists of rescoring of pieces by Bach, shows his taste in orchestral sonority more clearly than the original works, where it is involved in the stuff and substance of the music. The transcription is more luminous than his own scores are.

Of his originality it is enough to observe how difficult it is to trace any affiliations in his music. There are occasional traces of other men's music—an echo of Elgar, a flavour of Sibelius, a rhythmic hint from Stravinsky, a near-quotation from Rimsky-Korsakoff (or Rossini), but these incidentals signify nothing since they are only superficial traces not hereditary features. Walton was uninfluenced by homebred folk-song; he flirted with no foreign schools; he had next to no formal training; and from his early cathedral experiences he seems to have brought away no more than an aptitude for choral writing. His big works seem in an unusual degree to be self-conditioned creations of an individual mind, a mind moreover that emerged almost fully formed, or at any rate found its maturity with extraordinary speed and certainty. It follows from this that there is less continuity of development to be traced in his thought than is commonly the case with composers, though it is true that from the Viola Concerto onwards a greater intensity of feeling, a gradual broadening of sympathies, and a consolidation of character are discernible in his scores. Every one of them bears the most scrupulous marks of expression, accent, and phrasing. Indeed some are a little over-done and could produce their own immunity—all these graded accents, > — *ffp*, *fz*—but they do cumulatively produce the effect of rhythmic high tension. To the same end contributes his way of writing ♩♪♩ for ♩♪

When in the thirties Walton had revealed himself as a twentieth century romantic, that the witty play-boy of *Façade* was also the composer of the Viola Concerto, and that he was of this century, not of the last—the pressures of *Belshazzar's Feast* were not of the steam but of the electrical age—his modernism was accepted as a phenomenon of contemporary life. But when *Troilus and Cressida* came twenty years later the complaint was heard that he was still the same and so behind the times. In the sixties when the avant-garde of the day were busy exploring serialism, fragmentation, and indeterminacy, Walton was reproached as a back number. But he writes the sort of music he wants to write. It may suit Stravinsky to experiment with styles, putting them on and off like so many suits of clothes—which admittedly he fits to his figure and which do not conceal his personality—but for other men such quick-change artistry might seem like a loss of integrity. Vaughan Williams similarly went about his business, keeping his own counsel and doing what he had it in him to do regardless of pressures, fashion, and of the bubble reputation. So Walton keeps himself to himself, remains a dogged Lancastrian, writes what he wants to write in the way he wants to write it, develops his style slowly if at all, as in the casual look he takes at serialism, and does a composer's job, which is to write music to the best of his ability.

In more ways than one he resembles Elgar. Musically in that he is predominantly an orchestral composer but has produced choral music in the oratorio tradition; his concertos have attracted soloists of international repute; and there is a ceremonious side to him that has produced the equivalent of *Pomp and Circumstance* marches in his two Coronation marches: *Cockaigne* has its opposite number in the Johannesburg overture; there are two symphonies and curiously enough a *Wand of Youth* orchestral Suite. Elgar and Walton have one other characteristic in common in that they were both virtually self-taught English provincials who escaped academic training. But these remarkable parallels have no ulterior significance—at the utmost only to the extent of both being products of similar environments in English life. The existence of an opera, which Elgar never achieved, may be attributed to the radical change in our national attitude towards that art-form which crystallized in 1946, a revolution instigated by the various labours of Thomas Beecham, Edward Dent, Lillian Baylis . . . and Mussolini. For it is my belief that the decisive factor that tipped the precarious balance in its favour was the invasion of Italy by a large British army in the Second World War, which discovered to its delighted surprise opera as a going concern, 'like going to the cinema at home', as one private soldier said to me. We have signified our gratitude to Italy by lending on lease (at Ischia) to Italy Sir William Walton, the composer of an opera in the grand tradition of La Scala and San Carlo.

Chronological List of Works

1916   'A Litany' (part-song)
1918   'The Winds' (solo song)
1918–19   Pianoforte Quartet
1920   'Tritons' (solo song)
1921 & 1923   String Quartet
1922   *Façade* Entertainment
1924   'Bucolic Comedies' (five solo songs including 'Daphne', 'Through Gilded Trellises', and 'Old Sir Faulk')
1925   *Portsmouth Point* (overture)
1926   *Siesta*
       Façade: 1st suite for orchestra
1927   Sinfonia Concertante for piano and orchestra
1929   Concerto for viola and orchestra
1931   *Belshazzar's Feast*
       'Make we joy now in this fest' (part-song)
1934   Ballet from *Escape me never*
1935   Symphony No. 1
1936   Incidental music to *As you like it*
1937   *In Honour of the City of London*
       'Under the Greenwood Tree' (solo song from *As you like it*)
       Crown Imperial (Coronation March)
1938   'Set me as a seal upon thine heart' (part-song)
       Façade: 2nd suite for orchestra
1939   Concerto for Violin and orchestra
1940   *Duets for Children*
       Scapino (overture)
1941   *Music for Children*
1943   Prelude and Fugue for orchestra ('Spitfire') from *The First of the Few*
       The Quest (ballet)
1944   Incidental music to *Henry V*
1946   'Where does the uttered music go?' (part-song)

1947 String Quartet in A minor
1949 Sonata for violin and piano
1951 Two Pieces for violin and piano
1953 *Orb & Sceptre* (Coronation March)
      Coronation Te Deum
1954 *Troilus and Cressida*
1955 Incidental music to *Richard III*
1956 Johannesburg Festival Overture
1957 Concerto for Cello and orchestra
1958 Partita for orchestra
1959 A Queen's Fanfare
1960 Symphony No. 2
      Anon in Love (song cycle)
1961 Gloria
      'What cheer' (part-song)
1962 *A Song for the Lord Mayor's Table* (song cycle)
1963 Variations on a theme by Hindemith
1965 *The Twelve*
1966 *Missa Brevis*
1967 *The Bear*
1968 Capriccio Burlesco
1970 Improvisations on an Impromptu of Benjamin Britten
      'All this time' (part-song)
1972 Sonata for string orchestra
      Five Bagatelles for Guitar
      Jubilate

The dates given are those of composition, not of first performance.

Walton has composed music for a number of films. Only those are listed above from which music for concert use has been derived.

Index of Works

(Entries in heavy type refer to the main discussion of the subject.)

243

ORCHESTRAL WORKS

SONGS

General Index